D1612819

# A SECULAR EUROPE

# A Secular Europe

*Law and Religion in the European*
*Constitutional Landscape*

DR LORENZO ZUCCA

OXFORD
UNIVERSITY PRESS

# OXFORD
## UNIVERSITY PRESS

Great Clarendon Street, Oxford, OX2 6DP,
United Kingdom

Oxford University Press is a department of the University of Oxford.
It furthers the University's objective of excellence in research, scholarship,
and education by publishing worldwide. Oxford is a registered trade mark of
Oxford University Press in the UK and in certain other countries

British Library Cataloguing in Publication Data

Data available

ISBN 978–0–19–959278–4

Printed in Great Britain by
CPI Group (UK) Ltd, Croydon, CR0 4YY

Links to third party websites are provided by Oxford in good faith and
for information only. Oxford disclaims any responsibility for the materials
contained in any third party website referenced in this work.

A Beatrice

# *Preface*

The cover is a detail from Michelangelo's Sistine chapel fresco and depicts Minos, the king of Crete, and son of Zeus and Europa. Michelangelo takes the image from Dante who placed Minos at the gate of Inferno to judge the sins of the souls and send them to the right place in hell. Minos expresses his sentence by circling his tail the number of times corresponding to the exact emplacement of the soul. In this world nothing is open to chance, Minos's judgment is just and rigorous and flows from the correct application of Christian principles. The beauty of Dante's vision is its unique and perfect structure where everything hangs harmoniously. Christian faith gave unity and order even where there was chaos and fragmentation. The real world was the afterworld; life on earth was just a chaotic parenthesis.

Today's Europe is at first sight equally chaotic and fragmented, and in addition to that, nothing seems fit to give a meaning and an order to our lives. The waning of religion from public affairs, many claim, has brought more fragmentation and chaos and individuals of different religious and non-religious groups have competing allegiances from which they have to choose when they need to decide how to behave in any given society.

This book aims to provide one clear legal-political framework and to do so it develops a new model of secularism suitable for Europe as a whole. The new model of secularism is concerned with the way in which modern secular states deal with the presence of diversity in society. This new conception of secularism is more suited to the European Union whose overall aim is to promote a stable, peaceful, and unified economic and political space starting from a wide range of different national experiences and perspectives. The new conception of secularism is also more suited for the Council of Europe at large, and in particular the European Court of Human Rights which faces growing demands for the recognition of freedom of religion in European states. The new model does not defend secularism as an ideological position, but aims to present secularism as our common constitutional tradition as well as the basis for our common constitutional future.

# Contents

# List of Abbreviations

| | |
|---|---|
| AKP | Adalet ve Kalkınma Partisi: Justice and Development Party (Turkey) |
| BVG | Bundesverfassungsgericht: German Federal Constitutional Court |
| DPP | Director of Public Prosecutions |
| ECHR | European Convention on Human Rights |
| ECJ | European Court of Justice |
| EctHR | European Court of Human Rights |
| EU | European Union |
| LSD | liberal secular democracies |
| MAT | Muslim Arbitration Tribunal |
| NAB | neutrality-as-blindness |
| NAD | neutrality-as-deafness |
| OED | Oxford English Dictionary |
| TCC | Turkish Constitutional Court |
| UK | United Kingdom |

# Introduction

The resurrection and rise of religion in recent years triggered an ambiguous response in Europe. On the one hand, some have sided with a hard-line secularist position—often associated with French *laïcité* (translated, problematically, as 'secular' or 'secularity')—which sharply separates public and private spheres and firmly relegates religion to the latter. On the other hand, some have felt the need to reassert the Christian roots of Europe as a non-negotiable starting point. Either way, we witness Europe's struggle to grapple with its identity and in particular with its foundational values: rule of law, democracy, human rights, and, last but not least, secularism. Each one of them is asserted as an article of faith, rather than defended with cogent arguments. The European Court of Human Rights (ECtHR), for example, does not always articulate the reasons that lead it to a decision, in particular when it deals with secularism.[1] Moreover, European institutions and societies are increasingly at pains to accept that religious minorities would use those tools to advance their own agenda. Human rights are a good illustration: if freedom of religion holds true it applies to all religions and not only to the religion of the majority. This means for example that Muslims have the right to build their own religious buildings and to wear the clothes prescribed by their own religion. The claims may even go further: some parts of private life, because they are private, may eventually escape the rule of secular law to the benefit of the rule of religious law. Increasingly vocal claims of religious minorities have triggered the reaction of religious majorities who would want to preserve a central role in society; an example of this may be the litigation on the crucifix in the classroom in Catholic countries. This string of cases, which has inundated European courts, illustrates a potential collision course between law and religion in Europe.

The central question that I explore in this book is the following: is there a conflict between law and religion? The question is crude and in need of further elaboration but it conveys my central preoccupation well. At first, law and religion may be seen to be dealing with different domains. It may thus seem far-fetched to ask that question. After all, religion is firmly rooted in the transcendental perspective, while law is quintessentially immanent: God and

---

[1] See eg *Lautsi v Italy*, 18 March 2011, Application no 30814/06.

Caesar have always had two separate kingdoms. Religion aims at the salvation of people in eternity, whereas law aims at peaceful coexistence here and now. Religion promotes one specific understanding of the good life, whereas law attempts to be neutral about it and promotes as many ways of life as possible. Yet both law and religion regulate behaviour of large constituencies in different yet overlapping areas of life.

There is no complete overlap between law and religion, nor is there clear-cut separation. Law and religion meet at different points, be it the regulation of family life, the edges of life, or educational matters to give a few important examples. So the question becomes: what if law and religion issue incompatible norms? Does law have to give in to religion or vice versa? Or is there a space within which religion can ask for exemption? Or is it law that has to justify its divergence from religion?

Past answers to these questions are instructive and show the extent to which the relationship between law and religion evolved throughout the years. In medieval Europe, the dualism between immanent and transcendent world-views was clearly resolved in favour of the latter. The justice that mattered most was divine justice in the afterlife. The ultimate adjudicator was God and it mattered little from his viewpoint that an individual was a good law-abiding citizen if he was not a good Christian. Greek philosophers who happened to be born before Christ had no access to paradise for example. Dante's limbo is populated with virtuous people who have been excluded from the possibility of salvation.

Religious wars between Christians brought into sharp relief the necessity of a secular law firmly detached from religious considerations. If Christians of different denominations wanted to live together in this world, they had to put aside for a while their doctrinal disagreements. Law thus acquired the independent status of pacifier between religions in the whole of Europe. Europe was broken down into homogeneous areas where one majority religion enjoyed the support of the law, while acknowledging its toleration vis-à-vis other religions. This brought us to the age of nations: the conflict became one between the nation state and the national church both vying for predominance over a discrete territory. In France the conflict was particularly bitter following the Revolution since the new elite attempted to strip the church of its wealth and benefits. It took more than a century to settle legally that conflict with the famous *Loi de 1905*, establishing a legal separation between church and state.[2] Contemporary debates have been dominated by the

---

[2]  For a magisterial historical account of the church and state relation in Europe and in France in particular, see René Rémond, *Religion et société en Europe aux XIXe et XXe siècles. Essai sur la secularization* (Éditions du Seuil, 1998).

church and state framework, constantly redrawing the boundaries between the two.

The idea of separation between church and state has the appeal of simplicity. It nonetheless shows in practice great weaknesses due to the numerous exceptions and provisos that accompany that position. Moreover, it is not a universal stand since many states in Europe opt for a system of establishment (Greece, Norway, United Kingdom (UK), etc). Today, it may be more accurate to depict the church–state relationship as one of collaboration on different fronts.[3] Not only that: the state has to accommodate and possibly collaborate with leaders of religious minorities who have the ability to reach communities that are alienated from ordinary political processes.

One of the theses of this book is that the church–state model is out-dated and does not provide guidance as to the relationship between law and religion. In each European state, there is more than one church and each one of them is competing for followers. The state no longer sees churches as enemies but as charitable entities that can assist with some social problems and sometimes with the delivery of education. I suggest in this book that we should look beyond the church–state paradigm and begin to think of the presence of religion in the public sphere differently. First, religion is not confined within national boundaries, so its presence should be studied, evaluated, and recorded not just at the national level, but also at the supranational and international level. Secondly, the state has a strong interest in the community-building function of religion. Thus, at the European level, I will suggest that political institutions should promote a marketplace of religions where religious institutions compete for faithful while delivering their societal goods.

Moving beyond the church–state debate, the book offers a new understanding of secularism at the European level. When we speak of secularism the risk is to opt for a specific and very contingent conception of secularism that would have to be extended to the whole European constitutional landscape. So, for example, many claim that French *laïcité* provides the clearest and strongest statement of secularism and as such it should be embraced at the supranational and, perhaps, at the international level. This would be a mistake for several reasons: firstly, French *laïcité* as it is commonly understood—ie as a doctrine that protects religion only in so far as it is in the private sphere—is highly problematic as it creates an asymmetry between religious and non-religious people to the detriment of the former. Secondly, French *laïcité* as expounded above is a misrepresentation of the original intent

---

[3] See on this point, Norman Doe, *Law and Religion in Europe: A Comparative Introduction* (Oxford University Press, 2011).

of the *Loi de 1905*, which aimed to end the conflict between church and state by creating a legal separation between the two. Thirdly, the uncompromising character of French *laïcité* makes it a much easier target for those who want to criticize European secularism.[4] It has come to represent a rigid, divisive position which heartily pleases its followers and uncompromisingly repels its enemies. For these reasons, it is not helpful to extend one contingent historical experience to the whole of Europe.

A more promising starting point for constructing a viable conception of secularism for Europe is by paying attention to the changing socio-legal political landscape. If the Peace Treaty of Westphalia had established national kingdoms within which one religion was superior to any other, the secularization of power went hand in hand with the dismissal of the monopoly of one church. Instead of religious homogeneity, Europe is now characterized by religious (and social) heterogeneity. No one religion can claim supremacy over any other; if anything they may lend a helping hand to each other when facing the secular authority. Secularism can therefore be understood today as a way of maximizing religious diversity, while creating a unitary legal framework that would allow disagreement between religious and non-religious people to be settled peacefully.

I hasten to add that the new model of secularism is not a fully fledged philosophy, nor is it a new ideology or a world-view. It is instead a legal doctrine more properly called 'inclusive secularism'. It is easier to say first why inclusive secularism is not any of the things mentioned above. Secularism has many separate—and sometimes competing—layers. Secularism can be a whole system of thought, an epistemic stance, a world-view, an ideology, or a legal-constitutional approach. As a system of thought secularism is all-encompassing and aims at explaining the world as it is without reference to God. As an epistemic stance, secularism is meant to offer a disclaimer on what we can know and what is beyond our reach including religious knowledge. As a world-view, secularism provides a possible political viewpoint through which we are meant to look at human institutions. As an ideology, secularism is a corrupted form of a political world-view and aims to provide a dogmatic normative position as to what society should look like. Finally as a legal-constitutional doctrine, secularism attempts to provide a framework within which religious and non-religious people can live together. Inclusive secularism belongs to the last category.

---

[4] For a wonderful examination of the French debate, see C Laborde, *Critical Republicanism: The Hijab Controversy and Political Philosophy* (Oxford University Press, 2009).

Inclusive secularism, as I understand it, is the art of devising institutions for plural societies so as to maximize religious diversity, while preserving a unitary legal-political framework. No doubt there are competing understandings of secularism (see chapter 2). The conventional view presents secularism as a solution to the church and state problem mentioned above. The secular state in Western democracies has to organize the relationship between itself and the church. Some states elect a regime of separation (US, France, etc), other states elect a regime of collaboration if not establishment (UK, Greece, etc). The choice between separation and establishment is largely contingent and depends on discrete constitutional histories: a dominant church may contribute to the obedience vis-à-vis established power. A dominant church generally represents a social majority for whom the religious institution is desirable; however, it does not mean that minorities will be well treated under one dominant religion.

Both regimes of separation and establishment face the dilemma of how to treat minorities. Interestingly, where the dilemma is more evident it is not necessarily more serious. In England, the Church of England is the established church of the land. Anglicans are obviously fine with this, but what about Catholics or other Protestants? Law, and in particular the constitution, evoke for many the myth of neutrality. The constitution is a pact for all—it does not exclude anyone; to the contrary; it attempts to bring everyone into the legal fold. Law being equal for everyone, there is no risk of treating people unfairly, or so the story goes. Yet, secularism thus understood faces the dilemma of neutrality: how do secular states show equal respect to religious and non-religious people if the constitution seems to privilege a non-religious perspective?

My version of secularism does not attempt to solve the dilemma; instead it takes it seriously as a symptom of a widespread malaise: the inability of the secular state to cope with diversity. It is hard to believe that a secular state is neutral between religious and non-religious views. However, it is possible to suggest that the secular state should strive to be agnostic in matters of conscience. The secular state can thus be portrayed as being equally distant from religious and non-religious people; it does not assume any truth or any vision of conscience. Instead it painstakingly attempts to promote mutual understanding and nudge towards practical compromises between different constituencies. A secular state should not silence religious voices, it should allow for their participation in the public sphere, while setting out conditions for participation for all. Crucially the option to participate in democratic life should be wide open, but the final product of deliberation—secular law—can only employ a language that everyone can understand without the need to appeal to transcendental-metaphysical considerations that are not shared by all.

Inclusive secularism should be understood in a very broad sense since it encompasses different layers at the domestic, supranational, and international level. I refer to those layers separately and as a whole; in the latter case I loosely talk of a European Constitutional Landscape constituted by European states, the European Union (EU), and the Council of Europe, all contributing to different extents to the elaboration of secularism at different levels. It may even be the case that at the international and supranational level, secularism acquires a different meaning from domestic secularism which is inescapably rooted in national constitutional histories.

In the last fifteen years or so, the ECtHR has taken a keen interest in the application of Article 9 European Convention on Human Rights (ECHR) that deals with freedom of religion. Several cases from European states led the Strasbourg Court to examine the practices of states with established churches (Greece), as well as strictly secular states (Turkey). Recently, a high-profile case from Italy led the Court to consider whether the presence of the crucifix was compatible with secularism. Regrettably, the Grand Chamber came to view secularism as an ideological conviction of some people, rather than the precondition for coexistence through law.[5]

The EU has had to grapple with its own position vis-à-vis religion. The high point of the debate was reached with the preamble to the European Constitution. The question was whether or not Christian values should be inserted in the preamble. Meanwhile the constitutional ambition collapsed, while the preamble refrained from referring to Christian values. However, the question of the constitutional identity of the EU remains open and this book also aims to discuss the implications of such a quest. Domestic states are obviously concerned with religion, both in relation to their majorities and minorities alike. Examples of friction between the secular state and religion could endlessly be multiplied: think of the headscarf debate in France; the crucifix in the classroom in Italy, Bavaria, and Spain; the place of sharia law in Britain; the Mohammed cartoons in Denmark; the racist murderer in Norway and so on. More importantly, there is no existing secular model that is able to create a peaceful space for religious people in Europe. Inclusive secularism as I present it in this book aims to carve out a place for religion, while maintaining the secular nature of the law.

---

[5] See *Lautsi v Italy*, 18 March 2011, Application no 30814/06.

# The Structure of the Book

The book follows a tripartite division: Inferno, Purgatory, and Paradise, as in the famous work of Dante Alighieri, *The Divine Comedy*. However, *A Secular Europe* is neither divine, nor is it a comedy. If anything, it attempts to explain a deep-seated tension between religion and the secular state. Dante's Europe aimed to be unitary under the practical authority of the emperor and the theoretical authority of the church. There was no doubt that Europe was Christian, the only issue was whether or not the pope should also exercise temporal power—that is, power over the mundane business of politics and day-to-day life. Dante believed that the pope should not mingle with such issues and leave to Caesar the task of ruling over the terrestrial world. The task of the pope, after all, was much more important: he had to prepare people for the world of the afterlife. In that world, moral and legal standards would not be arbitrary and contingent. The world of the afterlife would be breathtakingly ordered and ranked. Everyone would have his place in the architecture of that world and there would be no room for deviation within it. The world of the afterlife is the real Christian world where Christian moral principles are laid out and implemented as clearly and coherently as possible. The world of the things as they are pales by comparison; this world is fragmented, disorderly, and at times meaningless—especially when void of Christian meaning.

The journey through Hell, Purgatory, and Paradise is a journey towards transcendental knowledge for Dante. In *A Secular Europe*, the journey is towards immanent knowledge instead. This does not preclude the possibility of religion. If Dante postulates a deep unity in the afterlife on the basis of a strict interpretation of Christian theology and Aristotelian teleology, *A Secular Europe* attempts to present secular law as the tool with which we can aim at unity in this world. Christian morality was the glue which bound people together in medieval society. Secular law is what binds people together in today's Europe, or so I suggest. It provides a framework within which religious and non-religious people can live together.

The journey in *A Secular Europe* begins with religious wars of the seventeeth century, when the schism within the Christian world caused people from all over Europe to clash with and slaughter each other. The political unity of Europe was shattered and destroyed over three decades of brutal conflicts. That is as close as it gets to Inferno in this world. Peace in Europe could only be reached at the price of engineering states with homogenous religious majorities in order to avert clashes between religious groups. Dissent and diversity were stifled and suppressed in exchange for order and authority. Within this landscape, toleration was the main instrument that would enable the survival of religious minorities. To be tolerated was not a privilege, but a mere pact of non-aggression (chapter 1).

It took Europe three centuries to shake the order established by Westphalia in the most violent way. Brutal wars in the nineteenth century were followed by global conflicts in the twentieth century. European nations fought bitterly amongst themselves until they understood that something had to be done in order to prevent murderous conflicts. The post-war period paved the way for a new political scenario in which certain national interests were pooled together. It is only since 9/11 that Europe has started rethinking itself as a Christian bloc as opposed to other blocs of civilization. The rise of religions has provoked a reassertion of secularism in aggressive and exclusive terms (chapter 2). Thus, the road seems to be leading towards a clash between secular law and religion (chapter 3).

The headless search for European identity is discussed in the section entitled Purgatory, where Europe purges its sins of nationalistic hubris and attempts to get to grips with itself. To grapple with its Christian identity, however, is more a sign of uncertainty and inability to articulate a new vision for the future rather than a genuine foundational exercise (chapter 4). After all, Inferno was the result of a Christian Europe torn between various religious families and sects. Something important was lost in that struggle. Europe moved from a unitary empire, through a bipolar Christian world and has now arrived at a stage of deep social and religious pluralism. Diversity is the central factor of today's Europe, which cannot be reined in by a reaffirmation of monolithic religious roots. Religion may still have a place in Europe but no religion should have a monopoly over other religions or over the morality of a state (chapter 5). European institutions are still in Purgatory searching for their real soul. Meanwhile their questioning is further prompted by the presence of Muslim minorities whose place in Europe is still unclear. Their religious and cultural background seems to be at odds with European conceptions of life in common and coexistence. In particular it seems hard to reconcile being Muslim with being European where the former stands for belonging in a community of belief whereas the latter stands for belonging in a political community which rejects belief. The tension materializes with the question of the place of sharia law in European legal and political systems (chapter 6).

Paradise is the last step of the journey where European fragmented reality meets with what I take to be the pillars of a shared European future. Diversity is the central idea that informs this part. European secularism should not be about the relationship between one state and one religion. Instead European secularism is about the relationship between plural religions among themselves and between various political entities ranging from the national to the supranational and international. The relationship between religious and non-religious people should be informed by the quest for mutual knowledge as organized by the secular state in appropriate *fora*, such as the school classroom which is the very first place where cultural differences can emerge and merge (chapter 7). More generally, the ethics guiding the relationship between people should be receptive and attentive to the protection of diversity (chapter 8). Finally, the instrument through which diversity can be maximized, while tensions between different people can be minimized, is secular law (chapter 9).

# PART I
# INFERNO

The Inferno is characterized by conflicts between religious and non-religious people. Conflicts in themselves are not a bad thing. They testify of the vitality of a community and are a sign of dynamism. However, the escalation of conflict can lead to the polarization of a community and to violence between different groups. It is therefore necessary to devise mechanisms that maximize constructive conflicts while minimizing destructive ones. Europe's legal and political history can be presented as a constant attempt to negotiate the boundaries between the church and the state as well as between religious majorities and minorities.

There are three different types of conflict explored in the Inferno. Firstly, I deal with conflicts between religions, like for example the struggle between Catholics and Protestants in seventeenth-century Europe (chapter 1). Secondly, I deal with the conflict between two versions of secularism, one which is inclusive and one which is exclusive (chapter 2). Thirdly, I deal with the conflict between law and religion (chapter 3).

# 1

# Tolerance or Toleration? How to Deal with Religious Conflicts in Europe[1]

## 1.1. Introduction

Europe is once again beset by religious conflicts. There are several examples of unrestrained opposition against, and by, religious minorities and majorities alike. Think of the ban on minarets in Switzerland which is spreading like wildfire in Germany, Italy, and beyond. Think also of the veil saga that has occupied French politicians and their society in the last two decades. The target of opposition can be religious majorities as well; one example is the litigation on the crucifix in the classroom.[2] Needless to say, opposition calls for an equal reply, and so religious minorities and majorities respond with individual actions or campaigns against secular societies and their states. Religious conflicts are not new in Europe. Religious wars in the seventeenth century were the bloodiest and most violent confrontation on the continent. The Treaty of Westphalia of 1648 put an end to them, and organized Europe in such a way that states could rule over religiously homogenous communities.[3] There were Catholic and Protestant states; religious pluralism within each state was limited as much as possible.

Religious conflicts in the seventeenth century were about belief, more precisely about the best Christian faith. Their starting point was theological disagreement.[4] Religious conflicts today are about political disagreement. They are conflicts about whether or not a faithful person can bring to bear

---

[1] This chapter is a revised version of my essay 'Tolerance or Toleration? How to Deal with Religious Conflicts in Europe' in Macksymilian del Mar (ed.), *New Waves in Philosophy of Law* (Palgrave, 2011).

[2] *Lautsi v Italy*, 18 March 2011, ECtHR (Grand Chamber), Application no 30814/06.

[3] According to the principle devised in the Treaty of Westphalia: *Ejus Regio, Cujus Religio.*

[4] See J Ratzinger, *Truth and Tolerance: Christian Belief and World Religions* (Ignatius Press, 2004). The Archbishop of Canterbury would also welcome more theology in public debates, see the conclusion to his lecture, 'Archbishop's Lecture: Civil and Religious Laws in England: A Religious perspective', <http://www.archbishopofcanterbury.org/1575>.

her religion in the public sphere in order to regulate her own behaviour (in a classroom, in parliament, in courts, or in the streets). Religious pluralism has not been a characteristic trait of European nation states after Westphalia. In the Council of Europe, there are still many states with an established church and fairly homogeneous societies.[5] This is markedly different from the United States of America (USA), for example, where non-establishment is constitutionally protected and religious pluralism is at the foundation of the state.[6] But European societies are changing at a fast pace and are becoming increasingly more pluralist.[7] This makes conflicts more, rather than less, visible.

Toleration emerged in the seventeenth century and was portrayed as the best response to religious conflicts. It was recognized as a key political virtue, which the state imposed as a legal obligation. A famous example of such a legal implementation is the so-called Act of Toleration 1689.[8] Liberal thinkers also promoted toleration. Locke, for example, argued that: 'the toleration of those that differ from others in matters of religion is so agreeable to the Gospel of Jesus Christ, and to the genuine reason of mankind, that it seems monstrous for men to be so blind as not to perceive the necessity and advantage of it in so clear a light'.[9] Locke regarded toleration as an imposition of reason, and the lack thereof is explained in terms of being carried away by 'irregular passions.'

Both the Act of Toleration and Locke's Letter of Toleration are examples of a moralizing attitude of the political and intellectual elite towards the masses. Toleration is regarded as one chief virtue of morally enlightened people who are capable of regarding wrong beliefs as conditionally acceptable. Most liberal theories that promote toleration follow this path of imposition of reason from an ideal moral viewpoint. These theories are normative through and through and rely on heavy assumptions about the wrongness of some religious beliefs and the rightness of some liberal values. The question is whether toleration as a moralizing attitude provides a good enough way of coping with conflicts that involve religion. The short answer is that toleration

---

[5] Andorra, Armenia, Denmark, UK Church of England (since Toleration Act 1689, *c*.13) and Church of Scotland (Church of Scotland Act 1921), Finland, Georgia, Greece, Iceland, Liechtenstein, Malta, Monaco, Norway.

[6] See M Nussbaum, *Liberty of Conscience: In Defense of America's Tradition of Religious Equality* (Basic Books, 2008).

[7] Here pluralist means non-homogeneous.

[8] The subtitle says: 'An Act for Exempting their Majestyes Protestant Subjects dissenting from the Church of England from the Penalties of certaine Lawes.'

[9] John Locke, 'A Letter on Toleration' in *An Essay concerning Toleration and Other Writings on Law and Politics, 1667–1683*, JR Milton and Philip Milton (eds) (Oxford University Press, 2010).

might have dealt with seventeenth-century conflicts, but does not seem to provide a sound basis to deal with present day conflicts.

Recent historical accounts show that the master narrative of toleration as a virtue emanating from the elite and spreading through the masses as a solution to religious conflicts is not so accurate as a narrative and not so promising in today's context. Those historical accounts show that tolerance was practised on the ground long before the elite's appeals for toleration. By this I mean that as a biological, physiological, and psychological matter every individual has a disposition to cope with a certain amount of diversity—tolerance of a non-moralizing kind—that does not depend on sophisticated moral reasons.[10] The practice of tolerance does not depend on a prior decision to refrain from opposing some categories of beliefs or people.

I shall argue that non-moralizing tolerance should be distinguished from moralizing toleration and should be understood as the human disposition to cope with diversity in a changing environment. Tolerance thus defined is the basis for an alternative approach to deal with religious conflicts. Such an approach is less dependent on normative assumptions and more responsive to empirical data, including psychological insights as to the human ability to deal with difference. In what follows, I will first present toleration as a moralizing attitude. Then I will show the limits of liberal theories based on such an understanding of toleration. I will suggest, instead, that we should pay more attention to tolerance understood as the natural disposition of every individual to cope with difference as the best basis for dealing with religious conflicts.

## 1.2. Toleration as a Moralizing Attitude

I will start with one definition of religious toleration given by the *Oxford English Dictionary* (OED): 'Allowance (with or without limitations), by the ruling power, of the exercise of religion otherwise than in the form officially established or recognized.'[11] One of the striking elements of this definition is the suggestion that there is an established religion to start with. According to this definition, toleration implies an act of establishment of a religion. Albeit striking, this is not inconsistent with the present existence of an established Church of England and with many other *de jure* established

---

[10] See Benjamin J Kaplan, *Divided by Faith: Religious Conflict and the Practice of Toleration in Early Modern Europe* (Harvard University Press, 2007).

[11] OED Online, definition 4a, <http://dictionary.oed.com/cgi/entry/50253991?single=1&query_type=word&queryword=toleration&first=1&max_to_show=10>.

churches in Europe, not to speak of *de facto* established churches. The second, closely connected, element of the definition is that there is an asymmetry between the majority and the minorities. The religion of the majority is free by definition, while minority religions are permitted by political fiat. Here lies the third element of the definition: this allowance is given out by the ruling power: it is a top-down concession that can be revoked whenever the ruling power decides to do so. And the ruling power can also decide (fourth element) whether or not to impose limits to the allowance which they have graciously granted.

There may be disagreement about the scope of toleration, but there is agreement as to its point. Toleration carves out a space between right and wrong beliefs. It is the space of tolerable wrong beliefs. In the Act of Toleration 1689 Anglican beliefs are held to be the right ones. Protestant beliefs are tolerable wrong beliefs; Catholic beliefs are plainly wrong and therefore unacceptable. In many European states, including the UK, this implied that one religious faith is recognized as official truth and the other faiths as wrong. Toleration thus defined is an act of establishment of right beliefs, and as such it is deeply problematic. The wrongness of religious (or secular) beliefs is only postulated but not argued for. Any imposition flowing from such a postulate is likely to be regarded as irrational and unfair.

Toleration is a political *ideal* allegedly imposed by natural reason that requires people to put up with a certain amount of wrong beliefs.[12] However, not all wrong beliefs are tolerated: some are considered intolerably wrong. In this context, it is certainly better to be tolerated than not, but it does not mean that being tolerated should be regarded as a privilege.[13] The key to toleration is that the state singles out morally right beliefs which attain the status of official truth. Other beliefs, despite being officially wrong, can be tolerated either out of principled respect or out of prudential calculation.

Liberals of different stripes disagree about toleration. More generally, they disagree as to how to create and maintain a cohesive society given the fact of pluralism. Two main strategies appear to characterize liberal attitudes towards religion: one is instrumental and the other is principled. The instrumental approach starts from the inevitability of conflicts amongst religious people or between religious and non-religious people. It is rooted in seventeenth-century Europe and its experience with religious conflicts.

---

[12] Here an important caveat is 'a certain amount'. Not all wrong beliefs can be tolerated according to this version of toleration. There are beliefs that are considered to be intolerably wrong. The state differentiates between right beliefs, wrong beliefs, and intolerably wrong beliefs.

[13] A very promising criticism of toleration is offered by L Green, 'On Being Tolerated' in M Kramer et al (eds), *The Legacy of HLA Hart* (Oxford University Press, 2009), 277–98.

The instrumental approach can take two forms. The first calls for peaceful coexistence for the sake of a more secure and conflict-free society and despite major disagreement on issues of belief. If someone does not comply with the laws, then the sovereign authority is entitled to punish her for intolerance. We can call it the coexistence conception of toleration (Hobbes). The second relies on the fact that the state cannot coerce people into revising their beliefs and that is why one has to accept them, however grudgingly. We can call this the permission conception of toleration. I have already mentioned that both the Act of Toleration 1689 and Locke's Letter of Toleration are paradigmatic examples of the permission conception of toleration, which involves a moralizing attitude that divides beliefs and behaviours into right, wrong, and tolerated.

An illustration of the coexistence conception of toleration is the so-called ideal of *modus vivendi*.[14] This ideal can only be met when competing groups in a society are roughly in a situation of equality, lacking which instability between the two is likely. *Modus vivendi* theories start from the conviction that it is impossible to reach consensus about few selected values, since disagreement about basic values penetrates decisions at every level. Given the fact of persistent disagreement, the only possible moral attitude that would avoid violent conflict is one which calls for a duty of coexistence. People live in the same space, but pass each other like ships in the night. They are requested to disregard each other's behaviour in order to guarantee peace and security within a society. This approach relies on the possibility of devising common institutions that exercise power fairly while maintaining pluralism of values and beliefs. The problem with this moralizing attitude is that it is bound to be very unstable: what happens, for example, when political elites themselves call for unrestrained opposition towards religious minorities in order to foster and spread negative feelings vis-à-vis Muslim immigrants? In these cases, political institutions find themselves in a dilemma: either they uphold their commitment to free expression as a paramount value of democracy, accepting that this is likely to foment more social conflicts and fears, or they curtail some forms of expression on the basis that is not respectful of minorities, thereby opening the debate over the real value and limitations of free expression. European societies face the double threat of extreme right-wing parties banking on fears and extreme religious groups becoming more popular and emboldened in the face of adversity.[15] A mere moral attitude of coexistence can hardly bridge the gap between those two constituencies.

---

[14] See J Gray, *Two Faces of Liberalism* (Polity, 2000).
[15] See eg *Le Pen v France*, 20 April 2010, Application no 18788/09.

Principled approaches attempt to show that there are some moral reasons that require us to take into account religious beliefs in terms of respect or even esteem. According to some authors, the American tradition of religious liberty relies on a principled attitude of respect towards religion, though there is disagreement as to what respect really means.[16] In any case, it is possible to suggest that one major strand of the American tradition of religious liberty relies on *rational consensus* theories, which argue that it is possible to devise well-crafted procedures with a view to obtaining agreement on a selected number of values that will constitute constitutional bedrock for everyone.[17] This theory relies on the hope that there will be convergence on a few universal moral truths.

Rational consensus theories often promote the moral attitude of respect rather than that of toleration. In Europe, Republican France promotes respect towards individuals independently from their religious beliefs. This can be deemed formal respect and contrasted with substantive respect, which seems to characterize the American experience.[18] The *République* represents the union of all the people within the territory. There is no mediation between the individual and the *République*: the values of one must correspond to the values of the other. There is no space for intermediate communities to represent individuals. Given this outlook, every citizen is regarded as strictly equal in a formal way. Here lies the difference with the American conception of respect which postulates that everyone enjoys equal citizenship and freedom *of* religion. In France, everyone enjoys equal citizenship and freedom *from* religion. In France one has to accept *legal laïcité* as the precondition for participation in public life.[19] The *République* does not recognize cultural differences within its own territory. In public institutions everyone is

---

[16] See the exchange between Martha Nussbaum and Brian Leiter. See Nussbaum, *Liberty of Conscience*. Brian Leiter argues with that view in B Leiter, *Why Tolerate Religion?* (Princeton University Press, forthcoming). Both authors define toleration and respect as mutually exclusive. By taking this position, one narrows down toleration to a notion of coexistence at best. Here I suggest that there are at least four conceptions of toleration following from Rainer Forst, 'Toleration', *Stanford Encyclopaedia of Philosophy*, <http://plato.stanford.edu/entries/toleration/>. Forst distinguishes between four types of toleration: permission, coexistence, respect, and esteem.

[17] See J Rawls, *Political Liberalism* (Columbia University Press, 1999). Even if it was possible to come up with such a list, it would still be unclear whether that agreement at the abstract level prevents disagreement at the level of implementation of those values.

[18] See Nussbaum, *Liberty of Conscience*. Nussbaum defends the idea of thick respect which requires a positive attitude of esteem towards religion: not only do we recognize each other as an equal member of the community, but we regard each other's position as likely to bring something to all of us.

[19] See C Laborde, *Critical Republicanism: The Hijab Controversy and Political Philosophy* (Oxford University Press, 2007). See also Olivier Roy, *La Laïcité face á l'islam* (Stock, 2005), translated into English, *Secularism Meets Islam* (Columbia University Press, 2007).

formally equal and must be seen to be formally equal. Hence, for example, no conspicuous religious symbols are allowed in public schools.[20]

In other parts of Europe, coexistence is still the preferred basis for the moral attitude of toleration and informs multicultural practices in the north of Europe. British and Dutch multiculturalism are partial illustrations of such theories. Society in the UK and Holland is constituted by plural communities that do not overlap and live separately in the same territory. Each community has a limited power to regulate some aspects of the life in common within that smaller unit. Each community regards itself as culturally independent, while recognizing the moral and political need of toleration in order for everyone to maintain his own lifestyle. Conflicts within communities are in principle settled internally, but they may be dealt with by ordinary institutions if the community is unable to find a compromise. This poses various problems, as the standard applied by ordinary institutions will invariably be different from the standards applied within a community. All these models appear to face serious problems in practice. French republicanism is not able to solve a major tension between its commitment to formal equality and the lack of substantive equality. Muslim pupils in French schools often come from underprivileged backgrounds. If you exclude them on the basis that their presence breaches formal equality, you will reinstate their economically disadvantaged status, thereby creating a vicious circle. Accepting them under the conditions that they remove their religious symbols is not a solution as this simply reinforces their belief that they are not equal to other people.[21] The central problem with this position is that the moralizing attitude of respect for all is paid at the very high price of giving up one's beliefs in the public sphere.

Dutch and UK multiculturalism appears to be too thin and presently very strained.[22] Religious minorities may enjoy greater freedom, but they do not enjoy the same access to opportunities provided by the society. Moreover, their voices are not sufficiently represented and are often mis-portrayed. To live in a community bruised and battered is a good recipe for creating antagonistic feelings that can only grow when left unaddressed. The existence of separate-but-equal communities pushes them far apart from one another and creates less than optimal conditions for future coexistence.[23] It may be

---

[20] See Laborde, *Critical Republicanism*.

[21] See Laborde, *Critical Republicanism*.

[22] See I Buruma, *Murder in Amsterdam: The Death of Theo Van Gogh and the Limits of Tolerance* (Penguin Press 2006).

[23] Behavioural economics shows that radicalization of individuals happens when they are segregated. Separate groups tend to think more radically rather than more moderately. See C Sunstein, *Going to Extremes: How Like Minds Unite and Divide* (Oxford University Press, 2009).

that these examples do not represent the full gamut of constitutional frameworks that aspire to maintain a cohesive society. Nevertheless, the weakness of these major models is demonstrated by a general trend in Europe whereby the relationship between religious and non-religious people is strained. These approaches require varying moral attitudes towards religion: permission, coexistence, respect, or esteem. Instead of opting for one or the other alternative, I argue that it is necessary to change fundamentally the viewpoint from which the issue is assessed. A fresh start involves a better understanding of the psychology of tolerance and promotes a different role for the state in promoting tolerant behaviour that is not informed by moral requirements.[24] Before moving to that point, let me illustrate with an example how different approaches of toleration fall short of coping with religious conflicts.

## 1.3. The Limits of Moralizing Attitudes: *Lautsi* as an Illustration

A recent landmark case of the ECtHR can serve as an illustration of the limits of moralizing attitudes towards religion. The case is *Lautsi* and since it is already widely known and discussed, it does not require a lengthy presentation. The basic issue concerns the presence of crucifixes in Italian school classrooms. Mrs Lautsi argued that the presence of the crucifix infringed her secular conviction, whereas the Italian state claims that the crucifix stands for the values of secularism. Put this way, the disagreement is between two forms of secularism, but in reality the question is whether religious symbols and traditions have a place within the secular public sphere.

So far we have distinguished two main moralizing attitudes towards religion: toleration as a basis for *modus vivendi*, and toleration as a principled position that is sometimes reinterpreted as respect. Regarded from the viewpoint of respect, the issue is not simple: does the moral attitude of respect help to tip the balance one way or the other? The plaintiff is pointing out that the right to education includes the respect of parent's religious and philosophical convictions. But of course, the Court must also respect the existence of social and cultural traditions. The issue of respect from a moralizing perspective is problematic because it is highly individualistic and insists only on respect for individual convictions. But everyone in society has an interest in having their cultural and social traditions respected as well.

---

[24] Spinoza's *Tractatus Theologico-Politicus* provides a great inspiration for this endeavour. See B. Spinoza, *Complete Works* (Hackett Publishing, 2002), in particular ch. XX.

The reasoning of the Court does not take this into account but simply leans towards an individualistic morality of rights: principled approaches regard rights as individual entitlements to use against the state. The problem is that there is something missing from the picture, which cannot be accounted in terms of rights: it is the power of any nation state to define its symbols of cultural and political allegiance.

From the viewpoint of instrumental toleration the issue is slightly different and focuses on the role of the symbol itself. Is the display of such a symbol conducive to an environment where all the pupils can coexist without feeling emotionally disturbed by an exclusive environment? Instrumental approaches regard rights as side constraints on the power of the state, but also on the rights of other people. From this viewpoint, they are more inclined to accept that there may be conflicts between two rights in given circumstances. Interests protected by rights can reasonably clash one against another. It is easier to see that the state can have interests at odds with those of an individual claimant. However, instrumental approaches do not offer a viable alternative to the vacuum they create. They may be powerful arguments against displaying one given symbol, but does that mean that no symbol can promote coexistence? Instrumental approaches of the multiculturalist stripe end up promoting the existence of various institutions which promote their own values separately. This is the system of multi-faith schools that pays lip-service to diversity but does not do much to promote convergence.

Both toleration and respect involve the evaluation of the costs of having a plural society. The justification of such solutions differs. For principled approaches, equal citizenship means that each individual should divest herself of any social or cultural attachment other than the republican one when living in a public space. It is not pleasant, but this is the price to pay for having a plural society in which everyone has an equal voice. Instrumental approaches stress the difference between people rather than one identity. Minority groups have different needs compared to the majority. They therefore have to be accommodated so that their rights protect their needs even if this waters down important values in some instances.

Neither approach, however, is able to fully cope with the conflict between religious and non-religious people. Either solution entails more polarization rather than less. The republican position leaves no room for diversity, while the multicultural position leaves no room for convergence. Both approaches over-rely on rights as encapsulating liberal values that can potentially be accommodated either through ranking or through definitional balancing. Neither approach captures the day-to-day practice of living together (as opposed to the moralizing attitudes of coexistence or respect) which is a much more reliable basis for an approach that attempts to cope with the existence of religious conflicts.

## 1.4. A Fresh Start: Tolerance Distinguished from Toleration

English is the only European language to draw a distinction between tolerance and toleration. In German (*Toleranz*), French (*tolérance*), Italian (*tolleranza*), and Spanish (*tolerancia*) there is only one name for those concepts. Not that the distinction in English is clear and easily applicable. Tolerance and toleration are used as synonyms in the literature; often one finds the two used interchangeably. But I do believe that it is possible to draw a distinction between toleration-as-a-moralizing-attitude and tolerance-as-a-natural-disposition. The former is a normative concept, while the latter is descriptive. A similar distinction is drawn by historian Benjamin Kaplan: '[This book] begins from the crucial premise that tolerance was an issue not just for intellectuals and ruling elites, but for all people who lived in religiously mixed communities. For them tolerance had a very concrete, mundane dimension. It was not just a concept or policy but a form of behaviour.'[25]

Here, I propose a *stipulative* definition of tolerance distinguished from toleration. I am not suggesting that the distinction mirrors ordinary language closely, although it has a link to it. However, I argue that this distinction illuminates both theory and practice. It puts the latter in a better light by showing how people behave when confronted with difference; it improves the former by pointing out what should be the role for the state and for individuals in light of practice. As we saw, conventional understandings of toleration as a general approach start from a political ideal of a peaceful society and draw from that ideal some conclusions as to the appropriate moral attitude towards religion. The alternative approach based on tolerance-as-a-disposition starts from the emotional reaction towards diversity in order to build up some correctives where the practice shows weaknesses.

Tolerance, as I see it, focuses on the *disposition* of an individual or a group of individuals to put up with an external agent of disturbance. This notion is much more biological and psychological and does not depend on prior moral judgement although it forms a more solid basis for further moral

---

[25] Kaplan, *Divided by Faith*, 8.

deliberation. To illustrate the notion of tolerance I have in mind, I will take a few examples from the OED:

The action or practice of enduring or sustaining pain or hardship; the power or capacity of enduring; endurance. More widely in *Biol.*, the ability of any organism to withstand some particular environmental condition. *Biol.* The ability of an organism to *survive* or to flourish despite infection with a parasite or an otherwise pathogenic organism.[26]

Tolerance is the *disposition* of putting up with external agents of disturbance; it involves a psychological attitude that strikes a middle ground between wholehearted acceptance and unrestrained opposition.[27] In a fairly stable society, most people lean towards that attitude; tolerance as a disposition carves out a space for every individual to flourish according to one's own beliefs alone and relatively unencumbered by the multifarious emotional inputs that derive from other people's beliefs and behaviours. If one did respond to each external stimulus, then the ability to flourish independently would be seriously hampered. Life would boil down to an emotional rollercoaster whereby our beliefs and behaviour are always defined in opposition to, or in emulation of, other people's beliefs and behaviours. Needless to say, this already is the case in many circumstances but it cannot possibly be the norm of our lives otherwise we would be unable to develop and flourish autonomously. Tolerance thus defined is not about drawing a priori moral lines and imposing them on issues of conflicting beliefs, but it is about the ability to cope with them in a way that does not prevent individuals from flourishing. Of course, tolerance is a matter of degree. It can only work when an individual or a society is in a condition of mental and physical stability, rather than being embroiled in unproductive conflicts. The healthier the individual or the society, the greater the ability to cope with external agents of disturbance and vice versa. To see tolerance in this way amounts to a Copernican revolution in matters of organizing a plural society as it requires that we radically change the basic question. Toleration as a moralizing attitude asks us to focus on how to regulate society in order to avoid conflicts or to respect each individual voice. Tolerance as a non-moralizing attitude asks us to focus on what are the root causes of individual and social malaise that lead to aggression of the religious other.

---

[26] OED Online, definitions 1 a, b, c, d, <http://dictionary.oed.com/cgi/entry/50253982?query_type=word&queryword=tolerance&first=1&max_to_show=10&sort_type=alpha&result_place=1&search_id=SXRt-jMaiTJ-7777&hilite=50253982>, accessed 30 September 2010.

[27] See TM Scanlon, 'The Difficulty of Tolerance' in *The Difficulty of Tolerance* (Cambridge University Press, 2003), 201. Scanlon also calls it a middle way between wholehearted acceptance and unrestrained opposition.

## 1.5. Tolerance as a Non-moralizing Approach

My approach starts from tolerance-as-a-disposition rather than moralizing toleration. It is different and can be distinguished from both principled and instrumental approaches that promote toleration as a moralizing attitude. There are three main differences between a moralizing and a non-moralizing approach.

Firstly, tolerance is not a principle to be imposed by legislation or a virtue to be preached by elites, but a human disposition that needs to be understood. Tolerance is not a behaviour that is *imposed* either by a moral or political doctrine, but it is a behaviour that *emerges* as a natural human response to difference. It is not the moral or political means through which religious conflicts are solved and dispelled, but the innate response to the fact that each one of us experiences conflicting emotions when faced with diversity. When a society is stable and healthy, there is little talk of the practice of tolerance. It is when things go wrong that intolerance is on everyone's lips.

Secondly, tolerance as a disposition can only flourish in an environment where freedom of thought is protected above everything else. No thought is to be considered as right or wrong from the outset, as it is the case from a moralizing viewpoint. Every person, be they religious or non-religious, should be free to advance their own ideas and beliefs and argue for them. Disagreement between people can only help to sharpen thought and allow truth to emerge. This is only possible, however, if no assumption or presupposition is considered to be dogma. A healthy polity will devise ways to cope with disagreement, but will never find a way to solve an issue once and for all.

Thirdly, a non-moralizing approach insists that negative emotions towards diversity are the result of lack of appropriate thinking. How can one possibly hate something or someone just because he or she is different? Negative emotions are more likely in the case of a moralizing approach that states a priori which beliefs are right and which are wrong. Wrong beliefs can sometimes be tolerated, but others are firmly opposed as a matter of stipulation. For example, polygamy is considered morally wrong and unacceptable in our societies, but I would argue that it is not necessarily morally wrong and unacceptable. Why would it be unacceptable to have a relationship between several people when this is the result of open and rational deliberation? The only reason why polygamy is perceived as intolerably wrong is because the institution of marriage as defined by Christian norms does not accept any other form of union beyond monogamy.[28]

Now that the three main differences have been set out, it is possible to elaborate a more articulated approach to cope with conflicts between religious and non-religious people. The starting point is the acknowledgement of clashes within each of us: we all oscillate between wholehearted acceptance and unrestrained opposition when we are first exposed to people whose behaviour and symbols markedly differ from ours. If each individual simply followed those emotions unreflectively, we would constantly go through a rollercoaster that leaves no time for flourishing. Tolerance is a naturally devised disposition that helps us to mediate between strong emotional reactions. As a matter of practice, each one of us is prepared to put up with a great deal of behaviour that may appear to be inconsistent with societal values or individually held beliefs. This is explainable in terms of the drive to survival that characterizes our self-development.[29] We would not be able to concentrate on our own flourishing if we were constantly pulled in one or another direction.

Of course, one does not tolerate murder. The emotional reaction to murder is of unrestrained opposition and there is no space for tolerance of such an action. Most relationships and actions, however, do not fall at the extremes of the spectrum. They provoke mixed reactions which pull in different directions. Through a process of reflection about those reactions individuals come to regard most of them as part of their world without fully accepting or rejecting them. Here begins the practice of tolerance: human beings qua reflective beings are able to form ideas about those emotions and as a result of this reflective process they tend towards a balance between opposite reactions, without which their lives would be an endless and meaningless series of confrontations.[30]

Each individual projects his internal clashes onto the external world and brings them to bear on the life of his group. His family, his community, his city, and his country—as long as they strive to be one—also experience a number of clashes vis-à-vis other people or actions. The root of any conflict of values is the original clash within, understood as an emotional response to someone or something that is not fully well known. A non-moralizing

---

[28] Divorce may be said to have introduced diachronic polygamy: it is permitted to have more than one wife/husband provided that this is done one at a time.

[29] Spinoza calls it *conatus:* the striving for individual empowerment and development. See B Spinoza, *Ethics* in *Complete Works*, passim.

[30] This is what biologists call Homeostasis, that is the natural tendency to regulate one's body so that it adapts to environing surrounding circumstances, see eg A Damasio, *Looking for Spinoza: Joy, Sorrow and the Feeling Brain* (Mariner Books, 2003).

approach based on tolerance rejects the idea that conflicts of values can be solved in a way that the clash within is removed from the individual altogether. Those clashes within that attest to an emotional reaction towards unknown people or things are inevitable. In fact, those clashes within are necessary for cognitive process as they stimulate the will to know the external world. Only negative feelings, such as fear, can constitute a limit to the knowledge of the external world in so far as they push individuals towards a defensive approach rather than a cognitive one.

A non-moralizing approach based on tolerance does not rely on prior judgements as to what can be the object of toleration and what should be firmly opposed. This would assume that one has already made up one's mind about rightness or wrongness often without properly getting to know the object of intolerance. Clashes within are more complicated than that and have various layers. First of all, one responds to the broader issue of a known or unknown phenomenon. If it is known appropriately then the clash within will not be very hard to deal with. It is when the phenomenon is unknown that things are complicated. Individuals and societies tend to simplify those matters by applying ready-made values to the unknown phenomenon and by filing it away in the right or wrong boxes. A non-moralizing approach based on tolerance resists that categorization and pushes for more knowledge before making a judgement.

Human beings have worked out a great number of collective responses to clashes within. Religion, for example, is a given response to a peculiar clash within. We feel that we are eternal, when we reflect about our souls, and yet we know that we are mortal. Religion assuages this clash by postulating a separation between the life of the soul and the life of the body. By privileging the former over the latter, religion offers consolation to a split individual. The spiritual clash within addresses the damning problem of the meaning of life—what are we doing in this world? This explains why religion is still so fundamental in the life of the great majority of people all over the world. It is because it does give an answer and allows people to get on with their lives in the meanwhile. Individuals and groups care a great deal about the precise answer they have been given. They care because they believe it is true. And as a consequence, they must believe that any other answer is false. How is it possible to tolerate a false claim on something that is so important to people's lives?

The spiritual clash within—mediated through institutional religion—is sometimes projected onto the external world. It becomes a social conflict between individuals, groups, and even nations. Europe as a whole was devastated by such a conflict in the seventeenth century. The political response to it was to carve out religiously homogeneous regions within which people would not be requested to tolerate other religious views. Toleration as a political virtue applied to relationships between nation states following the Treaty of Westphalia 1648. Homogeneity, however, is itself unstable because the natural freedom of thought with which we are endowed pushes us in different directions (as it was the case for Luther, Zwingli, and Calvin for example). Moreover, homogeneity has never been truly met amongst the people. Historical accounts of life in Europe show that different religious communities had to live side by side and the important lesson is that they generally found ways of doing so.[31]

Tolerance as defined here supports a non-moralizing attitude towards diversity rather than one that divides the world in right and wrong beliefs a priori. But unfortunately there are instances in which tolerance leaves its place to unrestrained opposition and this entails a spiral of social polarization and ultimately violence. In these cases, I don't believe that it is helpful at all to preach the attitude of toleration as a political ideal that would solve those conflicts. The most important thing to begin with is to reflect on the causes that led to intolerance. Political and economic considerations are obviously important. These undermine self-confidence and hope. When fears enter the scene, it is almost impossible to avoid the consequence that our clash within between acceptance and opposition will be resolved in favour of the latter.

## 1.6. Knowledge of Fear

Tolerance as a disposition informs the relationship between individuals belonging to different groups in a society. The instinctive mechanism of tolerance, however, can be hampered by the existence of entrenched prejudices and fears flowing from misunderstandings about other people. A racist, for example, is not able to tolerate because his conception of the other will be clouded by a set of prejudices formed a priori. Mutual knowledge that dispels prejudices is, therefore, absolutely necessary to promote and encourage a flourishing practice of tolerance. Unfortunately, it is often the case that prejudices are associated with fears; these two together make the possibility of mutual knowledge very difficult.

Knowledge of fear allows every individual to form reflective ideas about emotions; the process of subconscious enquiry is a good instrument for keeping emotional reactions under control. The smooth working, and development, of tolerance-as-a-disposition depends among other things on the

---

[31] See Kaplan, *Divided by Faith*.

knowledge of one's own fears. But, of course, this investigation is a matter of individual choice and cannot be imposed on anyone. Individuals who oscillate between competing emotions without being able to find a middle ground are in a difficult position and can hardly flourish under these conditions. If each one of us was able to inspect our subconscious and dig out the root causes of fear, then we would oscillate much less perilously between opposing emotions towards diversity. Of course, on a grand societal scale it is impossible to promote this; so each one of us has to put up with a certain amount of entrenched emotions that cannot be explained away rationally. Institutions can nevertheless nurture and protect the natural disposition to tolerate in many other ways and in particular through education.

Fear is not only negative. It performs a very valuable role in the life of human beings. It averts the mind to an impending danger and calls for a cautious attitude towards an unknown object or person. Fear warrants against immediate reaction or engagement. It generally nudges the individual towards further examination as to the actual danger faced. It also promotes a cognitive attitude geared towards the knowledge of the external world. When you know the object or person that is feared, you are able to apprehend it in a way that is not dangerous anymore. Perhaps our fear will disappear altogether as knowledge will have shown that there is no danger intrinsic to the external object or person triggering fear. So not only does fear protect us from danger, but it may also stimulate our knowledge of the external world which is yet unexplained.

Sometimes, however, fear overwhelms us and temporarily clouds our reason. We are frozen into inaction and we refuse to know the object of our fears. This is the case for example with Muslim minorities in Europe. Many consider them as a threat to Europe and depict them as such in the media. The mass reaction to those minorities is dictated by such fears and entails unrestrained opposition to some or all aspects of the behaviour of the minority. Most of the time, this reaction is not supported by actual knowledge but is simply based on a stereotypical description of the target of hatred. Fear can become phobia when left uncontrolled by reflective attitudes. Phobia is a systematic fear against persons or objects that has become entrenched and cannot be removed by the usual cognitive process that leads our minds to apprehend the external world. It is quite plain to see that today in Europe there is a widespread Islamophobia—that is, a systematic fear towards religious minorities that pits them against secular Western society. The general reaction towards those minorities is unrestrained opposition and there does not seem to be an easy way out of this deadlock.

How can we break the spell of Islamophobia? Some say by effectively protecting minority rights. I do not think that this is the correct response.

I believe that the state should instead promote mutual knowledge. We can take sharia law as an example. The conventional reaction is one of unrestrained opposition. Think of the emotional reaction faced by the Archbishop of Canterbury when he defended the possibility of having Muslim arbitration tribunals applying sharia law to private disputes.[32] He was then supported by the now President of the UK Supreme Court, Lord Phillips.[33] Both genuinely hoped that by engaging with sharia law, part of the mystery and fear that surrounds it would be dispelled. And when fear lifts its hold and gives away the place to further knowledge, then we can finally learn that sharia law is not that different from legal codes of behaviour that are closer to those observed in the Western world. Some elements of sharia law will remain incompatible with ordinary law; in particular physical punishments will be at odds with our practices. But those punishments are not the core of sharia law: they are perfectly detachable elements of a general system of rules that can be regarded as compatible with ordinary laws.

This is not to say that we are under an obligation to wholeheartedly accept sharia law. After some examination, we may still conclude that we disagree with its fundamental tenets, and we consider it as not being fully acceptable. But this is not a ground for unrestrained opposition either. This is a case where tolerance is emotionally possible once the cognitive prerequisites have been fulfilled. It is important to be clear at this point: in a secular state, it is possible to be tolerant to people who follow sharia law to guide their behaviour in certain domains. It is also possible that a conflict between two religious people can be solved by an arbitrator whom they both accept. But it is not permissible to allow for rules of behaviour that are incompatible with ordinary laws.

## 1.7. Law and Tolerance (*Lautsi* Again)

The best way to illustrate the practical difference of my approach is to use the *Lautsi* case again. There are three main aspects to take into account from my perspective: Firstly, the conflict should be regarded as an opportunity for knowledge. Is the crucifix in Italy a symbol of secularism as the state claims? The Italian government, for example, 'attributed to the crucifix a neutral and secular meaning with reference to Italian history and tradition, which were

---

[32] Archbishop's Lecture: 'Civil and Religious Laws in England: A Religious Perspective'.

[33] Lord Phillips, Lord Chief Justice, 'Equality before the Law', speech at the East London Muslim Centre, <http://www.matribunal.com/downloads/LCJ_speech.pdf>, accessed 4 October 2011.

closely bound up with Christianity'.[34] One may object that the crucifix is neutral, but it is hard to dismiss the role played by Christianity in Italy in shaping the social and political space in many ways. It is of course possible to suggest that secularism developed in opposition to religious values, but it would be churlish to claim that secular and religious values are mutually exclusive since their history is one of exchange and dialogue rather than competition and denial. The role of reason in promoting knowledge is, however, limited and it cannot be held that deeper knowledge of conflicting interests leads to a better solution in practice. This leads us to the second element of my approach.

The limits of knowledge through reason give rise to the necessity of imagination as a way of finding a new solution for the future. Can we really deal with this issue by applying old standards? Is it possible to solve the conundrum posed by *Lautsi* simply by applying a conception of secularism that does not take into account social and cultural traditions of one country? The presence of a symbol can be the starting point of a creative debate. Pupils may be asked whether they want to complement that symbol or whether they want to remove it. In either case, they should be asked to provide an explanation. Those who take the crucifix for granted would have to review their position, while those who oppose it or never even thought about it are encouraged to think about it from a completely free viewpoint. The crucifix could be considered as a starting point for reflection rather than an end point. This may truly put the students in a position where they can empathize with other students. This leads to my third point.

Knowledge and imagination must be supported by an ability to put oneself in other people's shoes. This was arguably very difficult some years ago in Italy when the vast majority of the population was Catholic. In such a context, it was difficult to appreciate the viewpoint of a divergent position. Immigration and further secularization today have created a more diverse environment in the classroom and in society. It is therefore more important than ever to engage in an empathic process that leads people to know their mutual starting points so that negative emotions and passions can be ruled out from the beginning.

To sum up, law can promote tolerance and a healthy environment by providing three essential services: it can and should stimulate mutual knowledge by providing genuine platforms of cultural exchange, starting with primary education where one can learn about religious differences. Secondly, it can and should stimulate freedom of thought through creative and

---

[34] *Lautsi v Italy*, 3rd November 2009, Application no 30814/06.

imaginative channels rather than imposing a ready-made set of values. Thirdly, it can and should encourage each and every individual to put themselves in someone else's shoes so that negative emotions towards diversity can be effectively reined in.

Solon claimed that each society deserves the laws that it can bear.[35] Let me explain why this makes sense: a society that is ridden by conflict and hysteria will only be able to bear laws that do not upset the majority. As a consequence the minority will be silenced and suppressed. Contrariwise, a society that is strong and stable will bear much more easily internal conflicts without breaking into pieces. Those conflicts will be regarded as opportunities to engage in further knowledge. They will also push us all to reinterpret creatively our traditions so as to accommodate as many diverging views as possible.

## 1.8. Conclusion

Religious conflicts will not be solved or explained away once and for all. They will keep coming back and present difficult decisions for all the European states, as well as for European institutions. The master narrative of toleration is not capable of dispelling all the issues that arise between secular majorities and religious minorities. It may well be that toleration was the right answer to religious conflicts in the seventeenth century. In a world that was little secularized, the major issue was to create a space for both religious minorities and majorities. Toleration presented a reason to oppose aggression against religious minorities that held wrong beliefs from the viewpoint of the majority.

However, the price to pay for toleration was high: the entrenchment of official truth about right beliefs, and the subsequent creation of a trichotomy between right, wrong, and tolerable beliefs that is not easy for the state to police without major inconsistencies. Such a trichotomy could only come with a moralizing attitude between majorities and minorities, an isolation of minorities, and a huge limitation on the dissent about majority values. Social homogeneity achieved stability at the price of freedom of thought on the fundamental issues of the society. Europe remained homogeneous for a long time and enjoyed periods of stability followed by instability until it broke down completely with the events of World War II. In the last fifty years, Europe has enjoyed great stability but social homogeneity has been replaced

---

[35] See C Montesquieu, *L'Esprit des lois* (Paris: Flammarion, 1995).

by a great deal of social and religious pluralism. Religious pluralism poses formidable challenges for secular authorities.

Europe is today largely secular. Religious beliefs have been banned from the public sphere and cannot constitute a source of an official truth supported by the state. Instead, the state has embraced conceptions of power and truth that do not depend on religious beliefs. The separation between theology and philosophy put reason on a pedestal and religious beliefs were relegated to the private sphere. Power and truth have been secularized, but this does not mean that they now enjoy any stronger foundations. Secularism no doubt has achieved much, but it can itself fall prey to criticism. In particular, secularism can be established as the new official truth of the state and this is not necessarily desirable as it entrenches and imposes a rigid interpretation of what is right and what is wrong, whereby religion is classified as being on the wrong side if it aims to voice its opinions in public.

A non-moralizing approach requires from each individual that no official truth be taken as written in stone (including the truth of *laïcité*). It also requires the state to create the preconditions for mutual knowledge, which is an important goal in order to nurture the natural disposition of individuals and groups to cope with difference. Such an approach is sceptical about conceptions of secularism that rule out altogether the possibility of a public role for religion. Instead it believes in a secularism that is committed to a plurality of goals in order to best deal with diversity. Not that religion should enjoy an unlimited access to the public sphere or special protection as it makes its voice heard. It nevertheless cannot be excluded from participation in political affairs as a matter of principle because it may capture some important messages that should be taken into account. Secularism should be regarded as a default framework within which disagreement (about the best political regime, as well as about the best kind of life) is widely protected. Developing this conception of secularism will be the object of chapter 2.

# 2
# Two Conceptions of Secularism[1]

## 2.1. Introduction

The failure of the European constitution ignited two apparently independent debates: what is the future of the European secular states, on one hand; and what is the place of Christian values in the European public sphere, on the other.[2] In recent years, the latter question has become more and more urgent—so much so, that the future of European secular states is considered to be very much dependent on their ability to cope with the alleged threat of religion. This is the way in which aggressive secularists perceive the problem. They would like to ban religion from the public sphere and relegate it to the private domain. I believe instead that the issue for secular states is how to cope with diversity and I put forward an understanding of secularism that is more understanding of religious reasons and more inclusive of religious people.

Aggressive secularism attempts to provide both an explanation for the weakness of secularism and a response to it. I will take as a representative of aggressive secularism, András Sajó (AS), who is a professor of constitutional law and a judge at the ECtHR.[3] AS begins by pointing out that strong religion is back in the public sphere.[4] The threat posed by religion, he argues,

---

[1] This chapter is based on a revised version of my essay 'The Crisis of the Secular State: A Reply to Prof. Sajó', International Journal of Constitutional Law, 7(3) (2009), 494–514.

[2] Joseph Weiler, *Un'Europa Cristiana* (Rizzoli, 2004). For a response, see Srdjan Cvijic and Lorenzo Zucca, 'Does the European Constitution Need Christian Values?', Oxford J Legal Stud, 24 (2004), 739.

[3] I will take as main target András Sajó, 'Preliminaries to a Concept of Constitutional Secularism', Int'l J Const L, 6 (2008), 605, which I take to be a paradigm example of aggressive secularism. My response 'The Crisis of the Secular State: A Reply to Prof. Sajó'. He wrote a final reply here: 'The Crisis that Was Not There: Notes on a Reply', Int'l J Const L, 7(3) (2009), 515–28.

[4] In what follows, I will not use Sajó's notion of strong religion. Instead, I will simply speak of religion, as I do not believe it is possible to draw a clear line between the two. An otherwise peaceable religion may very well claim an exception or a compromise that appears to some as a strong challenge to the secular constitution of the state. For example, some hard-core secularists believe that wearing the veil in public poses a threat to secularist principles. See *Leyla Şahin v Turkey*, 41 Eur HR Rep 8 (2005). It is important to distinguish between the claims made by religious people and the nature of religion itself.

is real, and secularism does not provide enough guidance to keep religion at bay. The reason for this weakness is to be found in the contingent and local nature of secularism, which developed within each secular state in a way that is too much open to compromises and concessions. As a response to this state of affairs, AS argues that secularism should rediscover its constitutionalist roots in order to become more assertive and aggressive vis-à-vis the claims of religion.

My aim in this chapter is to show that AS's diagnosis of the threat constituted by religion is only partly accurate. My suggestion is that religion is not a threat in itself but, rather, is simply a symptom of a greater malaise: the inability of secular states to cope with diversity. Moreover, AS's prognosis, entailing an aggressive notion of constitutional secularism, is wrong both in theory and practice. Wrong in theory, because it assumes that secularism is just about the strict separation between state and religion; in practice, because it believes that the best way to deal with religion is to silence it in the public domain. What unites AS's diagnosis and prognosis is the belief that strong religion is a disease to be eradicated and that secularism can be the cure. I believe, instead, that the central problem to be analysed here is the crisis of the secular state in its different European versions. All European states have experienced similar, though not identical, problems when regulating the place of diversity—religious or non-religious—in the public sphere. The crisis emerges as European states becomes less and less homogeneous and more and more diverse. To cope with the crisis, the secular state should develop a twofold strategy. On the one hand, it should promote, as far as possible, active communication and mutual understanding among all the groups of a society.[5] On the other, it should accept that in some specific cases we face conflicts between secular values that are intended to make diversity possible. If a genuine conflict arises, it will not be possible to find a one-size-fits-all solution. For example, it may be extremely difficult to please both those who believe in strong freedom of expression and those who would like to limit it when it expresses hatred of someone. In these limited cases, we have to agree to disagree, and the default position, therefore, will have to promote a thinner notion of coexistence among different groups and individuals on the basis of clear rules of the game.[6]

[5] Jürgen Habermas, *Between Naturalism and Religion* (Polity Press, 2008).
[6] John Gray, *Two Faces of Liberalism* (Polity Press, 2000). I am aware that this double strategy may be regarded as not very neat, since it combines a more substantive idealist perspective that promotes communication with a thinner realist perspective that promotes coexistence. To put it in Gray's terms, I suggest that the two faces of liberalism can be reconciled by assigning them different roles at different stages of deliberation and adjudication on the place of religion in the public sphere. More concretely, when devising general policies one should strive to promote communication while

The chapter is organized in the following way: in the first section, I will compare and contrast AS's diagnosis of strong religion as a threat to secular states with my diagnosis of religion as a symptom of the crisis within secular states. In the second section, I will compare and contrast AS's prognosis, consisting in ruling out religion in the public sphere, with my own position, consisting in promoting communication and mutual understanding, over the long run, and securing coexistence in cases of persistent disagreement and conflict.

## 2.2. Two Diagnoses

### 2.2.1. Religion as a threat

AS is principally worried about religious movements that challenge secular arrangements directly. In particular, he fears that religion may undermine 'the legal arrangements that claim to be neutral and generally applicable to all people living in the national community'.[7] In a nutshell, the challenge is as follows: religion forces secular legal systems to agree on compromises and concessions that imperil the integrity and coherence of secular laws. An example would be the growing encroachment on freedom of expression for the sake of protecting religious sensibilities. As a sign of the half-hearted and meek response of secularism, AS adduces the continued existence of blasphemy laws that partly excuse the blurred boundary between free expression and the protection of religion. The saga of the Danish cartoons teaches us, AS argues, that secularism is weak and open to compromises and concessions that European secular states should firmly and clearly refuse to make, and that they should so refuse on the basis that religion does not have a place in the public sphere and that we should protect what we really value. As a consequence, he welcomed the abolition of the blasphemy law which, following a thirty-year campaign, the UK government finally introduced/ implemented on 8 May 2008.[8]

---

offering a default position in case of a breakdown. When deciding precise cases, one should evaluate the attempt to promote communication and mutual understanding. However, when disagreement is persistent and turns into a deadlock, then one should rely on the default rules of the game and accept coexistence as second best. Much of this position depends on the definition of genuine conflicts between religion and secular states. I attempt this exercise in ch. 2.

[7] Sajó, 'Preliminaries to a Concept of Constitutional Secularism', 605.

[8] Sajó, 'Preliminaries to a Concept of Constitutional Secularism', 611 n. 13 (referring to the Criminal Justice and Immigration Act, 2008, *c.* 4, par 79 (Eng)).

Yet, there is something lost in translation in this picture. As far as the UK is concerned, the abolition of the blasphemy law must be read in conjunction with the Racial and Religious Hatred Act 2006, which deals with the balance between free speech and the right to be shielded from hatred. In section 29J, after having defined what amounts to expression and behaviour that stirs up religious hatred, the act states:

Nothing in this Part shall be read or given effect in a way which prohibits or restricts discussion, criticism or expressions of antipathy, dislike, ridicule, insult or abuse of particular religions or the beliefs or practices of their adherents, or of any other belief system or the beliefs or practices of its adherents, or proselytising or urging adherents of a different religion or belief system to cease practising their religion or belief system.

The Racial and Religious Hatred Act 2006 defines away the conflict by setting what I call a presumption of priority. Free speech still sets the tone for the context in which we express ourselves. We presume that our words are free even when we want to criticize or ridicule another religion. The Act, nonetheless, carves out an egregious exception, which concerns behaviour and expression that intends to provoke religious hatred. How do we know what falls in the latter category? This is part of a longer story that has yet to unfold in the years to come and concerns the relationship between various groups in a society. The best we can do is to avoid predetermining that relationship as a conflict.

In Europe, it is true that free speech and secularism play a paramount role in society, and that there is a presumption in favour of liberty. However, courts do draw a line at a certain point; the ECtHR, for example, confronted the issue of blasphemy in the seminal case, *Otto Preminger Institute v Austria*.[9] The case concerned a film that portrayed the Christian holy family in highly derogatory terms. The ECtHR had to decide whether the administrative sanction preventing the screening of the movie was in breach of Article 10 of the convention, or whether it was justified on the ground of protecting religious feelings. Strasbourg argued that the administrative sanction was justified because the film risked provoking a strong reaction within a predominantly Christian population.

Critics of this decision argue that there is no tension between free speech and the right not to be offended in one's own religion because the latter is not a right, properly speaking.[10] If there is a right not to be offended or harmed by other people's words, this must apply to any feeling, not only religious

---

[9] *Otto Preminger Institute v Austria*, 295 ECtHR (ser A) (1994).
[10] See Ronald Dworkin, 'The Right to Ridicule', *NY Rev Books* (23 March 2006), 29.

ones. We can be offended as football supporters, political partisans, and so on. There is nothing special about religion that warrants an ad hoc protection. This may be true on political grounds. It is arguably hard to single out an independent political reason for religion's special protection. After all, other forms of association could claim equal protection. In other words, it is difficult to show why, as a matter of principle, religion should receive different treatment. However, it is not so difficult on prudential grounds. Religion can inspire large crowds by stimulating their deepest feelings of attachment and identity. Religious people are particularly susceptible to offence and are very keen on responding to the perceived harm with any means, be they legal or illegal.

We learn, quickly, that part of the problem lies with the notion of secularism itself. AS bemoans the fact that we lack a strong normative theory of secularism to underpin our legal systems, and he attempts to fill this gap by offering his own brand of constitutional secularism. He begins this endeavour with an anatomy of secularism and secularization. Secularism is defined by AS as a social fact and as a feature of constitutionalism. We also learn that it stands for an ambiguous social reality, and that it is uncertain as a legal concept. AS then defines secularization as 'a historical project still in the making'. In essence, for AS, it is about religion and its organizations 'ceding some of their power over various aspects of life in favor of the state'.[11]

To define secularization as a historical project is problematic. Yet, as Olivier Roy points out, secularization is 'a social *phenomenon* that requires no political implementation'.[12] It takes place gradually as religion loses its position at the centre of human lives. Understood this way, secularization is not about the power relation between state and church but about the gradual waning of religion in society. The advantage of this definition is that it explains the difference between secularization, as a process, and the notion of secularism, which is a political project with a set of normative claims concerning the way in which the state deals with diversity. Secularism and secularization may go hand in hand, as was the case in Europe until the end of last century. The resurgence of religion, however, raises doubts as to the direction of the political project, on one hand, and of the social process, on the other.

One illustration of secularism in its strongest and most aggressive form is the French notion of *laïcité*. This is characterized by two separate elements: legal *laïcité* and ideological *laïcité*. The former consists of 'a very strict

---

[11] Sajó, 'Preliminaries to a Concept of Constitutional Secularism', 609.
[12] Olivier Roy, *Secularism Confronts Islam* (Columbia University Press, 2007), 7 (emphasis added).

separation of church and state, against the backdrop of a political conflict
between the state and the Catholic Church that resulted in a law regulating
very strictly the presence of religion in the public sphere (1905)'.[13] The latter
'claims to provide a value system common to all citizens by expelling religion
into the private sphere'.[14] AS suggests that a preferable version of constitutional secularism would be an aggressive type (close to *laïcité*) capable of
responding to religion and its presence in the public sphere. But in Europe
*laïcité* is clearly an exception. No state other than France has an equally strong
commitment to both the legal and ideological elements of separation between
church and state. No other state has entrenched a secularist principle,
constitutionally, except Turkey.[15] In northern Europe, secularism is not
present as a legal or constitutional doctrine (in fact, many states have an
established church, as in the UK or Denmark). But these societies were
gradually secularized, without open confrontation with religious institutions.

   An additional problem for a comparative constitutional theory of secularism is that it can hardly account for experiences outside of the Western world.
The notion of secularism is deeply intertwined with local practices and
histories in the West, as Charles Taylor has powerfully demonstrated.[16]
In addition, to propound a truly general theory of constitutional secularism
becomes an uphill struggle. AS, no doubt, is aware of the importance of local
history and other contingencies in the formation of the Western understanding of secularism. In fact, he explains the weaknesses of secularism in terms
of its many different facets, which makes it a 'fuzzy constitutional concept'.
But for AS this does not constitute an obstacle for the definition of a concept
of constitutional secularism.

   If secularism is weak and uncertain because of its local rootedness, secularization is only a half-hearted compromise, according to AS. In the majority of
legal and political systems the project of secularization has never been coherently conceived and brought forward. The relationship between church and
state has been dealt with, typically, through numerous compromises and
concessions thought to be compatible with secularism itself. Unfortunately,

---

[13] Roy, *Secularism confronts Islam*, xii.
[14] Roy, *Secularism confronts Islam*, xiv.
[15] The Constitution of the Republic of Turkey mentions explicitly the principle of secularism
ten times in the main text, <http://www.hri.org/docs/turkey>.
[16] Charles Taylor, *A Secular Age* (Harvard University Press, 2007), 15. As a consequence, it
scarcely makes sense to speak of Indian secularism as something *comparable* to Western experience.
For a different perspective, see Rajeev Bhargava, 'States, Religious Diversity, and the Crisis of
Secularism', *The Hedgehog Review*, <http://www.opendemocracy.net/rajeev-bhargava/states-reli-
gious-diversity-and-crisis-of-secularism-0>. Bhargava argues that the West should learn from the
Indian experience of secularism.

AS argues, the project of secularization does not lead us anywhere, given that it fails to display the intellectual consistency required to achieve any project for freeing the public sphere from religion. The problem with this position, as already pointed out, is that secularization is not an intellectual project but an organic development of a society in response to the gradual waning of religion in people's lives. Secularization does not set standards according to which the public sphere can be considered a neutral space. Rather, it mirrors a gradual development; thus, by definition, it will always be a less-than-fully-realized process. Moreover, local contingencies, to a great extent, shape national policies concerning religion.

Indeed, European secular states respond very differently to the alleged threat of religion. Some believe in top-down strategies, where secularism is imposed as a necessary medicine. So, for example, France was quick to enact a statute on the ban of Islamic headscarves from public institutions. Others have a more laissez-faire approach. They believe that we should leave ample room for manoeuvre by individuals and communities. Bright-line rules in this area look suspicious and limit freedom in a perilous way. Thus the UK, Denmark, Holland, and the Scandinavian countries are reluctant to tighten the screws on expressions of religious fundamentalism. AS is disappointed with the latter responses more than with the former. He advocates a stronger, more aggressive, more self-confident form of secularism.[17]

Recent events seem to vindicate his concerns. In the UK, the issue of the veil was brought out in public by then Foreign Affairs Minister Jack Straw (in 2006), while in Denmark the cartoons of Mohammed created much unrest in the population, and the state had to take this into account. In Holland, the murder of Theo Van Gogh made the Dutch people question their own liberal attitudes towards religion. Does this mean that the right response to religion is a more aggressive attitude on the part of the secular state? This is hardly the case. France has not responded to the threat posed by social instability in the suburbs. More generally, France is still struggling with its social problems. The country seems incapable of assimilating a large majority of its immigrants despite its aggressive integration policies. *Laïcité* was strong when its legal and ideological elements worked in unison. If the state and society agree that religion is to be kept out of the public sphere, then *laïcité* works fairly smoothly and effectively. But that is not the case anymore, when legal *laïcité* imposed by the state is not immediately accepted by the whole of society. The fact of imposing on all a single precise view of the world only exacerbates the divisions among the different elements of society.

---

[17] Sajó, 'Preliminaries to a Concept of Constitutional Secularism', 615.

European secular states are incapable of responding effectively to the increasing claims of religion. AS's diagnosis consists in singling out strong religion as a discrete threat that needs to be tackled head on. I want to suggest that there is something wrong with AS's diagnosis. The actual problem is not religion but the secular state's inability to cope with diversity. The secular state is unable to foster mutual understanding and create an appropriate framework of coexistence for the whole society under conditions of pluralism.

Religion's revival is not a disease but simply a symptom of the crisis confronting the secular state. Religion understands that the next challenge is not at the level of the state but at another level. Supranational pressures increasingly reveal that the state is no longer the best form of organization for our societies. The struggle for the soul of Europe has moved from the level of the state to the European level. Hence the heated debate provoked by the reference to Christian values in the European Constitution. As Olivier Roy rightly points out: 'Religion today is participating, in the same way as the construction of Europe is, in the disassembly of the spaces that created the modern nation-state.'[18] Perhaps the European patient suffers from a deeper disease than religion. It would not be enough to eradicate that putative cancer when the whole of the European body politic is ill. Thus, one is compelled to ask: what is the nature of this crisis?

## 2.2.2. Religion as a symptom of the crisis of the secular state

The secular state is in a difficult position. It barely copes with diversity and the fact of pluralism. And yet there is no alternative. Economically, this state is dependent upon immigration. Politically, it can hardly create barriers and walls of separation between the West and the rest of the world. Socially, the state is unable to keep together its own population, which is increasingly atomized. It does not come as a surprise that religion is not welcome; yet, it keeps knocking at the door with increasingly more difficult demands. And the impossibility of satisfying them only increases the gap between different segments of society, which is thus more and more polarized. This is, in a nutshell, what can be called the crisis of the secular state.

European secular states vary considerably when it comes to the management of diversity. France firmly believes in the assimilation of everyone under the umbrella of republican values.[19] Unfortunately, believing is one thing;

---

[18] Roy, *Secularism confronts Islam*, 12.

[19] For an excellent study of France's republican position see C Laborde, *Critical Republicanism: The Hijab Controversy and Political Philosophy* (Oxford University Press, 2008).

succeeding, another. Assimilationist strategies want to minimize cultural difference in order to maximize social unity at state level. Article 1 of the French Constitution 1958 is crystal-clear: 'France shall be an indivisible, secular, democratic and social Republic. It shall ensure the equality of all citizens before the law, without distinction of origin, race or religion. It shall respect all beliefs. It shall be organized on a decentralized basis.' The unity of the nation, its indivisibility, is the paramount principle of the Constitution. In order to guarantee unity, the republic proclaims itself to be blind with regard to religion. The second principle, tellingly, is that of *laïcité*. As a consequence, the law is also blind when it comes to differences of origin, race, or religion. One may think that all of this is desirable, that we can only be truly free and equal if everyone is treated as a free and equal person by the neutral state. However, to turn a blind eye to the reality of difference is deeply problematic.

If the state, as an abstract entity, can pretend to be neutral, it does not go without saying that the people constituting the state and society will behave in like manner. Discrimination in all spheres is widespread in France. One example, above all, is the failure of the dream of 'les cités'—the building blocks erected in the suburbs of cities all around France. Initially conceived as living experiments where everyone would become French, they slowly became ghettos, where the lowliest people in society are now gathered. The crisis of the assimilationist state begins here in the *banlieues*. Here, religion has its strongest pull. Thus fundamentalism grows in places where the secular state wanted to erase diversity and propagate republican values. By involuntarily creating these new communities in the *banlieues*, the French state shred its 'Rousseauist myth of a republic where there is nothing between the state and the citizen-individual in his isolation'.[20]

At the opposite end of the spectrum lie multicultural strategies. Diversity matters in this case. Cultural communities are allowed to form and flourish. The state does not impose a single model or a set of republican values. It protects a general freedom to live according to one's own cultural and social norms so long as nobody abuses his or her freedom or interferes with someone else's lifestyle. Recent events, however, have challenged this model, probably even more than they have the French model. Multicultural states such as Britain, Denmark, and Holland have witnessed events that have made them ponder their own commitment to cultural diversity. After the terrorist attacks in London perpetrated by British Muslims, the reaction was clear and painful. The then prime minister was reduced to insisting on British values,

---

[20] Roy, *Secularism Confronts Islam*, 97.

as if to rekindle the French Rousseauist myth, hoping to instil those values in all of society.[21]

The fact of pluralism is beyond dispute. Yet, it is a double-edged sword; it has advantages but also drawbacks. Western societies have become less parochial and have opened up to an ever-greater range of cultures and experiences. Within this framework, each individual is capable of choosing the life that best suits his values. But communication among the various groups and individuals is not always easy to achieve. The starting premises are, more often than not, different and the risk of talking at cross-purposes is high. Can we really agree on what dignity entails if one person believes it is an eminently religious notion and another believes that it is at the foundation of secular morality? For the former, God is the ultimate source of good. For the latter, God is absent from the picture, and all that matters is the self-determination of the individual. The greatest risk is polarization exacerbated by a breakdown in communications.[22]

It is important to stress, however, that such polarization is not a consequence of the rise of religion. Of course, religion contributes to it; in fact, it thrives in this environment in which it exploits division and disagreement. But religion is not the cause of polarization. The real cause is to be found in the inability of the secular state to cope with the fact of pluralism, or, to put it differently, with diversity. The unity and cohesion of our Western societies is not threatened by external agents; it is threatened, principally, from within. It is not a clash of civilizations; it is a clash within.[23]

A clash within is characterized by an oscillation between passivity and aggression. AS defends the swing of the pendulum towards a more aggressive assertion of our values vis-à-vis religion. He believes that secularism, as we presently understand it, is fraught with uncertainty and shabby compromises; he seeks, instead, a more aggressive and self-confident constitutional secularism which will be up to the task of coping with any (strong) religion that undermines the unity and cohesion of our polities. AS's position is explicable in the present context, as we move from an essentially tolerant state to an exclusive one. In part, he acknowledges the weaknesses of the secular state but then wants to remedy these by appealing to a common notion of

---

[21] See Tony Blair, UK prime minister, Address on Multiculturalism and Integration (8 December 2006), <http://ukingermany.fco.gov.uk/en/news/?view=Speech&id=4616073>.

[22] Even a liberalism of coexistence à la Gray accepts that there are ruptures in communication; however, he believes that the general legal, political framework will suffice. I believe that that can only work as a default position when communication breaks down, and disagreement is pervasive and persistent.

[23] See Martha Nussbaum, *The Clash Within: Democracy, Religious Violence, and India's Future* (Harvard University Press, 2007).

constitutional secularism the task of which would be primarily to police the area of reasonable positions and exclude those that do not meet these standards of reasonableness. However, the problem is that the less-than-reasonable positions thrive because the secular state has failed to integrate them in the first place. So our failure to include people becomes a ground for excluding them.

Part of the problem is that from the outset we never acknowledged the fragmentation of our values. We still believe that we live in fairly harmonious societies, in principle at least, and we point to our constitutions when we need support for this claim. Lacking a cohesive society, we agree that our fallback position—which, after all, is what unites us—is our constitutional order. After all, people do display constitutional patriotism. AS stretches this idea to bear on the question of the place of religion in the public sphere. He believes that behind our local and historical differences in religious matters, we do share a common constitutional commitment to secularism.[24]

Conflicts of values, and of world-views, have shaped all our societies since their inception. We oscillate between the proliferation of conflicts and their adjudication. When they become unmanageable, we resort to an external adjudicator that interrupts the conflict by the use of force. AS, following Richard Rorty, calls it a conversation stopper.[25] If we need to resort to this strategy, however, we have already accepted the decadence of our society and of our secular state. A good sign of a healthy polity is to be able to cope with disagreement without falling to pieces. AS proposes to exclude religion, the *agent provocateur*, so that we can put those pieces back together. By suggesting that, he misses the target. The European patient requires a different medicine.

What can secular law achieve under these circumstances? It all depends. If we were to follow AS's diagnosis, then secular law can do very little. It may raise its voice and impose bright-line rules on how to use religious arguments in public. However, it does not seem able to cope with pluralism and diversity in the matter of values. We will see, in the next section, that the prognosis offered by AS is all about eradicating the threat of religion. But this will not solve the larger problem plaguing the secular state: its inability to accept responsibility for its failure to manage diversity. If one accepts this diagnosis, religion may be regarded more as a symptom than as an illness. It is a symptom that we nevertheless have to tackle and to which we must respond.

---

[24] More on this in the second section of this chapter.

[25] Sajó, 'Preliminaries to a Concept of Constitutional Secularism', 629. Sajó does not acknowledge, however, that Rorty changed his own position on the matter. See Richard Rorty, 'Religion in the Public Square: A Reconsideration', Journal of Religious Ethics 31 (2003), 141.

However, the strategy cannot be local and aimed solely at the eradication of that symptom. The stakes are much higher: they involve reasserting the conditions for cohabitation, on one hand, and communication, on the other.

## 2.3. Two Prognoses

Any response to religion will be based, inevitably, on an evaluation of the threat that it represents. AS's diagnosis insists that religion is the major problem for society, one we have to tackle head on. His prognosis demands that we perform a surgical operation to remove religion from our public spaces. The intervention would take place at two levels, involving a more self-assertive notion of secular reason as the sole expression of legitimate authority and a reaffirmation of popular sovereignty as the sole source of legitimate authority. This double medicine, AS argues, is mandated by secularism.

An alternative prognosis follows from an acknowledgement of the crisis of the secular state in Europe. Religion cannot be regarded as the sole culprit in social tensions and unrest. The problem is much deeper and more complicated, and it needs to be addressed with a holistic and innovative attitude that should be fully capable of embracing the facts of pluralism and diversity. This prognosis can only work on a long-term basis. It is not an intrusive operation going to the core of our society to eradicate evil; it is a cognitive process that requires everyone's participation. One problem remains, and it concerns a strategy adopted in the present cases. Conflicts about what secularism entails are real and cannot simply be dismissed. At times, it will be possible to reach a sound compromise. On other occasions, we will have to agree to disagree and resort to a default position that aims at coexistence on the basis of the clear rules of the game. In what follows, I will sketch and compare these two strategies.

### 2.3.1. Constitutional secularism as a direct response to religion

AS's notion of constitutional secularism could also be called strong or exclusive secularism. Its central concern is to exclude religion from the political realm. To achieve this objective, it is prepared to use strong remedies and to draw bright lines, where religion asks for compromise or concessions. Before studying what constitutional secularism requires, we need to know what constitutional secularism means.

After complaining about the weaknesses and ambiguities of secularism resulting from its uncertainty, AS takes us by surprise when he suggests that it is possible to identify a common core to the concept. This is all the more surprising, as AS repeatedly acknowledges that secularism '*has no clear standing among constitutional values*'.[26] This means two things: on the one hand, it means that secularism does not figure as a constitutional norm but for one very limited exception. On the other, it suggests that secularism does not correspond to any other values of constitutional status. Despite all this, AS still firmly claims that 'certain fundamental demands of constitutionalism propose and demand secularism'.[27] Now, this may well be true from a purely normative viewpoint. But it does not tell us anything about the way in which different constitutional practices converge towards that common core.

The theoretical path proposed for reaching a definition of the concept of constitutional secularism is as follows: the starting point is represented by the many different local conceptions of secularism, which do not seem to have much in common. The end point is the concept of constitutional secularism as 'there seems to be enough commonality among these [conceptions] to allow us to construe the shared principles that form secularism'.[28] It is very hard to understand how AS comes to this conclusion since, in the first part of the Article in question, he has stressed the importance of local contingencies and histories. It is unclear, therefore, whether the concept of constitutional secularism is a top-down, purely normative concept, which comes from AS's own peculiar understanding of constitutionalism and its fundamental requirements, or whether it is a bottom-up, experience-based concept, which derives from the distillation of discrete local constitutional attempts to regulate the relationship between law and religion. It would be possible to speculate endlessly on this ambiguous starting position. It is better, however, to move on and ask what animates AS's position and what its central question is.

The central issue for AS is political. This seems to be a more promising context in which to analyse the problem. A more precise question could be the following: what is the place of religion in the public sphere? Of course, there is little agreement on how to define the public sphere.[29] Nonetheless, many people in Europe would agree, at least, on this initial question because of our histories and practices. The question, as pointed out, is political. It is not theological or philosophical—that is, it is not about testing the theological or philosophical assumptions behind one position or another. It is about us, deciding what kind of polity we want and, with it, what kind of law

---

[26] Sajó, 'Preliminaries to a Concept of Constitutional Secularism', 621 (emphasis in original).
[27] Sajó, 'Preliminaries to a Concept of Constitutional Secularism', 621.
[28] Sajó, 'Preliminaries to a Concept of Constitutional Secularism', 621.
[29] Habermas, however, makes a monumental effort to paint a subtle picture of it. See J Habermas, *The Structural Transformation of the Public Sphere* (MIT Press, 1991).

and what kind of institutions it requires. AS is right to point out that this is the central question. He is wrong, however, when he claims that the answer should be biased in favour of secular positions, as this is already the case. In Europe, we know already that a statute or a judicial decision cannot be prefaced or justified on any religious ground. But crucially, the fact that the official public sphere is religion-free does not and cannot imply that religion should stay out of any public space. It is because Europe is already biased in favour of secularism that we have to be particularly careful when we strike the balance between secular law and religion.

AS's constitutional secularism, however, strikes the balance in the harshest way: religion should stay out of the public sphere and, in particular, out of politics. AS suggests that we should reassert political authority as religion-free. Without secularism there is no constitutionalism, AS tells us. This position presents three problems. Firstly, it seems to universalize a local understanding. AS's constitutional secularism, with its strong legal and ideological components, reminds us of the French version of *laïcité*. However, as I argued previously, French *laïcité* is a very peculiar exception in Europe, and there are no reasons why other European states would be better off with it. Secondly, it does not provide a solution for the tension between constitutional abstract principles and local, contingent understandings of secularism. AS merely asserts that there are enough commonalities to construe a concept of constitutional secularism. Yet there is neither evidence nor argument to this effect. If anything, AS convincingly persuades us that local contingencies and histories are extremely important to the understanding of secularism. Thirdly, it presents a chicken-and-egg problem: does constitutionalism mandate secularism or vice versa? AS suggests, at one point, that constitutionalism mandates secularism,[30] only to assert, later on, that secularism is a precondition for the existence of a constitutional order.[31] Is there, then, a concept of constitutional secularism? The answer so far seems to be negative. But let us assume that constitutional secularism represents a common European position. What would that require the secular state to do?

Two main requirements characterize AS's constitutional secularism. Firstly, it mandates secular reasoning to the total exclusion of religious arguments as the only form of expression; secondly, it asserts popular sovereignty to the

---

[30] Sajó, 'Preliminaries to a Concept of Constitutional Secularism', 620 ('secularism as a dictate of constitutionalism').

[31] Sajó, 'Preliminaries to a Concept of Constitutional Secularism', 626 ('Secularism mandates a constitutional arrangement where autonomous critical reasons are to be respected as foundational for communal coexistence and self-regulation').

total exclusion of any other source of power, in particular divine power. Let us examine these in turn.

Secular reason, AS tells us, springs from the Enlightenment. It requires that a polity be based on reasons open to acceptance by all. Since religious reasons are not accessible to non-religious people, this would constitute a burden for them and communication would be impossible. As a result, AS tells us, we should exclude categorically religious reason from the public sphere. Moreover, secular reason rules out religion from legislation and other official pronouncements. Secular reason is also central to the comprehension of human rights as these refer to a 'homocentric world and to ways of thought freed from transcendentalist premises'.[32]

There are several problems with AS's understanding of secular public reason. First of all, he fails to draw an important distinction between secular reason and public reason, which is clearly drawn, at least by John Rawls, in 'the idea of public reason revisited'.[33] Secular reason is based on comprehensive non-religious views. Secular reason and secular values are much broader than public reason. Public reason is based on political conceptions that meet Rawls's carefully crafted conditions: 'their principles apply to basic political institutions; they can be presented independently from comprehensive doctrines of any kind; they can be worked out from fundamental ideas seen as implicit in the public political culture of a constitutional regime'.[34] Even if Rawls's distinction is not accepted by everyone, AS does not seem to disagree: 'Secularism—and not only because of its intimate relation with the Enlightenment—mandates a constitutional arrangement where autonomous critical reasons are to be respected as foundational for communal coexistence and self-regulation.'[35] He genuinely believes that secular public reason is our common comprehensive doctrine at the foundation of Western political systems.

The trouble is that secular reason, as a comprehensive doctrine, is not shared by everyone in our societies, as there are other competing comprehensive doctrines, mainly religious ones. How does one find a compromise between religious and non-religious comprehensive views without appealing to secular reasons? That is the question that preoccupies Rawls, though it does not seem to preoccupy AS in the least. This explains why AS does not hesitate to call religious arguments a burden on non-religious people. But the

[32] Sajó, 'Preliminaries to a Concept of Constitutional Secularism', 625.

[33] John Rawls, 'The Idea of Public Reason Revisited' in Rawls, *The Law of People* (Harvard University Press, 1999), 143–4.

[34] Rawls, 'The Idea of Public Reason Revisited', 143.

[35] Sajó, 'Preliminaries to a Concept of Constitutional Secularism', 626.

problem is that our societies impose secular burdens on religious people without paying the slightest attention to religious arguments. Hence, AS's suggestion to exclude religious arguments totally has an authoritarian ring.[36]

If it is true that official legislation and case law should not display religious arguments, this clearly does not apply to all the arguments in the public sphere. Habermas successfully distinguishes between different layers of the public sphere. The most general distinction is that between an official and a non-official public sphere. In the latter, the presence of religious arguments should be accepted. In due course, religious arguments should be translated or supported by non-religious reasons so that other people may also benefit from them. These two provisos have been advanced by Habermas and Rawls, respectively. They both acknowledge, however, that this does create an asymmetry between religious and non-religious people. Habermas, therefore, adds that non-religious people should be required to confront arguments originating from religious views with a more open mind and a greater willingness to learn from them.

Ultimately, AS's suggestion that secular public reason is the only ground for human rights is deeply controversial. In Western democracies, there is no agreement on the issue of the foundation of human rights. Many scholars, however, recognize that human rights do have much in common with our Christian roots, even if they depart from them.[37] For all these reasons, AS's notion of secular public reason is highly problematic.

Let us now examine the second requirement of constitutional secularism: popular sovereignty as a source of power to the exclusion of religion. AS argues that 'popular sovereignty means that all power in the state originates from people, therefore *it cannot originate from the sacred*'.[38] The connection between secularism and popular sovereignty is not a common feature of European states and certainly not universal. In the UK, for example, the idea that sovereignty is deeply linked to secularism is simply not true: the Queen is also the head of the Church of England.[39]

---

[36] See Camil Ungureanu, 'The Contested Relation between Democracy and Religion: Towards a Dialogical Perspective?', Eur J Pol Theory, 7 (2008), 405.

[37] See eg Michael J Perry, *Toward a Theory of Human Rights: Religion, Law, Courts* (Cambridge University Press, 2006).

[38] Sajó, 'Preliminaries to a Concept of Constitutional Secularism', 627 (emphasis in original).

[39] To explain the connection between popular sovereignty and secularism, Sajó resorts to the example of post-revolutionary France. See Sajó, 'Preliminaries to a Concept of Constitutional Secularism', 627. Needless to say, this example is based on a local history that hardly represents states other than France itself. This confirms, if need be, that Sajó's constitutional secularism is a disguised generalization of the French experience.

More importantly, the argument from popular sovereignty hardly resists criticism. What if the people themselves were to seek a greater role for religion in the public sphere? Of course, they would not be able to alienate their own sovereignty, but they certainly would be able to appoint more religion-friendly officials. The story of Turkey, where secularism in a strong form has been constitutionalized since the times of Ataturk, is paradigmatic in this context. The conflict between religion and the secular state is at its peak when it involves political parties. The role of religion in politics is often ambiguous. Christian parties are a traditional feature of European political systems. But what would be the legal status of Islamic parties? Are they all to be banned because they promote sharia law and Islamic values? Or should we distinguish between moderate and authoritarian parties? It would seem logical to allow for the representation of Muslim Europeans through political parties provided they respect the basic conditions of our political orders: democracy, fundamental rights, and rule of law. Against this background, it is somehow perplexing to observe a string of cases coming from Turkey and dealing with the dissolution of Islamic parties. The leading case is *Refah Partisi*.[40] However, the currently ruling party, Justice and Development Party (Adalet ve Kalkınma Partisi, the AKP), has also been the object of scrutiny of the Turkish Constitutional Court (TCC).

In conclusion, AS's prognosis is problematic for several reasons. The concept of constitutional secularism has shaky theoretical foundations and cannot represent a truly common European position. Moreover, its pre-requisites, namely secular reason and popular sovereignty, yield very controversial positions that do not take seriously religious people. In the following, I will suggest that a better prognosis follows from an altogether different diagnosis. Religion is not the prime problem of the secular state. The secular state itself is in search of a better foundation. Religion is there to remind the state that it constantly needs to articulate its normative premises. From this viewpoint, religion may even help the state in its endeavour of becoming stronger vis-à-vis growing numbers of conflicts between various constitutive parts of society.

## 2.3.2. The secular state and diversity

To suggest that religion is the problem, and its exclusion from the public sphere the solution, is misleading—indeed wishful—thinking: misleading,

---

[40] *Refah Partisi (The Welfare Party) and ors v Turkey*, 13 February 2003, Application nos 41340/98, 41342/98, 41343/98, and 41344/98.

because it misses the real problem, that is, the crisis of the secular state; wishful, because it promises to resolve a major social problem of communication between groups simply by imposing a conversation stopper. The secular state is unable to cope with the fact of pluralism. Rawls's agonizing question captures the mood well: 'How is it possible—or is it—for those of faith, as well as the nonreligious (secular), to endorse a constitutional regime even when their comprehensive doctrines may not prosper under it, and indeed may decline?'[41]

Secular and religious views can scarcely coexist without clashing with one another. AS suggests that the game should be won by the secular side. However, it is difficult to see how this squares with his claim that constitutional secularism is more than freedom from religion. It is also necessary for the maximization of freedom of religion. Even if this appears at first as an attempt to present constitutional secularism as an all-encompassing doctrine, it is clear that so many different goals are not jointly achievable. Here lies the weakness of constitutional secularism and of any other comprehensive view that attempts to reconcile many different and competing interests. The most egregious ones are protected by fundamental rights. The conflicts arising between them serve to illustrate the problem.

Freedom of religion clashes with freedom from religion, the case of the Islamic headscarf providing a possible illustration. Freedom of expression clashes with the right not to be offended in one's own religious feelings; think of the Danish cartoons. Freedom of association for political parties based on religious views clashes with secular constitutional requirements; this is what happened in several Turkish cases involving the Refah Partisi and subsequently the AKP. And so on. Some of these conflicts can be defined away or avoided. Many strategies are available and do produce local results. But is a common strategy possible?

Many still believe in the possibility of reaching an area of consensus, where we free ourselves from our ideological assumptions and exchange arguments on a level playing field. Rawls's attempt to carve out a space for reasonable political views fits that bill precisely. Yet it is unclear whether he succeeds in this attempt. And more importantly, the stakes of this game are unclear. Political liberalism aims at a political level playing field. But religion in Europe may be interested in something more than the political game. It does not really want to conquer political institutions because it understands the crisis of the nation state and contributes to it by pushing the boundaries and by playing with the state's many contradictions and potential conflicts.

---

[41] See Rawls, 'The Idea of Public Reason Revisited', 151.

However, religion is very much interested in the social game. It wants to conquer the people. It thrives in local communities and aspires to create global ones. An example is the idea of the *Umma* as a global community of believers. Another example is Pope Benedict XVI's suggestion that Christian values should be at the core of the European civil society.[42]

Religion may even leave to the state the political arena of institutional exchange and official communication. In this domain, reasonableness applies all the way through and excludes, in principle, comprehensive views that cannot be shared by all. Religion, however, does not give up its pursuit of truth and the relevance of its comprehensive doctrine for humanity. So it claims a place, and already plays a role, in the unofficial public sphere. It promulgates its message on a global level, not at state level. The real problem is that the secular state, at the national level, is struggling with the fact of pluralism and does not appear to be able to provide viable solutions. Inevitably it resorts to the next level, the European level. At the judicial level, the ECtHR has already been solicited in a growing number of ways to address the claims of religious minorities. The response has not always been satisfactory. The court started well with the *Kokkinakis* case, where the ban on religious proselytism in Greece was limited on the ground of respect for religious freedom: one religion cannot hold and control a monopoly on the sacred. But lately, strict secular arrangements prohibiting the political association of moderate religious people in Turkey were upheld, at least in the *Refah Partisi* case.

The goal of constitutional doctrines should be modified. They all aim at consensus and struggle to impose a model that would create the conditions for reaching it either procedurally or substantively. The more we insist on building consensus and convergence, the more we end up with shabby compromises, at best, and with alienated minorities, at worst. Our societies have too many overlapping and competing interests to defend. We have to accept that diversity and dissent are the underlying themes of our societies. The goal should not be to promote consensus at all costs. The goal should be dual and complex. Consensus should be sought as far as possible, on one hand. But, on the other, diversity should also be promoted and dissent permitted as much as possible. In other words, Europe should accept the possibility of conflict as a way of life, as its central tenet, and as its engine for change.

It will not be easy to agree on fundamental values. Comprehensive views will not give up their exclusive claims to truth. It is also very hard to agree on

---

[42] See Joseph Ratzinger, *Without Roots: The West, Relativism, Christianity, and Islam* (Basic Books 2006). He stressed time and again that there is no tension between religion and the secular state.

a few selected values applying to the political realm from the viewpoint of reasonableness. However, it may be possible to agree on the rules of the game. The game is diversity and dissent, and the rules must be such that diversity and dissent do not produce violence and social strife. We already have those rules in the form of bills of rights and the case law they produced. These rules are broad enough, and yet specific enough, to include everyone without requesting any agreement as to background values.

Sometimes it will be possible to reconcile competing claims. At other times, we will have to acknowledge that certain conflicts of rights not only embody disagreement over basic values but that they also indicate the existence of a deadlock—a situation in which we cannot reach a solution without compromising something of value.[43] In these cases, we face a dilemma. How should the rules of the game deal with dilemmas? There is no fixed answer to that. Some legal systems will opt for legislative solutions; others for judicial ones. Others still will strike a balance between the two, or seek a solution using other methods such as direct democracy in the form of a referendum.

The way in which dilemmas are adjudicated, however, is only a contingent issue. What is more important is to acknowledge and accept the existence of dilemmas and conflicts between the values underpinning secularism. To do so, we will have to know more about religious claims and their background culture. In other words, we will initiate a process of mutual understanding. This would be a cognitive process that both could improve our understanding while maintaining an underlying diversity. Only after that process is in place, will one be in a better position to single out or define more precisely the normative conflict faced by the secular state. Neither will it always be possible to explain away the conflicts between such values. In these cases, one will have to agree to disagree and appeal to the rules of the legal political system to settle the conflict. An example will illustrate this process: the issue of hate speech in relation to religious minorities.

Free speech is often regarded as a paramount concern of our liberal democracies. In an age of Mohammad cartoons, one feels more compelled to pay a greater attention to this problem. It does not mean that there is a genuine conflict there. The case is presented as follows:

1. Free speech permits injurious and offensive statements.

2. Injurious and offensive statements against one religion are not permitted.

---

[43] Lorenzo Zucca, *Constitutional Dilemmas: Conflicts of Fundamental Legal Rights in Europe and the USA* (Oxford University Press, 2007).

This case appears very difficult at first. However, to test in a real context we can consider the way in which the Racial and Religious Hatred Act 2006 deals with the balance between free speech and the right to be screened from hatred. In section 29J, after having defined what amounts to expression and behaviour that stirs religious hatred, the Act states:

Nothing in this Part shall be read or given effect in a way which prohibits or restricts discussion, criticism or expressions of antipathy, dislike, ridicule, insult or abuse of particular religions or the beliefs or practices of their adherents, or of any other belief system or the beliefs or practices of its adherents, or proselytising or urging adherents of a different religion or belief system to cease practising their religion or belief system.

The Racial and Religious Hatred Act 2006 defines away the conflict by setting what I call a presumption of priority. Free speech still sets the tone for the context in which we express ourselves. We presume that our words are free even when we want to criticize or ridicule another religion. The Act nevertheless carves out an egregious exception, which concerns behaviour and expression that intends to stir religious hatred. How do we know what activity falls within the latter category? This will be part of a longer story that has to unfold in future years and concerns the relationship between various groups in a society. The best we can do is to avoid prefacing that relationship as a conflict.

What is possible to stress at this point, however, is the following. Fundamental rights adjudication tends to polarize positions into two opposing camps with two discrete arguments that are somehow decontextualized. But if we stop and think about the value of free speech for example, it is clear that everyone has an interest in a background environment free of phobias and prejudices. If thoughts and beliefs are exchanged in a phobia-ridden environment, then the quality of expression is bound to be low, and its nature partisan. If, on the contrary, free exchange of ideas happens in an environment conducive to mutual understanding, then the overall quality of expression will be much higher. If we keep in mind this overall goal, then individual expressions of hatred will somehow be permissible and yet immediately relegated to the dustbin of thoughts by the vast majority of people. Unfortunately, when we are living in a hysterical environment, expressions of hatred are only likely to raise the heat and lower the light.

## 2.4. Conclusion

Religion's place in the European public sphere is a relatively new issue that deserves more attention. AS's heartfelt position attempts to deal with many problems from a comparative constitutionalist perspective. This is, indeed, a good point of departure as the problem is common to most of the European states and cannot be reduced to a national issue. AS's diagnosis, however, can be supported only partially. The responsibility for the open conflict between religion and the secular state cannot be attributed to one side only, namely (strong) religion. AS is, in fact, aware of this and complains in equal measure about the growing claims of religion and the weakness of secular states. His prognosis, however, betrays a more one-sided perspective. The secular state should reassert itself with greater confidence and respond more aggressively to the threat posed by some forms of religion.

I disagree. I believe that strong religious claims are not an isolated cancer that can be removed from societies by adopting a more aggressive counter-position. The crisis of the secular state is deeper and more daunting than that. It requires a holistic response that blends a more substantive strategy, based on increased communication and mutual understanding, with a thinner strategy that works as a default position and aims at mere coexistence in order to respond to actual cases of conflict between religion and the secular state. Increased mutual understanding can only take place in the long term; in the meantime, it is possible to resort to clear rules of the game in order to cope with discrete problems.

My approach is preferable to AS's on two levels: the theoretical and the practical. AS exposed secularism's practical problems, only to claim that these could be solved by developing a stronger, more self-confident, and aggressive theory of constitutional secularism flowing from the mandates of constitutionalism itself. I claim, instead, that those practical problems—actual conflicts between values underpinning secularism—should be taken more seriously in order to modify the attitude with which the secular states respond to the fact of pluralism. Only then can we offer a better theory regarding the place of diversity in the public sphere. My position blends an idealist theory that promotes mutual understanding and a realist theory that promotes coexistence under conditions of prolonged and persistent disagreement. Inclusive secularism must be robust in many ways. Firstly it must be robust in the face of weak secularism that accepts too many shabby compromises: it should constitute a clear practical authority. Secondly, it must be robust in the articulation of its own fundamental tenets: it should be a clear theoretical authority. Thirdly, secularism must be robust but not aggressive. It cannot impose solutions but only propose them. It cannot use the force of violence, but only the force of reason. Finally, secularism must be robust in order to guarantee an environment free from fears and phobias. In the next chapter, the conflict between law and religion will be explored starting from the idea that it is the task of secular law to deal with practical conflicts.

# 3

# Law v Religion[1]

## 3.1. Introduction

On 1 January 2009, the Vatican reformed its system of legal sources. The Lateran pacts of 1929 established that Italian laws will be automatically transposed as valid laws of the Vatican state. Since the beginning of 2009, however, the Vatican has no longer automatically transposed Italian laws. Instead, it is to check each law, one by one, in order to establish whether or not Italian laws are in conflict with Catholic moral principles. The most important aspect of this constitutional revolution is the acknowledgement of an open conflict between secular laws and religious principles. Once this is established the next question is to ask how to deal with those conflicts and, even more crucially, who is to undertake the task of dealing with them. From this viewpoint, the Vatican aims at having the final word on the most pressing moral and political problems. Abortion, euthanasia, stem-cell research, and many other problems would be ultimately and authoritatively adjudicated by the Vatican.

It is necessary to stress at this point that there is a clear difference between a theoretical authority and a practical authority. A theoretical authority tells us what we should believe in; a practical authority tells us how to behave. The Vatican aims at regaining its status as a theoretical authority in moral matters. But it also aims at becoming a practical authority in situations of conflicts by claiming that its moral high ground should take priority over any legal compromise. The confusion between theoretical and practical conflicts should be resisted. To begin with, the search for the truth of theoretical authorities should not be burdened by local compromises imposed by the resolution of practical conflicts. Also, practical conflicts require different skills from theoretical conflicts: they are more about outcomes rather than

[1] This chapter is a revised version of my essay 'Law v Religion' in L Zucca and C Ungureanu (eds), *Law, State and Religion in the New Europe: Debates and Dilemmas* (Cambridge University Press, 2012).

premises. Finally, someone's absolute moral conviction may even be an obstacle to the resolution of a practical conflict that would satisfy individuals with incompatible world-views.

Law's business is to solve practical conflicts. It guides our behaviour in the public sphere and regulates our relationships. Practical conflicts can be very varied. They can be about how to keep a promise in economic transactions or how to guarantee privacy in a world in which communication is virtually limitless. The former is the realm of contract law and the latter is the realm of constitutional law. There are infinite examples, as any law attempts to give guidance under circumstances of conflicting interests. Religion, however, is not interested in every field of law (although this varies according to each religion). Religion is interested in the big moral problems of today's societies. Its natural field of intervention is constitutional law at the level of principles, in particular those principles embedded in constitutional rights. Of course it also deals with family law issues, and at times with criminal law problems. But constitutional rights penetrate every field of law, and they are more open to arguments from morality.

The conflict between law and religion is all-pervasive in the area of practical conflicts. But the relevant literature shows a lot of confusion about the nature of that conflict. The language of conflict is often abused and over-used. Commentators talk about conflicts of rules, principles, values, and even conflicts of identities or clashes of civilizations. In order to avoid such an unstable and vast terminology, I deliberately place my analysis within precise boundaries. The conflicts I am interested in here are practical conflicts—that is, those conflicts that deal with the issue of how to behave under certain circumstances. The core case of practical conflict is when a norm states an obligation to do something and another norm states an obligation not to do that very thing. A classical example is the religious norm that makes it obligatory to wear the Islamic headscarf and the (French) secular norm that makes it obligatory not to wear the Islamic headscarf in public schools. The gist of the conflict between law and religion can be identified with a conflict of obligations stemming from a range of different norms.

There are two main strategies that have characterized the management of practical conflicts between law and religion in secular democracies. The first strategy concerns the scope of law and religion. Modern secular states sharply distinguish between the public and the private sphere. Law rules in the public sphere, whereas religion does so in private assuming that an individual is a believer. This strategy has the advantage of simplicity. But the problem is that religion is asking for a more visible place in the public sphere, while the secular state does not seem to be armed with strong enough arguments to prevent that from happening. Moreover, simplicity is not synonymous with accuracy: religion has always played a role in the public sphere, but it was often considered as complementary to the state and was therefore never opposed. The rise of new religious demands that are at odds with secular laws makes the distinction between private and public spheres increasingly obsolete.

The second strategy deals with the stringency of legal or religious obligations. This requires from the adjudicator a difficult evaluation of the importance of obligations within constitutional frameworks. Sometimes, legal obligations will be deemed as paramount and religious minorities will have to yield to that. So for example, Jehovah's witnesses' refusal of blood transfusions is overridden when it risks jeopardizing one's life. Other times, religious obligations can be recognized as paramount and therefore justify exemptions to existing legal regimes. For example, the obligation not to carry knives is overridden by the Sikh religious obligation to carry their ceremonial knife. In a few cases the conflict is persistent as law and religion fail to justify successfully the priority of one obligation over another. Examples of this situation are many, but the most debated conflict involves the obligations stemming from the so-called right to life and its application to beginning- and end-of-life cases.

This chapter will explore the varieties of practical conflicts between law and religion, starting from the central idea that the core case of conflict is that between obligations stemming from legal or religious norms. The first section will ask the question: what are the conflicts between law and religion? Following on from that interrogation, I will try to deflate the possibility of conflict by suggesting that practical conflicts are better understood and dealt with by using a constitutional framework that understands law in non-transcendental terms. This will be the central question of the second section.

## 3.2. The Varieties of Conflicts

At the core of conflicts between law and religion are obligations. But of course each obligation originates in a different norm. We can build a typology by focusing on the norms that ground conflicting obligations (see Table 3.1.). The most general distinction to draw at this point is that between norms that belong to the same normative system and norms that belong to different normative systems. We therefore have conflicts from within and conflicts from without. An example of the former is the conflict between rights; an example of the latter is the conflict between domestic and foreign norms that requires a sophisticated adjudication based on conflict of laws.

**Table 3.1.** The variety of conflicts (between law and religion)

|                     | Duty-imposing norms  | Power-conferring norms                           |
| ------------------- | -------------------- | ------------------------------------------------ |
| Within the system   | eg conflict of rights | eg authority of arbitration tribunal            |
| Outside the system  | eg conflict of laws  | eg ultimate authority between church and state   |

A second helpful distinction may be that between duty-imposing and power-conferring norms. It is easy to understand how duty-imposing norms may be in conflict since they prescribe specific behaviours that at times are not jointly performable. For example, the right to free speech makes it possible to utter speech that may be injurious. But the right to be protected against racial or religious hatred makes that speech impermissible in principle. It is more difficult at first to see why power-conferring norms could give rise to a conflict between law and religion. However, if we accept that there are conflicts between duty-imposing norms then the next step is to ask who will adjudicate those conflicts. If the adjudicator is a religious institution working as an arbitrator according to the laws of its country, then this arbitrator is likely to reach decisions that impose obligations which conflict with obligations imposed by ordinary laws. For example, the Muslim Arbitration Tribunal may well reach a decision that recognizes *talaq* divorce as permissible, while our legal norms clearly prohibit it. In this case, the source of the conflict is the power-conferring norm granting authority to the institution, but the actual conflict is still between duty-imposing norms.

### 3.2.1. Fundamental rights and the conflict between law and religion

Fundamental rights are the main source of duty-imposing norms leading to conflicts between law and religion. One of the reasons for this is that fundamental rights lack a clear secular foundation. Disagreement between religious and non-religious people about the foundation of fundamental rights is endless and pervasive. A concept like dignity, for example, is very much open to arguments from both sides. The stakes are very high as the interpretation of such a concept is radically different if its foundation is God-based rather than human-based. A God-based conception of dignity would be very static and would essentially prescribe what is not permissible to do to humans. A human-based conception of dignity would be very dynamic and would essentially prescribe what is permissible to do to humans. The lack of foundation makes it impossible to establish a harmonious heaven of values underpinning fundamental rights. If we do not agree on what are the most important properties of fundamental rights that make them so central to our legal political system, we will have great trouble in ranking those rights when they prescribe incompatible behaviours. As a consequence, we will be compelled to accept that any system of fundamental rights is underpinned by a pluralist realm of values.

Another reason for which rights can be conducive to conflicts is their indeterminacy. Rights are cast in very broad and imprecise language that yields very little guidance as to the right way of articulating their claims under specific circumstances. This means that an extensive work of interpretation is necessary. It also means that the label of rights justifies almost any claim as long as one learns to use the language employed to one's own advantage. Religious groups are appealing to rights with increasing frequency in order to claim particular exemptions or privileges. Many secular people see this as a misuse of rights that are regarded as Trojan horses for religious people to encroach upon public policies. The truth is that fundamental rights are indeterminate and that they offer to everyone the possibility of making claims that are merely self-interested. What, then, are these conflicts of rights involving law and religion?

Even if Article 9 ECHR specifically protects religious freedom, the European regime of religion depends on a range of rights spanning Articles 2, 8, 10, 11, and 14 ECHR. Religion has a strong interest in policing the boundaries of life (Article 2) which conflicts with a secular interest in furthering individual autonomy (Article 8). Also, religious expression can be protected as any other form of expression (Article 10); more often than not, religion claims that other forms of expression which ridicule or offend religion should be limited; see for example the Mohammad cartoon saga. In addition, religion has a considerable interest in being able to assemble if not associate for political purposes (Article 11). This is not always easy to accept and often conflicts with secular norms of the constitution as was the case in Turkey with the *Refah Partisi* case. Finally, religion claims to be able to organize itself according to its norms; this creates a problem if those norms discriminate on the basis of gender or sexual orientation (Article 14). In what follows I will give some examples of conflicts between obligations stemming from fundamental rights.

### 3.2.1.1. Article 2 v Article 8

The scope of the value of life is bitterly contested. Some believe that to value one's life includes the recognition of one's ability to decide when to end that life. In most cases, this is not very difficult as suicide is always possible. But in some exceptional cases, a patient is trapped in a body wrought by illness and unable to carry out alone the ultimate act of her life. The question is whether we should allow such patients to do so by assisting them in their last informed decision to quit their lives.

Religious institutions and religious people want to resist this suggestion. They claim that our life is not our property as it has been granted by God, who is the only one in control of matters of life and death. Non-religious people disagree with the idea that God is the ultimate adjudicator. But they are uncertain as to whether we should assist people in dying. Whenever they do argue that assisted suicide is permissible, they generally rely on the value of individual autonomy, which allows room for decisional privacy on the part of the individual. Life is theirs and they certainly cherish it. But if for some reason they become detached from their life and only think about limiting the pain life protracts then they should be given a chance to end their life.

The leading European case in this area is *Mrs Pretty*.[2] Mrs Pretty had motor neurone disease which paralysed her completely. In addition, this disease was slowly, but surely, killing her. She asked the DPP (Director of Public Prosecutions) for her husband to be excused in the event that he accepted to assist her suicide. The DPP rejected her request arguing that the prohibition on killing could find no scope for excuse. She then embarked on the judicial route which took her to Strasbourg. The ECtHR examined her arguments under Articles 2, 3, 8, 9, and 14 ECHR. In particular, the Court examined her claim that the right to life includes a right to die, and rejected it. The Court also examined her claim that her right to privacy covers her right to decide on how to die. It rejected this claim too, arguing that the blanket ban imposed by the law was not disproportionate as it responded to a very pressing social need (namely, the protection of vulnerable people who could be pressurized into accepting an earlier death).

Interestingly, the Catholic Bishops' Conference of England and Wales filed a brief with the intent of supporting the ban on euthanasia:

They emphasised that it was a fundamental tenet of the Catholic faith that human life was a gift from God received in trust. Actions with the purpose of killing oneself or another, even with consent, reflected a damaging misunderstanding of the human worth. Suicide and euthanasia were therefore outside the range of morally acceptable options in dealing with human suffering and dying. These fundamental truths were also recognised by other faiths and by modern pluralist and secular societies, as shown by Article 1 of the Universal Declaration of Human Rights (December 1948) and the provisions of the European Convention on Human Rights, in particular in Articles 2 and 3 thereof.[3]

---

[2]  *Pretty v the UK*, ECtHR, 29 April 2002.        [3]  *Pretty v the UK*, para 29.

The Bishops' Conference claimed controversially that suicide and euthanasia were outside the range of morally acceptable options. Even more controversially, they argued that modern pluralist and secular societies recognize those fundamental truths. If anything, when talking about euthanasia we locate ourselves at the core of moral conflicts between deeply held values. And, by definition, modern pluralist societies are open as to the definition of the value of life and disagreement on this issue remains acute.

### 3.2.1.2. Article 9 v Rights of others

In Europe, the leading case is *Kokkinakis v Greece*.[4] This is also the first case dealing with freedom of religion at the ECtHR. Kokkinakis was a Greek Jehovah's Witness. He was sent to jail several times for acts of proselytism. On 2 March 1986, Kokkinakis and his wife visited the house of Mr Kyriakis, a Greek Orthodox priest, with the intent of presenting their views and distributing some religious materials. Shortly after their visit the police were called and Kokkinakis and his wife arrested, prosecuted, and convicted for proselytism. Before the ECtHR they claimed that the ban on proselytism was a breach of their fundamental right to religious freedom.

The problem is that the ban on proselytism is said to be compatible with the Greek Constitution—which establishes the Orthodox religion as the religion of the state—as it is meant to preserve a degree of religious coexistence and applies indiscriminately against all religious groups. Now, the apparent conflict faced by Greek courts was that between freedom of religion and the principle of an established church. Greek courts unanimously held that the ban on proselytism was perfectly consistent with freedom of religion. The plaintiff challenged the latter claim. The ECtHR found that the interference on religious freedom is disproportionate. In this case, the tension between freedom of religion and the prohibition of proselytism is made worse by the constitutional establishment of one religion. A secular state, in this case, has a better claim for religious pluralism as it aims to protect equally all different religions. Moreover, secularism should not be about polarizing the society.

However, secularism may polarize a society when it boils down to a normative position that rides roughshod over societal views. A good illustration of this issue is *Leyla Şahin*'s case. Leyla was a medical student at Ankara University. She was compelled to move to Vienna to continue her studies after her local university turned the screw on the headscarf ban. She nonetheless decided to challenge the decision of the university to ban the headscarf in public places on the ground that it violated her freedom of religion.

---

[4] *Kokkinakis v Greece*, ECtHR, 25 May 1993.

The Turkish Constitutional Court (TCC) held that the principle of secularism was of constitutional rank; it pointed out that secularism makes religious freedom possible by severing individual religious consciences from political interference: so far so good.[5] But the TCC made a mistake: when considering freedom to manifest one's religion in public it argued that religious dress can be held to be incompatible with the principle of secularism. In other words, it saw a conflict where there was none. It believed that secularism mandated absolute religious neutrality in the public sphere. By holding this, it actually undermined the very idea that secularism is there to support religious freedom including freedom to manifest one's own religious views in public. Secularism understood in such a rigid way is incompatible with other principles. Moreover, it is hard to square with religious practices in Turkey. If the society is predominantly Muslim, it is not desirable nor is it feasible to prohibit any form of religious display.

The TCC took an extreme view of the principle of secularism, one that divides and polarizes the society instead of creating the conditions for cohabitation. It is surprising to note that the ECtHR paid lip-service towards this highly problematic understanding of secularism. It simply afforded a great margin of appreciation to the Turkish institutions. But to do so neither supported secularism nor did it support freedom of religion. Yet it ascertained a political conflict, whereby the principle of secularism clashes with the principle of freedom of religion.

### 3.2.1.3.  Article10 v Article10

Free speech and religion give rise to a second important conflict. In a democratic society, free speech is often portrayed as paramount. However, its scope was recently questioned when free speech was stretched to protect religious insults and offences. The tension is that between the right to free speech and the right not to be offended in one's own religion.

In Europe, where free speech and secularism play a paramount role, there is a presumption in favour of liberty. However, courts do draw a line: the ECtHR, for example, confronted the issue of blasphemy in its seminal case, *Otto Preminger Institute v Austria*.[6] The case concerned a film that portrayed the holy Christian family in highly derogatory terms. The ECtHR had to decide whether the administrative sanction preventing the screening of the movie was in breach of Article 10 of the Convention or whether it was justified on grounds of protection of religious feelings. Strasbourg argued that

---

[5] *Leyla Şahin v Turkey*, 41 Eur HR Rep 8 (2005), para 39.
[6] *Otto-Preminger-Institut v Austria*, ECtHR, 20 September 1994, *Serie* A, 295.

the administrative sanction was justified as the film risked provoking a strong reaction within a prevalently Christian population.

Critics of this decision argue that there is no tension between free speech and the right not to be offended in one's own religion because the latter is not a right properly speaking. If there is a right not to be offended, or harmed, by other people's words this must apply to any feeling, not only religious ones. We can be offended as football supporters, political partisans, and so on. But there is nothing special about religion that warrants an ad hoc protection. This may be true on political grounds: it is hard to find a precise political reason why religion should be specially protected.

Perhaps it is just a change in social circumstances. Critics of the protection of religion claim that societies rush too quickly to regulate new social phenomena without paying enough attention to the underlying principles that would offer a solution if properly understood and interpreted. Even if they accept that hate speech should somehow be regulated, they contend that there is no authority that can police the line between free speech and hate speech effectively. This is open to disagreement.

### 3.2.1.4. *Article 11 v Secularism*

The conflict is at its peak when it involves political parties. The role of religion in politics is often ambiguous. Christian parties are a traditional feature of European political systems. But what would be the legal status of Islamic parties? Are they all to be banned because they promote sharia law and Islamic values? Or should we distinguish between moderate and authoritarian parties? It would seem logical to allow for the representation of Muslim Europeans through political parties provided that they respect the basic conditions of our political orders: democracy, fundamental rights, and rule of law. Against this background, it is somehow perplexing to observe a string of cases coming from Turkey and dealing with the dissolution of Islamic parties. The leading case is *Refah Partisi*.[7]

The conflict at stake in these cases is that between the principle of secularism and the principle of free association. The most obvious problem concerns the articulation of these principles in more precise directives. The trouble is that the task of articulating these principles lies in the hands of the TCC, which clearly represents, and is composed of, the members of the secularist elite. This means in other words that secularism will always be interpreted as being at odds with the association

---

[7] *Refah Partisi (The Welfare Party) and ors v Turkey*, ECtHR (Grand Chamber), 13 February 2003.

of political parties of religious inspiration. But what are the arguments for the dissolution?

In *Refah Partisi*, the case against the party was brought some time after its constitution. In fact, Refah had already spent one year in government in a coalition of other parties. The opponents to Refah contested that in its manifesto the party did not rule out the possibility of resorting to violence as a means of political action. Moreover, Refah advocated in its manifesto the establishment of plural legal systems whereby secular people would be subject to secular law and religious people would be subject to religious law, at least in the fields of private and criminal law. The latter claim was held to be at odds with the secular constitution that mandated the principle of one secular law for the whole society. The former issue was more generally held to be at odds with the integrity and safety of the constitutional order.

Now, in the one year of Refah Partisi's governmental experience there was no immediate sign of its willingness to either resort to violence or to push forward a plural legal system. There was, so to say, a gap between its deeds and its words that did not exactly warrant an action against the party. Nevertheless, opponents to Refah seized the first opportunity to ask the TCC for its dissolution. Based on a mere exegesis of Refah's manifesto, the TCC reached the conclusion that the party endangered the secular constitutional order and therefore had to be dissolved.

The case was referred to the ECtHR, where plaintiffs claimed that their right to political association had been unduly limited. In a rather controversial decision, the Grand Chamber of the ECtHR followed once again in Pilate's footsteps. After considering the legitimacy and proportionality of the interference with the party's right to political association, the ECtHR decided to leave to Turkey a large margin of appreciation when deciding the conformity of a political association to its secular constitution.

The story does not stop there. Refah's politicians, including the present prime minister, created a new party with similar aims but a more moderate style. The outcome was the AKP, which is now the ruling party in the country and has produced the prime minister and the president. The morale of the story is that a party's dissolution on grounds that it promotes values which are not shared by the whole society does not entail the curtailment of an association's political life. To the contrary, it may even encourage its success, as happened for AKP. Undeterred by this development, some opponents of AKP asked the TCC to step in again and dissolve also the present ruling party. In a recent decision, the TCC reached an odd compromise by which the AKP is maintained in power but the public funding it receives is halved. This time, the TCC was under too much pressure both from within and from outside its party lines. And it is arguable that the way in which the conflict between secularism and political association was dealt with in Refah's case did not serve as a good precedent. Secularism is still very much regarded by part of the elite as an article of faith that cannot accommodate for a religious party. Perhaps there is something wrong with the way in which the conflict has been presented. Perhaps it should not be regarded as an absolute principle unable to yield to political compromise. There is an area of conflicts where absolute lines are drawn even more firmly.

## 3.2.2. Power-conferring norms and the conflict between law and religion

Power-conferring norms confer power to an institution or a designated person to adjudicate a number of disputes. In Europe, the unequivocal principle is that legal disputes must be adjudicated by ordinary courts according to ordinary laws. There are, however, some exceptions which fall under the generic name of alternative dispute resolution. These include mediation, conciliation, and arbitration. The last is a particularly interesting case in the context of the conflict between law and religion, as some European countries give the opportunities to parties to have some of their disputes solved by an arbitrator who applies religious laws. In the UK, for example, there exist Jewish courts, of which the London Beth Din is a prominent example,[8] and from 2007 there is a Muslim Arbitration Tribunal (MAT) that applies sharia law in a few selected areas.

The MAT was established in 2007 to provide a viable alternative for the Muslim community seeking to resolve disputes in accordance with Islamic sacred law and without having to resort to costly and time-consuming litigation. The establishment of the MAT is an important and significant step towards providing the Muslim community with a real opportunity to self-determine disputes in accordance with Islamic sacred law.[9]

These methods of alternative dispute resolution raise possible conflicts between secular laws and religious principles. If religious principles were incompatible with secular laws, then the decision of the arbitrator enforcing those principles would be regarded as a way of smuggling in religious obligations that are incompatible with the norms of the legal system. But the principles of sharia law are generally not in conflict with the requirements of the law in Europe, as stressed by Lord Phillips, Lord Chief Justice.[10]

---

[8] <http://www.theus.org.uk/the_united_synagogue/the_london_beth_din/about_us>.

[9] <http://www.matribunal.com/index.html>.

[10] Speech by Lord Phillips, 'Equality Before the Law', delivered at the East London Muslim Centre, 3 July 2008, <http://www.matribunal.com/downloads/LCJ_speech.pdf>.

The Archbishop of Canterbury raised a similar point in his speech at the High Court on February 2008. His point was that individual personal conduct based on the principles of sharia law did not necessarily come into conflict with the laws of England. In certain carefully defined legal matters such as 'aspects of marital law, the regulation of financial transactions and authorised structures of mediation and conflict resolution', it would be desirable to give the choice of jurisdiction to the parties.

Where conflicts are possible is at the level of sanctions for non-compliance with sharia law. European legal systems uniformly prohibit severe physical punishment, which is sometimes prescribed under some interpretations of sharia law. It is clear that those sanctions would be banned from any European jurisdiction. This does not exclude more substantive conflicts between European laws and sharia law.

### 3.2.3. Conflict of laws and conflicts between law and religion

Ordinary courts are facing a growing number of cases in which two rules of different legal systems clash. Strictly speaking these are clear examples of legal conflicts: they involve two valid rules which prescribe incompatible behaviours; and we have to choose between the two, thereby putting one rule to the side. For example, rules in conflict may concern family law and have religious roots: can we recognize polygamy?; what is the legal status of *talaq* divorce?[11]

In principle European legal systems strictly prohibit polygamy. So if a second marriage takes place in Europe, it is customarily annulled. But what if the marriage has already taken place in another country where polygamy is allowed? In this case the conflict of rules is the following:

Rule 1 says polygamy is strictly prohibited.

Rule 2 says it is not the case that polygamy is prohibited.

When courts deal with problems of private international law rule 2 is a potential candidate for incorporation in the legal system of the litigation for the purpose of the adjudication of the present case. The judge will have to apply rules of conflict establishing which rule applies. In France, for example, a judge recognized that a polygamous relationship could yield some legal consequences such as the payment of children's benefits.

*Talaq* divorce is another feature of sharia law. When the husband pronounces three times the word *talaq*, the marriage is deemed to be dissolved.

---

[11] This section draws on the very interesting work of Pascale Fournier, *Muslim Marriage in Western Courts: Lost in Transplantation* (Ashgate, 2010).

As a matter of principle, *talaq* divorce is considered to be against the law in most European countries. However, some courts ascribe to it some validity if *talaq* divorce took place abroad and both parties can be present to confirm this fact before a judge. Once again the conflict between two rules is quite explicit in theory. In practice, there is some accommodation which becomes more and more necessary as our societies welcome a growing number of immigrants.

### 3.2.4. Church–state relationship and conflict between law and religion

Norms that regulate the relationship between church and state may also give rise to conflicts between law and religion, in particular when there exists a privileged relationship as is the case between the Vatican State and Italy. This is an interesting case as it has implications at three levels. Firstly, it concerns the mutual independence of two normative systems: Italian laws and Vatican laws. Secondly, it is about the relationship between two sovereign states. Thirdly, it is about the separation between church and state. The Vatican would like to free itself from these institutional burdens and focus on its status as an authoritative moral voice at the global level. The trouble is that in order to exercise effective authority one has to take into account institutional and other contingent burdens in order to reach the best possible compromise.

The aim of this exercise is to establish an autonomous body of laws, a *Corpus Vaticanum*, which would be firmly rooted in objective moral principles. Needless to say objective moral principles of the Catholic Cchurch would take absolute priority over conflicting laws of the Italian, and of any other, state or international organization. The Vatican has recently refused to approve a United Nations declaration decriminalizing homosexuality. The *Corpus Vaticanum*, albeit limited in dimension, aspires to offer a unique voice in the sphere of comparative law and a unique understanding of law at the global level.

In the words of José Maria Serrano Ruiz, the architect of this reform, the Vatican intends to become the ideal city state, a model for other states from a normative viewpoint. His main arguments for breaking free from Italian laws are threefold. Firstly, Italian laws are too numerous and simplification is required. Secondly, Italian laws, as with any other secular laws, are too unstable. The Vatican is instead committed to Aquinas' ideal of *lex rationis ordinatio*, which requires a stable framework of concepts and values for the law. Thirdly, there is a growing number of conflicts between Italian (or any other secular) laws and non-negotiable principles of the Catholic Church. The Vatican, given its privileged position as an independent state, clearly wants to become the ultimate authority on moral aspects of the laws. It aims to become an exemplary and universal authority in the resolution of conflicts between secular laws and religious principles.

There is a number of difficult conflicts between law and religion. To deal with them, secular states have to rethink their secular commitment afresh and articulate new responses to old problems. In what follows I do not attempt to provide detailed guidance on how to cope with those conflicts. To do so would be well beyond the scope of this chapter. Instead, I focus on the possibility of deflating the conflict between law and religion by embracing a constitutional framework that is rooted in this world and accepts its own fallibility while liberating the transcendental viewpoint that religion provides from the necessity of providing political compromises that would suit religious and non-religious people.

## 3.3. Practical Conflicts and Secularism

The conflict between law and religion I presented so far arises only if one establishes a link between theoretical and practical conflicts. Law and religion need not conflict if their domain of intervention were kept separate: law would aim at regulating behaviour, while religion would aim at directing beliefs. Things are of course not so simple. It is the very reform of the Vatican that testifies of the willingness of the church to intervene in matters of behaviour by positing the right moral standards. So the conflicts described above are conflicts because religion (the Catholic Church in this case) wants them to be regarded as conflicts. Once the conflict is ascertained, then one can offer his preferred way of resolving it. In the specific case of the Vatican, the conflict would be resolved by appeal to religious moral principles that have a superior status over human laws. From this viewpoint, the church has an interest in reading in conflicts rather than proposing possible accommodation. In fact, the message is that there is no accommodation possible in certain domains, such as abortion for example.

I am not interested in seeing conflicts everywhere, just to be able to offer my own preferred solution. I believe that genuine conflicts between values where compromise is impossible are rare, although they are not non-existent altogether.[12] When it comes to the relationship between law and religion,

---

[12] I defend this view in Lorenzo Zucca, *Constitutional Dilemmas: Conflicts between Fundamental Legal Rights in Europe and the USA* (Oxford University Press, 2007).

I think that we should be very slow to see conflicts everywhere. After all, much of European law is based on a broad understanding of Christian morality to start with. Moreover, it seems to be possible to define the domains of both law and religion in such a way that they do not overlap all the time so as to avoid tensions. The point of constitutional secularism as I understand it is not to silence religion altogether, but to organize a legal-political framework within which religious and non-religious voices can be equally well heard. Secularism is not meant to embrace any world-view in particular, but to protect them all as far as possible.[13]

Secularism does not aim to be a fully fledged philosophy that is in competition with religion for the explanation to the meaning of our lives. Nor is it in competition with any other secular philosophy that aims at providing a non-transcendental explanation of the meaning of our lives. Secularism provides an answer to the practical problems of life in common (practical conflicts) under conditions of moral and political pluralism. It does not, however, replace religion in its quest of meaning. It simply suggests that the transcendental (or non-transcendental) quest for meaning should be kept separate from the way in which life is organized in this world.

A way of looking at it is by appealing to Taylor's idea of an immanent frame. The basic idea is that social and political institutions have outgrown religious institutions in the organization and regulation of life in this world. Those institutions are more and more demarcated from religious influence, they have totally independent goals from religious ones, and they operate outside of the sphere of religious influence. Examples of this kind of institution could be endlessly multiplied: markets, schools, armies, agencies, governments. All of these exist and act in a framework that is detached from the transcendental world. The value and the meaning of those institutions are not measured by reference to transcendental goals. Instead, their value and meaning is defined by reference to the immanent frame of this world in which we live. The idea of an immanent frame attempts to explain social and political behaviour as it operates within our secular age. Both religious and non-religious people organize their behaviour in markets, schools, armies, agencies, and governments in a way that does not appeal to divine intervention; they accept that those human interactions depend entirely on the goodwill of human beings.

---

[13] Of course, any of those world-views could in theory be the right one, and therefore the others would be all wrong. In fact, any respectable world-view claims precisely to be the only one valid viewpoint. Lacking a method to establish this, we have to resort to a constitutional approach that protects all world-views as far as possible.

It is possible, and probably necessary, to regard the law as belonging to that set of social and political institutions that does not depend on divine intervention. Justice in this world entirely depends on the good-will of individuals to behave according to the laws of the community. The meaning and value of the law as a human institution depends entirely on our worldly experience and is not linked back to a transcendental ideal of justice (as was the case in the world Dante inhabited). Some insist, however, that the law cannot be purely secular in that way. They insist that positive law can be morally wrong and if that is the case, it should be resisted. Moreover, positive law has to respect human rights in any case and those rights can only be understood as being based on a conception of human nature that escapes a purely immanent explanation, especially when it concerns the edges of human life.

Human rights are sometimes regarded as the point of intersection between the secular and the natural understanding of law. That is where the church, and other religions, would like to play a role in the policing of human laws. This opens up the terrain for an open conflict between the law and religion. My final aim is to offer an understanding of law as purely secular.[14] By that I mean, a law that strives to be free from moralizing or naturalizing influences. Secular law only focuses on practical conflicts, while leaving theoretical conflicts untouched. At this point some will argue that if we do not give a foundation to fundamental rights, then it is not possible to explain why we protect the fundamental rights that we protect. The short answer to that is that it was only possible to agree on the vast majority of national and international bills of rights by bracketing out of the picture conflicting world-views that would have otherwise prevented agreement. The outcome is often not ideal, but that is precisely the point: there are no ideal solutions to practical conflicts, but we can nonetheless work towards reasonable accommodations that are in need of contextual implementation.

My position aims to deflate the conflict as it is set up by religious institutions. I do not want to disregard religious positions as to the importance of morality seen from those perspectives. It nonetheless remains the case that no religious or non-religious world-view can claim to provide a satisfactory and final position for the whole society, simply because nobody is prepared to give up his own world-view to embrace that of another. Any church can criticize human laws from its own perspective; but it cannot possibly have the final say as to the compatibility between human laws and moral principles. Law as a social and political institution aiming to regulate the behaviour of all people

---

[14] See ch. 9 below.

living in the same society is firmly rooted in the immanent frame as it developed hitherto; in addition to that there is no chance that we all agree on a transcendent frame of reference which is valid for everyone. It may be that law thus understood will not be always compatible with religious principles. However, the ultimate practical authority in this world as to whether that incompatibility is relevant for excusing illegal behaviour is a secular authority that is equally distant from religious and non-religious world-views.

If we understand law to be secular in this way, we do not oppose secular law to religion. Instead, we oppose two viewpoints: one is the viewpoint from eternity and the other is the viewpoint from a local and contingent world. Secular law attempts to address issues within a local and contingent world. It therefore does not prejudge the viewpoint from eternity. It simply leaves it untouched, and accepts that religious and non-religious world-views may still attempt to influence the process of legislation either by criticizing existing laws or by proposing new ones.

Religion is more often than not in an advantageous position. It does not have to take the responsibility of adjudicating concrete cases that arise when people disagree about laws and policies. It can just sit back and evaluate which laws are compatible with its own morality and which laws are not. It has a powerful voice with which to criticize this or that secular law that is incompatible with its own perspective. By doing so it performs an important social role, and a valuable one, in so far as it pushes law-makers to evaluate legislation from different perspectives. This is a privileged position that does not entail the burdens of political compromise.

It is much more difficult to be in the driving seat in fashioning policies that will have to pass the muster of religious and non-religious people. This does not happen very often, but an example can illustrate how hard and ultimately impossible it is to manage a legal system that declares itself as ultimately based on religious principles. The example is Ireland and the issue at stake is abortion. Secular laws in the vast majorities of European countries regulate abortion by way of compromise between the principle of respect for life of the unborn and the principle of respect for the autonomy of women's decisions regarding their body.[15] Secular laws can hardly claim that either principle enjoys absolute precedence over the other when they clash.[16] The Irish Constitution, however, does exactly that. It prioritizes the protection of life of the unborn to the exclusion of the respect for the autonomy of women's choice. This means inter alia that a woman who conceives a baby through an

---

[15] I am deeply aware of the unpalatable, yet necessary, character of these compromises.
[16] The overwhelming rhetoric in these cases is that of balancing between principles.

act of violence should carry a pregnancy to term. Of course, there is at least one major complication from a religious perspective. What if pregnancy threatens the life of the mother? Here the life of the foetus and that of the mother are pitted one against another and a choice between the two is inevitable. The Irish Constitution allows precisely for that exception to the absolute right to life of the foetus. It can thus be said that even such a rigid position allows for a minimum degree of choice on the part of the woman.

In the recent case of *A, B, C v Ireland*,[17] the Grand Chamber of the ECtHR condemned Ireland to pay damages to one of the three women who brought the case precisely because one of them could not fully benefit from that exemption as there was no clear legal framework to deal with the fact that her life was at risk because of her illness. More generally, the case is the last instantiation of a battle that has taken place in the last thirty years and one that will go on until a reasonable compromise between the right to life of the unborn and the right to decisional privacy is reached. In this world, the silent majority of women who are faced with the tragic choice of abortion feel that the Irish position is condemning them to carry out pregnancy against their will or to risk it by engaging in a poorly regulated trip abroad which does not always guarantee success as the *A, B, C* case shows. To have an absolute primacy of the right to life of the unborn over the right of decisional privacy cannot be regarded as a reasonable accommodation. One right is completely sacrificed on the ground that Catholic religious morality does not allow for any leeway as it states an absolute principle. Such a position is acceptable from the viewpoint of Catholic people. It is absolutely fine if they stick to it as strictly as they want. However, such a strict principle cannot be shared by non-religious people who do not share the premises of the argument protecting the life of the unborn.

The Irish abortion saga, which is by no means at the end, shows that a constitutional framework cannot be based on religious principles while guaranteeing reasonable accommodations at the same time. It is either one or the other. It seems that the church is better off as a critical observer of the constitutional framework rather than an active player directly involved in the game of constitutional adjudication. As I said, that does not mean that religion should be wholly absent from the process of negotiation. It simply means that secularism provides a default framework whose business is to allow for political compromise while untying the hands of competing religious and non-religious world-views that are then able to develop freely and exchange arguments to the maximum possible extent.

---

[17] [2010] ECtHR 2032.

## 3.4. Conclusion

The possibility of conflict between law and religion is actual and present. It must be thoroughly examined and understood before jumping at any normative conclusion as to how to solve those conflicts. As a matter of fact, some of the conflicts will not be resolvable in a way that does not involve sacrifices for either religious or non-religious people. A religion that claims exclusive truth cannot possibly reach a compromise on issues that involve the denial of those very truths. Yet, practical conflicts call for constant compromise. In order to avoid confusion it will be necessary to distinguish sharply between theoretical conflicts between comprehensive views on what to believe and practical conflicts between those views on how to behave. If conflicts can be freely allowed at the theoretical level, there must be a cutting point at the practical one. The cutting point does not have to follow orthodox lines between the public and the private sphere. A bigger role for religion in the public sphere can be allowed but it also has to be strictly regulated.

At the theoretical level, the best we can do is to promote mutual knowledge in order to understand why compromises cannot be accepted on comprehensive grounds. To know more about the way in which religions deal with general issues of morality can equally help everyone push their own boundaries in order to find better solutions. Theoretical conflicts should be welcomed as they provide a constant engine for finding better and more articulated responses to common present problems and challenges. Disagreement at the theoretical level can only be beneficial if it is a spur to further thinking.

At the practical level, however, conflicts are not tolerable if they push different groups of a society in totally different directions thereby giving rise to an unbridgeable gap or excessive polarization. Here again it is necessary to distinguish between micro and macro management of conflicts. At the micro level, it is desirable to leave individuals and groups free to decide how to behave by following one of the possible solutions based on comprehensive views of a religion or of any other system of thought. At the macro level, however, secular law must necessarily determine what happens if religious and non-religious comprehensive views are unable to give guidance locally on how to behave in case of conflicts of obligations.

Europe is blessed and cursed with the fact of pluralism. Each European should realize that the fundamental values in which she believes in are at the same time sacred and fragile. Liberty and equality, to take but two examples, are the outcome of many centuries of struggles and yet can be lost and compromised away very quickly. By deciding where one stands on conflict of values, one reaffirms and ranks those values. It is a particularly difficult exercise which needs to be carried out under the best possible cognitive conditions. If we let fear and suspicion guide those fundamental decisions, we would simply jettison our values. In particular, we would jettison our very premise of value pluralism. European societies must rise to that challenge and show that they can cope with disagreement and difference better than they do at the moment. This challenge takes us from the Inferno to Purgatory.

# PART II
# PURGATORY

Inferno was about the conflicts between religious and non-religious people in Europe. In particular, it criticized some prevalent attitudes towards religion in European nation states. Purgatory entails a change in perspective and attempts to cast a different light on the relationship between law and religion in Europe. The supranational and international layers allow for a certain amount of purification from the national experience, even if they involve their own challenges. European institutions have a great responsibility in redefining the place of religion at the supranational/international level. Europe's secularism must go beyond secularism as it was elaborated within nation states. European secularism is about preserving and promoting diversity, while maintaining one clear voice that speaks for the values of everyone, religious and non-religious people.

The EU Constitution saga showed the failure of a Christian-based identity for the EU. This does not mean that Christian values are simply irrelevant: rather, it means that the EU is committed to a form of secularism that promotes diversity overall and which aims to protect as far as possible religious and non-religious voices (chapter 4).

The Council of Europe through the ECtHR has managed to articulate the idea of diversity into discrete principles that are still very much at a trial phase. However, it is possible to discern Strasbourg's intention to carve out a marketplace of religions where religious monopolies are gradually dismantled and the neutrality of the state is applied contextually. In addition, Strasbourg attempts to give an interpretation of the law that is free from religious elements (chapter 5).

Finally, European states are faced with claims of minorities seeking to bring back religious norms into the lives of people living in Europe. The response to those claims is so far unsatisfactory as it is based more on prejudices and myth about the nature of religious norms rather than on the ability of secular law to frame and shape the application of religious law, such as sharia (chapter 6).

Purgatory shows that Europe is slowly trying to grapple with its growing social and cultural pluralism. The results are mixed and tentative since Europe does not offer a new identity that fills the gap left by the waning of religion as a social bond. The EU is like a Pirandellian actor in search of a new author. The Council of Europe through the ECtHR, on the other hand, is timidly sketching an understanding of freedom of religion broad enough to please its enormous constituency. Finally European states are struggling with immigrant minorities and their cultural claims in times where fear and economic unrest make it really difficult to abandon entrenched prejudices about unknown cultures.

# 4

# Does the EU Need Christian Values?[1]

## 4.1. Introduction

The Lisbon Treaty does not include a reference to God nor to Christian values. Instead it mentions a number of influences: 'Drawing inspiration from the cultural, religious and humanist inheritance of Europe, from which have developed the universal values of the inviolable and inalienable rights of the human person, freedom, democracy, equality and the rule of law...'

The Charter of Fundamental Rights of the European Union is also free from specific references to Christian values: 'Conscious of its spiritual and moral heritage, the Union is founded on the indivisible, universal values of human dignity, freedom, equality and solidarity; it is based on the principles of democracy and the rule of law. It places the individual at the heart of its activities, by establishing the citizenship of the Union and by creating an area of freedom, security and justice.'

Some have criticized such phrasings and have argued against the 'Christian deficit' or ideologically loaded 'thundering silence' with regard to the invocation of Christian values in the main legal instruments defining the EU's constitutional identity.[2] Others have welcomed the ability of the EU to strike a balance between competing influences, in particular between Christian and humanist ones.[3]

Those who are concerned about the apparently widespread 'Christophobia' gather around one clear and simple notion of Christianity as it would be too difficult to defend the unity of Christian values by representing all the Christian voices in Europe. Needless to say, those who would want Europe to speak with one Christian voice are thinking about the voice of the Roman

---

[1] This chapter is based in part on a highly revised version of S Cvijic and L Zucca, 'Does the European Constitution Need Christian Values?', OLJS 24(4) (2004), 739–48.

[2] See eg JHH Weiler, *Un'Europa Cristiana: un saggio esplorativo* (Rizzoli, 2003).

[3] See eg R McCrea, *Religion and the Public Order of the European Union* (Oxford University Press, 2010).

*Magisterium.*[4] The same goes for those attached to so-called humanist values: they present them as coherent and unified, but this merely rides roughshod over endless debates and dilemmas faced by people who are outside of the Christian camp while embracing a non-religious comprehensive view of the world.

The point of this chapter is to argue against the idea of constitutional identity on the one hand; on the other the idea is to argue that the EU is secular, and that its secularism is the only framework that makes the cohabitation of different world-views possible at the same time. As pointed out in chapter 2, secularism properly understood is not about the relationship between the state and religion, but it is about the way in which political organizations deal with diversity. From this perspective, to assert a *secular Europe* does not mean to deny a Christian Europe or a humanist Europe. A *secular Europe* is the approach that makes it possible for religious as well as non-religious beliefs to be heard and to share a peaceful future.

This chapter is organized in the following way. In section 4.2., I introduce a contemporary understanding of Christian Europe. In section 4.3., I argue that a constitution ought not to be concerned with identity. In section 4.4., I argue that the reference to cultural, religious, and humanist inheritance in Europe cannot be successfully interpreted as articulating a deeper identity of the EU: identity should be decoupled from European constitutionalism. In section 4.5., I consider the arguments in favour of mentioning Christian values in a constitution. In section 4.6., I dismiss the necessity of referring to Christian values and argue instead that the peculiarity of any secular state is to be committed to a set of values—namely on the indivisible, universal values of human dignity, freedom, equality, and solidarity—on which everyone can agree without sharing the deeper reasons for signing up to these values. In section 4.7., I defend a new model of European secularism and conclude that the EU is secular just in this sense.

## 4.2. Europe and Christianity

Those who defend a Christian Europe do not necessarily have a missionary purpose to make people believe in God. Neither do they seek the dismantling of the secular state and the institutionalization of religion in Europe. Moreover, those who advocated the inclusion of Christian values in the preamble

---

[4] Weiler, *Un'Europa Cristiana.*

of the Lisbon Treaty did not to want it to be interpreted as an excuse for refusing to proceed with the process of Turkey's integration into the EU.[5]

What would a Christian Europe look like then? Joseph Weiler distinguishes between Christianity in the thick and in the thin sense.[6] In the thick sense, Christianity stands for the whole theological package wrapped in the mantle of revealed truth, while in the thin sense Christianity represents an important social and cultural reality. The former is represented by practising believers, while the latter espouses Christianity in a broad sense, namely as a normative universe that captures the moral sensibility and social culture of the majority of Europeans. According to Weiler, the community of thin Christians practises religion only in vital moments of their lives (such as birth, marriage, and death). In his view, an outside observer looking at the EU could easily come to the conclusion that Christianity, understood in the aforementioned thin sense, presents a common denominator of the population living in the EU. The churches can remain empty, but one cannot ignore the fact that 'with their majestic beauty' they occupy a dominant position in European hearts and public space.

Weiler's suggestion to introduce God and/or Christian values in the preamble of the treaty was based on the idea of thin Christianity as being a dominant cultural element of the European constitutional landscape. I have several doubts as to the dominant nature of this phenomenon. Many would not hesitate in defining that heritage as a relic from the past, which symbolizes oppression as well as many other things. Others would detach the aesthetic value of churches from the spiritual role they used to play. Physically religion is very present all over the European territory, but this does not constitute an argument for the centrality of religion in European hearts.

More importantly, from a constitutional perspective nothing militates in favour of entrenching Christian values in the preamble only to preserve them against their waning status in the society. Weiler insists that thin Christianity is not only acceptable, but an indispensable element of the European constitutional project. In his words, Christianity cannot be eliminated from the historical heritage and the present identity of Europeans any more than one can remove the crosses from European cemeteries. Thus Weiler bemoans the fact that the Lisbon Treaty (former Constitutional Treaty RIP) builds an 'auto-imposed wall of separation between the European polity and Christian values'.[7] This suggestion is a caricature and, more importantly, it is wrong. The preamble explicitly draws from cultural, religious, and humanist influences. This can hardly be described as a wall of separation at the level of

[5] Weiler, *Un'Europa Cristiana*.     [6] Weiler, *Un'Europa Cristiana*.

[7] Weiler, *Un'Europa Cristiana*, 48.

principles. It is a major concession to those religious people who believe
that human rights have a religious foundation, for example. This belief,
which is part of a thick world-view, can only be entertained alongside other
beliefs which are incompatible with it if we presuppose a secular constitutional framework: one which guarantees a principled distance from any
other world-views that regard human rights as either being founded on non-
religious ideals or as representing a pure linguistic agreement on interests that
we happen to regard as very important, at least in their abstract formulation.

At an even higher level, it has to be added that Weiler's argument in favour
of Christian values assumes the validity of his communitarian position—one
which requires the existence of an historical memory and a common culture
for the purpose of the construction of an ethical community.[8] This approach
obscures the most important issues regarding the functions of constitutions,
which we can encapsulate in the two following questions: firstly, is the
function of the constitution to mirror the ethical community or to provide
the basis for its constant development?; and secondly, even assuming that the
constitution mirrors the ethical community, should the community's identity
and that of its normative system mirror the historical memory or rather the
present configuration? I for one believe that the constitution is an agreement
between disparate constituencies who want to lay the seeds of peaceful life in
common despite ethical disagreement. Following from this, I also believe that
modern constitutions should not aim at reflecting the historical memory
especially when the historical memory reflects a degree of social homogeneity
which is no longer the chief characteristic of the society.

## 4.3. The Functions and Point of a Constitution

A constitution has two main functions. Firstly, it organizes the state's institutional structure. Secondly, it defines the link between individuals and
the public authority. In addition to those two functions, the constitution
may or may not enshrine the values, ideals, and symbols that are thought
to define its identity. This is true in particular for national constitutions
anxious to establish a common heritage in order to justify their independence
from other nations. A constitution for Europe is by its very nature and scope
less anxious to establish that common heritage as its very idea and point
is to bring together different and sometimes disparate constitutional experiences. The point of a constitution for Europe is to guarantee that diversity in

[8] Weiler, *Un'Europa Cristiana*, 74.

social, moral, and political outlook does not constitute a ground for conflict. The point of such a constitution, and more generally the point of any constitution, is to reconcile competing interests, thereby preventing possible tensions and contributing to social peace. To put it with the very European motto: the point of the European constitution is to promote 'unity in diversity'.

The third identity-forming function of the constitution is not indispensable. Weiler himself suggests that that function can be achieved in an implicit or explicit way. An implicit way would be to express the values and commitments indirectly through the first two functions of the constitution. Thus, the institutional treaty or the Charter of Fundamental Rights could by themselves stand for the substantive values and ideals of the EU. The explicit way consists of declaring those values separately in a document that attempts to express the political unity of the community. This is meant to be the role of a preamble, if one decides to have one at all.

Since the Lisbon Treaty opts for a preamble which invokes a magic European identity, it ought not to be silent about the real cultural heritage of the polity, Weiler claims. There is a big difference, however, between the recognition of a monolithic identity in terms of precise religious values and the proclamation of an identity formed by many different religious and non-religious strands. European identity is an empty shell that still waits to be filled in by a core set of values. It may be suggested that European identity is really more of a short cut for the recognition of great diversity at the national level. Indeed the Lisbon Treaty affirms in Article 4.2 the respect of national identities which are not much clearer than their European counterpart: 'The Union shall respect the equality of Member States before the Treaties as well as their national identities, inherent in their fundamental structures, political and constitutional, inclusive of regional and local self-government.'

## 4.4. EU Constitutionalism and Identity: Decoupling the Two Ideas

Constitutional identity is nonsense upon stilts. Its meaning, scope, and strength are impossible to determine without injecting bias into the interpretation of the fundamental text. In the US, for example, Laurence Tribe points out that 'the very identity of the "Constitution"—the body of textual and historical materials from which [fundamental constitutional] norms are to be extracted and by which their application is to be guided—is . . . a matter that cannot be objectively deduced or passively discerned in a viewpoint-free way'.[9] In the EU, the same would certainly apply with some added difficulties. Firstly, there is no reference to constitutional identity but either to European identity or to national identities (there is also a reference to religious identities). Not only is it not possible to discern a constitutional meaning for these identities, but if it was then they would surely clash one against another.

In this section, I want to distinguish as firmly as possible between constitutionalism and identity (however defined). The obvious upshot is to deny any legal role to the notion of constitutional identity. This is not to say that identity is completely unintelligible: it is, but from viewpoints that should not matter legally. National identity, for example, matters politically and socially and it is often used as a way of motivating the masses to mobilize. More often than not, talk of identity mobilizes a subgroup in order to separate it from a bigger community (Scottish nationalism, for example, insists that Scottish identity calls for an independent state with its own constitution). The politics of identity is partisan and divisive, while constitutionalism is meant to be a framework for all and in this sense it is unifying.

There are different ways in which identity can be defined, none of which—I submit—is relevant from a legal constitutional viewpoint. To simplify, identity can be defined in relation to the person, the object, or the territory to which it applies. Table 4.1. shows a schematic illustration of what one may mean by identity in the European socio-political context.

In EU treaties, there is an explicit mention of European identity, national identities, and religious identity. But of course, the paradigmatic example of identity is personal[10] and some say that we can single out an identity of a

**Table 4.1.** The diversity of identity

| Scope/object | Wide | Narrow |
|---|---|---|
| *Ratione loci* | European identity | National identity |
| *Ratione materiae* | Religious identity | Ethnic identity |
| *Ratione personae* | Societal (cultural) identity | Personal identity |

---

[9] Laurence Tribe, 'A Constitution We Are Amending: In Defense of a Restrained Judicial Role', Harvard Law Review, 97 (1983), 433, 440. See for a defence of constitutional identity, GJ Jacobsohn, *Constitutional Identity* (Harvard University Press, 2010); M Rosenfeld, *The Identity of the Constitutional Subject: Selfhood, Citizenship, Culture and Community* (Routledge, 2009).

[10] Indeed the Court singles out a right to personal identity in Case C-168/91 *Konstantinidis v Stadt Altensteig* [1993] ECR I-1191. AG Jacobs finds such a right in the common constitutional traditions of member states.

society, which largely overlaps with national identity. Ethnic identity is not mentioned in the EU treaties because it is a source of great internal divisions and conflicts. These different types of identity point to the possibility of tensions between, say, European identity and national identities. This tension may be explainable by reference to the European motto: unity in diversity. Of national identities there are many, but they all contribute to form one European identity. If this might have a political sense, it can hardly be translated into a meaningful legal tool. So far Article 4(2) EU has been used once by the European Court of Justice (ECJ) in the case *Sayn-Wittgenstein* to recognize a margin of discretion in favour of the Austrian national identity. National courts, on the other hand, were quick to jump on the constitutional identity bandwagon as it widens their scope of influence and power.[11]

Those who insist on constitutional identity suggest that each polity has a bulk of very important rules that make up its identity.[12] Either this is a pleonasm, as we already refer to those rules as constitutional, or worse it is an ideological weapon for the courts to single out each time what is *really* important in a constitution. It is a pleonasm if by constitutional identity one refers to those rules that are *really* constitutional. Surely it is not the job of judges to say so, but they certainly would enjoy it, since this would be a formidable way to carve out their own protected terrain of supremacy vis-à-vis other jurisdictions. In the EU, respect for national identities means respect for national constitutional norms as it is the case in *Omega* where the ECJ respects the German conception of dignity.[13] To this extent, constitutional identity is a limitation of the primacy of EU law.[14] This interpretation, however, rides roughshod over the fact that if constitutional identity was an applicable legal tool, then it would have to benefit also the European constitutional identity, thereby strengthening the primacy of EU law rather than limiting it. If we wanted to push the logic (is there such a thing?) of constitutional identity to European identity, then there is little doubt that the duo of primacy/direct effect are part of such a constitutional identity. Why should

---

[11] These include the German Constitutional Court (BVG) and the French Conseil Constitutionnel.

[12] This seems to be the meaning that the BVG and the Conseil Constitutionnel attribute to constitutional identity. This is also the meaning that M Rosenfeld attributes to it, as well as GJ Jacobsohn: see Rosenfeld, *The Identity of the Constitutional Subject* and Jacobsohn, *Constitutional Identity*.

[13] Case C-36/02, *Omega Spielhallen- und Automatenaufstellungs-GmbH v Oberbürgermeisterin der Bundesstadt Bonn*, ECJ, 14 October 2004.

[14] A von Bogdandy and S Schill, 'Overcoming Absolute Primacy: Respect for National Identity under the Lisbon Treaty', CML Rev, 48(5) (October 2011). L Besselink, 'National and Constitutional Identity before and after Lisbon', Utrecht Law Review, 6(3) (November 2010).

national (constitutional) identities encroach upon the quintessential European (constitutional) identity?

### 4.4.1. European identity v National identities

Let us assume for a moment that it would be possible to define and use national identities as a legal-constitutional tool in the European constitutional landscape. Some European scholars do exactly that: they interpret Article 4(2) as defining national identities in constitutional terms.[15] They then go on to suggest that the ECJ should respect national (constitutional) identities in so far as it should leave a margin of discretion to national (constitutional) courts to interpret and protect core constitutional norms. In *Omega*, for example, the ECJ carved out a margin of discretion for the BVG to define its own understanding of dignity. Here constitutional identity is defined in relation to the interpretation of fundamental values.

Needless to say, this understanding of national (constitutional) identities raises a host of problems. First of all, what are fundamental constitutional norms and what are non-fundamental constitutional norms? Some suggest that national constitutional identity only covers some important norms, while others are regarded as trivial. For example, the norm in the Greek Constitution that explicitly prohibits media tycoons from obtaining public procurements is considered by the ECJ as not being a fundamental constitutional norm.[16] Commentators argue that that is an example of a non-fundamental constitutional norm—that is to say, of a norm which is not part of the constitutional identity.

The importance of such a distinction cannot be underrated, since it would define the scope of primacy of EU law over national law. When EU law touches upon national constitutional identities, its primacy is limited. This is not the case when EU law touches upon constitutional norms falling outside the constitutional identity. The obvious question is: who defines what falls within the walls of constitutional identity? The answer is that there should be one judge—or failing that a clear methodology—fit for that purpose unless we want to open a Pandora's Box of national identities, which all national courts would be tempted to exploit in their own favour. Given that the notion is so slippery and broad, it would open the door to never-ending litigation.

---

[15] See Bogdandy and Schill, 'Overcoming Absolute Primacy'; and Besselink, 'National and Constitutional Identity before and after Lisbon'.

[16] Case C-213/07, *Michaniki AE v Ethniko Simvoulio Radioteliorasis*, ECJ, 16 December 2008.

A further problem arises where national (constitutional) identity is incompatible with EU fundamental norms which are allegedly part of EU constitutional identity. Imagine that a national constitution defines citizenship in ethnic terms and this has the consequence of depriving some citizens of certain rights, say for example where eligibility for the highest offices depends upon certain ethnic conditions. In this case we have a conflict between a national constitutional norm (presumably being part of constitutional identity) and a fundamental EU norm that prohibits discrimination on ethnic grounds (this norm being part of European constitutional identity—I assume). Should the member state be granted a margin of discretion or should European law take primacy in this case? This riddle is not easily answered. To understand why, I shall try to disentangle identity and constitutionalism.

Constitutional identity has been used by national constitutional courts to erect a barrier around the national understanding of constitutions. The German Constitutional Court in the Lisbon decision and the Conseil Constitutionnel have already resorted to this notion. It is clear, however, that the recognition of diversity in terms of national constitutional identities can only take place against a unitary background without which there would not be clear, transparent, predictable application of European law—in other words, there would not be rule of law.

## 4.4.2. Personal identity v National identity

> What's in a name? That which we call a rose by any other name would smell as sweet.
>
> Shakespeare, *Romeo and Juliet* (II, ii, 1–2).

It is somehow ironic that the first time the ECJ refers to the respect of national identities is to limit the right to personal identity. In *Sayn-Wittgenstein*, the applicant complains of a restriction of her freedom of movement and her right to personal identity. The applicant had acquired by way of adoption the title *Furstin von Sayn-Wittgenstein* while leaving in Germany and she was using this name for many years in her luxury estate business. Austrian civil authorities argued that she was not entitled to use a title of nobility since nobility had been abolished with the creation of the republic.

On the one hand, we have a right that was recognized by the ECJ in the landmark decision *Konstantinidis*, where AG Jacobs singled out the protection of personal identity by looking at the constitutional traditions of member states. On the other hand, we have a national limitation on that right and on free movement on the basis that the Austrian Constitution

protects the principle of equality of citizens and the idea that its republican
status must be respected as being part of Austria's constitutional identity. In
other words, personal identity as acquired in one member state (Germany)
can be limited on the ground of national identity as protected in another state
(Austria). More precisely, on the side of personal identity there is also free
movement of people, while on the other there is the principle of equality
and Austria's national identity as a republic. By allowing Austria to protect
its own national identity, the ECJ undermines its own idea of common
constitutional traditions which are always likely to be put to a test by national
(constitutional) identities which necessarily pull in the opposite directions.
If common constitutional traditions are centripetal, national constitutional
identities would be centrifugal.

### 4.4.3. The constitution of identity: is the constitution like an identity card?

Identity cards are meant to tell officials who we are. A picture, a name, and
a few more details will give a snapshot of our image which is meant to
be unique. Constitutions have a similar function: they are meant to tell who
we are as a political society. Is the analogy between constitutions and identity
cards a sound one?

The answer to this question is not straightforward because there are several
assumptions buried in the previous question. First of all, it is assumed that
personal identity is comparable to social identity. What makes one a distinct
individual is not the same set of features that make a society. To start with,
societies cannot be immortalized in a snapshot. Thus, societal identity
depends much less than personal identity on physical appearance (physi-
ognomy). Societal identity is much more elusive as it deals with inner features
of the society more than with apparent ones: beliefs, traditions, histories
make up social identities in a way that is unique. Italian identity depends on a
very complex blend of religious and cultural events that have shaped our
being Italian in a graspable way. Even though each and every Italian person
has a distinctive personal identity, it is possible to say that at a very general,
and perhaps superficial, level what makes us all Italian is a blend of religious
history together with the fact that we all speak one language. As Manzoni, a
prominent Italian writer, put it in 1831: '*Una di lingua, di arme e di altare*', in
the heyday of national affirmation.[17] From this viewpoint Italian national

---

[17] Unity of language, of army, and religion.

identity precedes the formation of the Italian state; and the constitution of the state does not touch upon national identity.

Societal identity is often made up of two central elements that crucially take the lion's share: on the one hand, religion is a predominant ingredient of social identity. On the other hand, ethnicity constitutes a second highly important ingredient in the formation of social identities. Ethnicity is quite difficult to define, but for our present purpose I take ethnicity to be the collection of cultural events that have shaped societal histories, such as for example the formation and adoption of one given language. Ethnicity is usefully opposed to race, where race is a set of phenotypes that make up one's appearance whereas ethnicity has nothing to do with biological features and the method by which one discerns it is distinctively anthropological. That religion and ethnicity do take the lion's share does not mean that there are no other ingredients to the recipe of identity. It simply means that those two are much stronger and more visible and often trump other identity-forming elements.

The second assumption buried in the question above has to do with the function of a constitution. By comparing ID cards with constitutions one assumes that the chief function of each document is to depict—describe—a person or a society so as to single out its unique features. Constitutions, however, have other functions that are much more important. In a very succinct way, we can say that constitutions have an overarching normative function rather than descriptive: they tell us what the political society ought to be and not what the society looks like. When the French revolutionaries began the task of writing a constitution, they certainly did not want to tell us what their society looked like: they wanted to alter that society from its core. When we face a constitutional moment, the emphasis is on change rather than on preservation; the normative function is more important than the descriptive one. Here we have to add a note of caution: European constitutionalism has the weakness of not being born in a constitutional moment. When the project of a constitutional treaty was discussed and drafted, the point was more to organize existing documents, rather than to pave a new road to an ideal society.

On this point, identity and EU constitutionalism converge, although they do not coincide. If the constitution does not aim to be primarily normative, then its descriptive-symbolic function becomes more important. Indeed, the most animated discussions of the EU Treaty in the media dealt with the preamble of the constitutional treaty rather than with its long body of articles. In particular, the issue of Christian values was one of the main bones of contention. In other words, the main problem seemed to be the religious identity of the EU. This immediately raises the riddle of identity in constitutions: is identity constituted or declared? From what we have said so far, social (and personal) identities are a unique set of features of people, thus they can only be ascertained. But then why should a constitution bother to ascertain what is already visible to everyone? The elephant in the room in this debate is that the EU's religious identity is not discernible given the advanced state of secularization. To claim the contrary would just be a lame attempt to put the clock back. This in itself would neither be normative nor descriptive: it would simply be an exercise in constitutional archaeology. Constitutions engage in such an exercise when they have to fill a gap or promote a mythical, long-gone image of a country. They typically do so in emphatic preambles: the Hungarian one is a perfect illustration.

### 4.4.4. Identity crisis and religious identity

When a political society is too obsessed with its identity, it may point to one problem: an identity crisis. In Europe, this crisis begins to become very daunting. The EU, as we just saw, cannot avail itself of a strong religious identity, which has always been a paramount criterion. This is not because there are no religious roots, but because those roots have faded away. They do not define European identity anymore, in a positive way at least. Few Europeans would define themselves as *primarily* Christian. This is not to say that Christian roots do not work negatively: EU enlargement has largely coincided with its Christian borders stopping at the gate of Turkey and eyeing Bosnia with trepidation.

If we do not know who we are, at least we know who we are not. The EU's identity works very much in this way: the EU is not Turkey, nor any other Muslim state. The EU is not Orthodox Russia. The EU is not Africa. In this loose sense, the EU is Christian—primarily Catholic and Protestant. Religious identity therefore is not completely irrelevant. We cannot say the same for ethnicity, since it is hard to say that there is a common ethnic denominator in Europe. If anything, what is very visible is Europe's pluralism in terms of language, traditions, customs, etc. It may be suggested that there is something called European history. But in fact the history of Europe is marked by conflicts and never-ending assertion of diversity rather than identity.

The European constitution flirted very briefly with the idea of religious identity only to dismiss it. Beside the fact that the Constitutional Treaty never saw the light, the Lisbon Treaty's preamble only mentions abstractly the importance of spiritual values. In the Lisbon Treaty, there is no *Invocatio Dei*, there is no mention of Christian values, and there certainly is no reference to the Catholic Church. It is interesting to compare that with the new Hungarian Constitution which features all three elements: there is an *Invocatio Dei*, there is a reference to Christian Values, and, last but not least, the Catholic Church is invoked as spiritual guide. To this extent at least, EU constitutionalism and Hungarian constitutionalism are at the opposite ends of the spectrum. EU constitutionalism strives to preserve and promote its secular commitment, whereas the Hungarian Constitution blatantly throws it away.

The idea of secular constitutionalism prompts a few more points. Were we to embrace the idea of constitutional identity then the secular nature of the state would qualify as a candidate for recognition of what is *really* constitutional. Is it then possible to change the secular constitutional identity of Hungary and turn it into a religious one? Surely identity is not something that one can change on a whim and surely it is not enough to enact a mere constitutional amendment to change one's constitutional identity? There is a second point: what if, on the basis of its new religious identity, Hungary would like to entrench some norms that are inconsistent with Europe's fundamental norms? Say, for example, that Hungary discriminates on the basis of sex following a constitution that is not exactly gay-friendly as it is biased in favour of Christian values. Should Europe leave a margin of discretion or should it enforce its own commitment to equality?

To say that the two constitutional voices are at loggerheads does not mean that their actual identity is completely different. It is the case that the EU is Christian at least in a negative way as we saw above. And it is not the case that Hungary is a Catholic society even if the constitution says it is. Here we see that what constitutions say (or do not say) about identity is always at least partly misleading. And this is why constitutions should not be concerned with identity. An example that confirms the resistance to the constitutional change of identity is Kemal Ataturk's Turkish Constitution. Ataturk wished to transform Turkey into a modern Western secular state through constitutional action. It is possible to say that Turkey's religious identity cannot be easily squared with its alleged secular constitutional identity. This was the object of a major litigation and an ongoing process of constitutional transformation: the *Refah Partisi* case showed the initial resistance of secular institutions vis-à-vis Islamic parties, which culminated with the dissolution of Refah. But in the long run, a moderate Muslim party (AKP) took hold of power and only recently failed by a small margin to gain a big enough majority to initiate constitutional reforms unilaterally as had happened in Hungary.

The Lisbon Treaty does not mention ethnic markers either. The preamble states: 'Drawing inspiration from the cultural, religious and humanist inheritance of Europe, from which have developed the universal values of the inviolable and inalienable rights of the human person, freedom, democracy, equality and the rule of law . . .'; on top of this, the EU's motto is *Unitas in Diversitate*. It is not clear what gives unity to Europe yet apart from the primacy of the law, but it is clear that a central feature of Europe is its plurality and diversity which is celebrated in the European treaties.

Again it is useful to compare the EU's treatment of ethnic identity to the Hungarian one. The EU nowhere mentions strong ethnic markers; ethnicity is not used to enlarge the conception of citizenship; and more extremely, ethnicity is not used as a ground for discrimination. In the new Hungarian Constitution, ethnic markers are clearly spelled out by reference to the Magyar people. This category is used to extend the right to vote and participate in elections to Magyar who reside outside of Hungary. It is therefore a tool to extend citizenship in a fully ethnic way. Finally, ethnicity does not seem to be used as a ground of discrimination, as it was the case in the Bosnian Constitution. It is clear, however, that Magyars are first-class citizens while the others are 'those with whom we live': in essence, they are guests.

Despite these differences, what unites the EU and Hungary is the fact that they both suffer from an identity crisis. Hungary is perhaps paradigmatic in this sense: oppressed by Orthodox Russia, and the Islamic Ottoman Empire, it does not want to give up its identity altogether and defer to the EU which has its own problems of identity and much else besides. If the diagnosis is clear—the EU and Hungary suffer from identity crises—the constitutional prognosis is much more difficult: what can constitutionalism do for identity?

### 4.4.5. Preservative (backward) and transformative (forward) constitutionalism

Can a constitution rekindle the flame of identity? To do so it would have to bring back religion to its old role. This is not possible as traditional religion has lost its role in secular European societies. It has not disappeared altogether, but it is not a central element of political morality anymore. Is it possible then to insist on ethnicity to send a clear message of identity? Today, this does not sound like a smart constitutional move. A constitution should strike a subtle balance between preserving past achievements, while transforming the society so as to make it capable to meet future challenges. A constitution is there to map a road for the future, and not to entrench a glorious past that is long gone.

On this point, EU constitutionalism is searching. It does not only look backward in order to find European roots. It also tentatively looks forward and tries to meet future challenges even if it does not manage to state exactly what Europe is all about, or who does Europe want to be as a grown up? EU constitutionalism, at least, is not compulsively backward-looking. Unfortunately, the Hungarian Constitution is clearly an example of backward-looking constitutionalism. Identity will be found in the past: the glorious past of the Austro-Hungarian Empire. Hungarian constitutionalism is vintage: it would be fit for the nineteenth century. It is in this vein that the Hungarian Constitution refers to 'we the nation', rather than 'we the people'. The nation is broader and more abstract than the people. The nation uses ethnic criteria of belonging, whereas the people are blind to ethnic criteria: whoever happens to meet the necessary legal conditions in Hungary is part of the people. Nineteenth-century constitutionalism is obsessed with the magical unity of the nation and always attempts to ascribe mythical origins to it. The Hungarian Constitution also uses the myth of St Stephen who brought Hungary into Christian Europe 1,000 years ago.

The problem is that a constitution does not have the magic effect of bringing back to life a nation with its own identity. Either the spirit of the nation is there, in which case it does not necessitate any special mention in the constitution, or it is not there and a constitution will not bring it back. A purely backward-looking constitution misses out its very point of existence, which lies in the project of constructing a better future for the political society to which it is addressed. A constitution may have a limited symbolic function, but it will not be fit for resurrecting a national identity from the dead. So if the diagnosis is an identity crisis, the prognosis cannot be an injection of nineteenth-century constitutionalism to bring back national pride and identity.

Is European constitutionalism doing any better? If nineteenth-century constitutionalism is dead, what does twenty-first century constitutionalism stand for? Is it able to tell the world who Europe is and what it wants? EU constitutionalism cannot rely on a constitutional or a religious identity to send a message. Instead it has to rely on secularism: the EU is committed as much as its twenty-seven member states to secular rule as opposed to any form of theocracy. Here again, though, it seems as if secularism cannot fill the gap left by religion as a social glue and as a symbol of unitary identity. What keeps us all together if it is not religion? EU's secularism is somehow unique in a world where religion is still very prominent, including in the US. So it may well be that European secularism can become a defining trait of Europe. In order for this to be the case, however, we have to adapt and adjust its secularism. Secularism in the domestic arena used to stand for a sharp separation between church and state. In France, the conflict between them was solved by the law of 1905. But this understanding of secularism made sense within nineteenth-century constitutionalism where the nation state could benefit from greater social and political homogeneity. Nowadays we cannot talk of homogeneity anymore: Europe is characterized by deep social and political pluralism. There is still one state, but there are several religions competing in the market. Also, churches do not aim to undermine the state; they mainly want to collaborate and provide services. So the way in which church and state coexist only makes sense historically and from a domestic viewpoint. The EU is not there to replace domestic conceptions of church and state relations; however EU secularism can help to protect diversity (religious and non-religious) while minimizing conflicts. The point of EU secularism is again unity in diversity.

The protection and promotion of diversity stands in clear opposition to any thick conception of identity. If anything, we can talk of plural identities in a thin way, where the fact of being attached to several cultural markers makes us all more complex individuals in society. Diversity insists on the fact that we cannot talk anymore about a monolithic identity where religion or some other ethnic features have the lion's share. Thus European constitutionalism is meant to be based on the twin requirement of secularism and diversity.

EU constitutionalism is forward-looking in a thin sense, in that it does not put forward a substantive image of itself. It focuses on procedure and institutions, and perhaps that is exactly what constitutionalism should be about. The tendency is to overburden constitutionalism with several ambitious tasks. But perhaps a constitution should simply organize power horizontally and make sure that it does not impose itself arbitrarily over citizens. The rest is embellishment. In any case, any constitution should be aware of the past of the political society and be able to explore the future. In other words, any constitution should be both backward- and forward-looking. The Hungarian Constitution in its preamble is only backward-looking.

### 4.4.6. Between reality and ideals: Diversity v Identity

Diversity is a fragile state: how much diversity can we allow for before we witness a split society? It is an open question to know what provides unity beyond diversity. The European answer seems to be that law is to be regarded as the glue that keeps us all together. Of course, law does not have the symbolic power of religion. In this sense it is more difficult to move the masses to the love of law, or even worse to the love of a technocratic machine spouting regulative norms. It nevertheless is the case that law (and constitutional law in particular) has the task of creating a framework within which diversity can flourish. Constitutions provide unity which treats all identities on a par with each other. It would be paradoxical to claim that a constitution provides a unifying identity since the whole point of constitutions is to protect and promote diversity even in the field of identities.

Perhaps twenty-first century constitutionalism should abandon altogether the idea that it is possible to mirror a stable identity of a political society. EU constitutionalism cannot hope to reflect the identity of one political society because there are at least twenty-seven different political societies to represent. It also cannot hope to constitute one common identity because identity is not an artificial construct and there is no such thing as a minimum common identity. European identity can be an aspiration, a wish perhaps, but it cannot provide a serious basis upon which constitutional interpretation can be performed, nor can it provide a picture of what the EU really stands for. At best it can work negatively as a marker of the territory the EU occupies where the borders seem to be drawn in correspondence with clashing identities (Russia, Turkey) against which peace and security must be maintained. But in my mind even this function of identity is purely ideological.

I argued in this section that it is possible to decouple identity from constitutionalism. We cannot blame the latter for not enhancing the former; we cannot criticize the former for not inspiring the latter. It might have been the case in the past. In a long-gone Christian Europe, where religious wars decimated the continent, it was prudent to associate religious identity with political rule (*ejus regio cujus religio*). Unity was provided by a transcendental image of the world. Today, we have to accept that the world as we see it in Europe has lost its transcendental aspiration. Questions of religious identity have been bracketed out of the picture. Whether or not this is a good thing is a separate issue: what matters here is that we have to make sense of the world from within the immanent frame. Secular law as a tool for maximizing diversity while minimizing conflicts is the best thing we have to re-establish a solid constitutionalism without the talk of constitutional identity. Constitutional identity would bog down constitutions and make them too partisan. At the interpretative stage, it would not help constitutional courts to balance competing constitutional interests; it would instead add a further layer of complexity which judges should be happy to do away with. Regrettably, I expect that national and European courts will enjoin in this game.

The language of identity, be it national or religious identity, has certainly not disappeared. The Hungarian Constitution is the last example of a populist resurgence of nationalism in religious and ethnic terms. This is a sign of crisis rather than assertion. If national identity was established and flourishing, it would not need to be asserted in a constitution. Even in this case, however, it is unclear to what extent the language of identity could have a legal impact. If it did, and had negative consequences in terms of the protection of fundamental rights, it may be that Hungarian national identity would have to be appraised and evaluated in the light of European norms that clash with it. If, for example, the secular equidistance requested by constitutions was not secured, it would be the ground for an interesting litigation. All this is speculation, the kind of speculation that lawyers must avoid by turning away from the language of identity.

## 4.5. The Case for Inclusion of Christian Values

Weiler not only argues for the desirability of the inclusion of Christian values in the preamble but claims its necessity from three different perspectives. Firstly, he presents a constitutional argument. Secondly, he argues for a philosophical link between liberalism and Christian doctrine. Thirdly, he suggests a prudential reason for such an inclusion.

The constitutional argument is divided into a formal and a substantive argument. The formal argument claims that the lack of reference to God or to Christian values does not show respect for the constitutional traditions of the member states. For instance, according to Weiler, such a solution goes directly against the constitutional documents of several European states such as England, Malta, Greece, and Germany; and favours strong secular constitutions such as the French or the Italian texts. These examples, however, seem to me to be inaccurate. The law of organized religion in England is a compromise between secularism and establishment.[18] It therefore cannot be adduced as an example of a country with a non-secular legal framework. On the other extreme of the spectrum is France which entrenches in its very constitution a commitment to *laïcité* that cannot be found anywhere in the preambles of the Lisbon Treaty or the Charter of Fundamental Rights. So it seems that the EU is not choosing an extreme model of aggressive *laïcité* over and above a constitutional model of friendly accommodation. The EU is simply fashioning its own model which preserves and promotes diversity as Article 22 of the charter amply confirms: 'The Union shall respect cultural, religious and linguistic diversity.' This position seems to me the most desirable.

However, Weiler cites the preamble to the Polish Constitution as the ideal compromise solution that the EU could have followed. In that preamble the constitution proclaims:

---

[18] J Rivers, *The Law of Organized Religions: Between Establishment and Secularism* (Oxford University Press, 2010).

We the Polish Nation—all citizens of the Republic,
Both those who believe in God as the source of truth, justice, good and beauty,
As well as those not sharing such faith but respecting those universal values as arising
from other sources,
    Equal in rights and obligations towards the common good . . .

The suggestion is that this formulation represents both religious and non-religious people and their world-views. It is presented as being more inclusive than a secular preamble. On this point I sharply disagree since the notion of secularism I defended throughout is not to be opposed to religious people and not to be equated to the philosophical views of non-religious people. A secular approach as I understand it is equally distant from religious and non-religious people and their philosophical views. In fact, a secular approach makes their life in common possible by extrapolating common intermediate values from their competing positions. To this, one has to add that the Polish text is not meant to reflect a lofty ideal of respect but it has been the result of a 'hastily concocted opportunistic compromise between the Catholic Bishops and the centre-left political forces who dominated the parliament'.[19] This down-to-earth depiction of the Polish compromise suggests that, instead of reaching a noble ideal, the Polish *pouvoir constituent* reached a Solomonic decision that complicates the task for lawyers and politicians.

The substantive argument is even more problematic. Weiler explains that the EU and Christianity share the same commitment in tolerance and pluralism. Together they can collaborate to uphold those values; there is no need to keep church and state separate for fear that the former may push forward its own agenda: the agenda is the same in either case. As I argued in chapter 1, however, much depends on what is meant exactly by tolerance. The position of the church is much closer to what I call moralizing toleration rather than to the preferred non-moralizing tolerance.[20] The Catholic Church insists that there is only one truth, which means that whoever does not sign up to that truth is wrong, albeit only tolerably wrong in many cases. This is a clear example of moralizing toleration which is not easy to square with genuine pluralism, if by the latter one means not only that we disagree about values but also that we disagree as to their ultimate justification (or lack thereof). Tolerance and pluralism are compatible only if they both subscribe to an open attitude, and principled distance, vis-à-vis competing world-views. As a consequence, the substantive argument appears to be merely formulaic

---

[19] Wojciech Sadurski, 'Laundering Values', unpublished manuscript on file with the author.
[20] J Ratzinger, *Truth and Tolerance: Christian belief and World Religions* (Ignatius Press, 2004).

and inaccurate for Christianity and secularism do not have the same under-standing of tolerance and pluralism.

From the viewpoint of constitutional interpretation, such a reference would have made hard cases truly unpalatable. Weiler argues that the inclusion of Christian values in the European Constitution would not be the 'Trojan horse' of Christian morality into European law. The ECJ or other constitutional courts of the member states would not give an advantageous position to religious interpretation over other interpretations on issues such as abortion, euthanasia, or divorce. It seems, however, that upon reflection any explicit reference to Christian values is bound to have either of the two following effects: on the one hand, judges may be nudged into polarized positions defending either Christian or non-Christian interpretations of the constitution. On the other hand, a judge caught in the dilemma created by polarization may simply end up opting for his own personal convictions as a middle ground. Neither of these two outcomes is desirable from the viewpoint of a Europe that wants to protect and promote diversity by taking a stance that is equally distant from any specific world-view.

The more general philosophical argument deals with the relationship between humanism and Christianity. Weiler argues that the invocation of the traditions of humanism and enlightenment ignore their Christian roots and are as such imbalanced. Others have argued exactly the contrary claiming that the European public order strikes a good balance between religious, cultural, and humanist influences.[21] I insist that the point of a constitutional framework is neither to take into account specific world-views such as the Christian one, nor to balance them one with another in an effort to find a compromise. The point of a secular framework is to protect and promote each and every world-view from an equally distant perspective. This is otherwise called secular neutrality, which is sometimes mistaken for a nega-tive attitude towards diversity. In my definition, neutrality does not equate to an absence of judgement; neutrality is the doctrine with which the secular state protects and promotes diversity.[22] This means that neutrality requires a positive choice in favour of social diversity and to the detriment of social homogeneity which was artificially imposed on European states with the Peace of Westphalia.

Weiler's interpretation of the relation between liberal-humanist and Chris-tian values has a revisionist and simplistic flavour. Historians of the Enlight-enment have pointed out that there are at least two clearly separate trends

---

[21] McCrea, *Religion and the Public Order of the European Union.*
[22] For a discussion of neutrality, see ch. 5.

within Enlightenment thought.[23] One trend is radical and has always fought to establish a sharp distinction between philosophy and theology starting with Spinoza's *Theological-Political Treatise*. The other trend is more moderate and has always attempted to build a liberal understanding of politics that is responsive to Christian values as it is the case for Locke, for example. Thus, the link between liberal-humanist and Christian values cannot be reduced to an either/or proposition. The struggle has been complex and varied from country to country. It is better regarded as a dialectical relationship rather than a mutually supportive one. The dialectic varied from sharp opposition on the part of Catholic people to collaboration on the part of Protestant ones. In Spinoza's specific case, the elaboration of a secular ethics required equal distancing from the Jewish and the Protestant communities to which he had been previously attached. The reference that the Lisbon Treaty makes to both religious and humanist inheritance is more than sufficient and all encompassing to pay tribute to that dialogical relationship.

The third and final argument for inclusion is prudential: the 'Christian deficit' of the European Constitution could offend religious minorities. This may sound at first counter-intuitive but it certainly contains a grain of truth. Weiler argues that minorities would probably interpret the silence in relation to one's own religious traditions as an implicit unwillingness to recognize the religion and culture of minorities. From a religious perspective this is true under certain precise conditions: if the choice is between an aggressive laique state and a religion-friendly state, the religious person will choose the latter. Yet, as I have stressed time and again, a secular approach need not be exclusive of religion and aggressive towards religious views. From this viewpoint, I believe that it is an utter sophism to say that religious minorities interpret the failure to assert the religious values of the majority as an implicit refusal to accept other religious particularities. The opposition between a laique state and a religion-friendly state is asymmetrical and construed with the precise aim of nudging people towards the latter option. The real contrast is between a laique state and a strongly Christian state: between France and Ireland to give an example. Faced with these two choices, a Jewish or Muslim minority may well be more attracted to a secular state that is inclusive of religion. This remains of course in the realm of speculation, but the point is very important: the prudential argument is based on a false opposition.

The case for inclusion fails on the three fronts. Even if one were to accept the formal constitutional argument that the majority of European member

---

[23] J Israel, *A Revolution of the Mind: Radical Enlightenment and the Intellectual Origins of Democracy* (Princeton University Press, 2010).

states resorted to an invocation of God or Christian values in their constitutional preambles, the absence of Christian values in the EU Treaty and
Charter of Fundamental Rights is not to be interpreted as a thundering
silence, but instead it should be understood as a positive affirmation of a
secular approach that values diversity and cherishes all world-views while
refraining from embracing any of them. Jurgen Habermas makes a useful
distinction between two conceptions of toleration that is helpful to restate
the key point. On the one hand, there is the toleration of the outsider
described by the author as a simple expression of the patronizing benevolence
of a particular world-view that disagrees with another world-view but agrees
to tolerate it under certain conditions. Such an attitude providing for the
covert persistence of old prejudices is not on a par with the reciprocal
toleration of different religious doctrines as is required by the secular liberal.
On the other hand, a meaningful toleration that ought to characterize the EU
is based on mutual recognition and mutual acceptance of divergent world-
views. I would add that the secular state provides a neutral framework within
which mutual recognition and acceptance can take place. The type of
toleration Weiler suggests when proposing the inclusion of Christian values
corresponds to the first imperfect definition of toleration. To illustrate with a
final example, to claim for the inclusion of Christian values in the EU is
similar to claiming that a secular state like Syria should recognize Islamic
values more prominently in its constitution given its constitutional history.
To espouse this version suggests a lack of awareness of the disastrous effects of
the politicization of religion in the modern world, and in particular in the
Middle East. A secular Europe which is inclusive of religion should be
preferred over an aggressive self-assertion of either a laique or a Christian
Europe. Thus, the insertion of Christian values in the European Constitution
was correctly rejected.

## 4.6. Religious Temperament, Secular Philosophy, and the European Constitution

Does the rejection of Christian values in the preamble amount to the
embracing of a secular world-view or a secular philosophy for the regulation
of behaviour in the public sphere? It doesn't. A secular world-view which
excludes any other world-views from the political playing field would be self-
defeating: the point of secularism is to maximize freedom of thought and
belief, not to narrow it down to one single way of thinking the world. Nor
is it desirable to adopt a secular standpoint that creates a sharp distinction

between private and public sphere. To do that would impose an unfair and asymmetrical burden on religious people vis-à-vis non-religious ones. Why would a non-religious individual be able to appeal to all his beliefs and opinions in the public sphere (right and wrong ones), while religious people would have to appeal only to their non-religious beliefs?

To talk of different, competing world-views means that the way in which we understand our lives and the world surrounding us can be looked at from many different viewpoints that cannot possibly be collapsed into one. People, religious and non-religious, have different interests, priorities, and expectations. Inevitably, their viewpoints will be different and one of the main differences is whether or not they take a religious viewpoint as to the meaning of their lives and their place in this world. Many religious viewpoints do not believe that the term of life in this world is the most important thing: life beyond this world—eternal life—is so much more important. Pluralism of viewpoints is a fact that needs to be taken into account when we deliberate about policies. Thus it is not possible to speak of a single, fully developed secular world-view which would work as a unique benchmark against which one can assess whether beliefs can be accepted as a basis for policy-making or legislation. A secular world-view, if it is possible to speak of it as such, would only be one of the many viewpoints, with no special claim of validity over other viewpoints.

The position I defend in this book is not a secular world-view but a legal secular approach. The latter is a doctrine on how to organize institutions so as to preserve a political sphere that embraces diversity of world-views, while avoiding violent tensions between them.

The secular approach expounded here does not equate to a secular philosophy either. A secular philosophy very broadly defined is a philosophy that avoids all explanation by reference to a transcendental world. Interestingly, few philosophical positions qualify fully for that title. An example of a fully secular philosophy is John Searle's: 'We do not live in several different, or even two different, worlds, a mental world and a physical world, a scientific world and a world of common sense. Rather, there is just one world; it is the world we all live in, and we need to account for how we exist as a part of it.'[24] This secular philosophy fully embraces a scientific methodology and posits as objects fit for explanation only those facts that have been scientifically ascertained. The technical level and sophistication of this type of philosophy is undoubtedly very high, but it nevertheless is unable to explain the religious temperament as this cannot be scientifically explained or singled out.[25]

---

[24] J Searle, *Mind* (Oxford University Press, 2001), 304.
[25] T Nagel, *Secular Philosophy and the Religious Temperament* (Oxford University Press, 2010).

Yet, many philosophers starting with Plato believe that the 'world as it is' is only a pale copy of the world of ideas. Such philosophy displays a distinctive religious temperament that secular philosophy is unable to explain simply because it regards it as being completely irrelevant.

This book's secular approach is neutral between purely immanent and transcendental philosophies. The point is not to understand the 'world as it is' or the world of ideas; rather, the point of my secular approach is to regulate relationships between people with different world-views and different religious or non-religious temperaments.

## 4.7. Conclusion: EU's Secularism

The EU adopts a secular approach. Its secularism is not about the relationship between church and state; this is obvious enough: the EU is not a state. EU's secularism is about diversity. This, however, does not mean that the EU attempts to mirror faithfully all the constitutional approaches of its various member states. Nor does it mean that it strikes a balance between them. To take diversity seriously the only possible approach is to keep a principled distance from any of the national positions.

EU's secularism stands for a complex set of requirements expressed in the preambles to the Lisbon Treaty and to the Charter of Fundamental Rights: the Lisbon Treaty talks of 'the universal values of the inviolable and inalienable rights of the human person, freedom, democracy, equality and the rule of law'; the charter refers to 'indivisible, universal values of human dignity, freedom, equality and solidarity; it is based on the principles of democracy and the rule of law'. The French Trinity of *liberté, égalité,* and *fraternité* is the obvious model of both preambles with only minor variations. Indeed, secularism must protect freedom of belief of religious and non-religious people; no coercion whatsoever can be justified when it aims to influencing people's beliefs. Freedom also covers religious exercise: no one can interfere or curtail the liberty to practise one's own religion. Equality is also a very important goal: religious and non-religious people have symmetrical rights and duties. Moreover, the state cannot favour any world-view (religious or non-religious) and/or adopt it as its own preferred standpoint. Fraternity requires that the EU should hear all the voices of religious and non-religious people when deliberating about its political identity and on the way in which rights and duties should be defined. On top of these political values, which are secular values, there is another goal worth stressing which emerges from the EU's insistence on democracy and the rule of law. Both democracy and the rule of law are means to achieve and maintain a maximum degree of peace and harmony amongst the various constituencies of a society. So the fourth, paramount, element of secularism is the goal of social peace through democratic deliberation and law.

The legal order of the EU has the task of reconciling different, at times diverging, interests with the aim of preventing or dissolving possible tensions and thereby contributing to social peace. The fourth goal is particularly important from the legal viewpoint as it defines its very point. Secular law is about taking different interests into account and mediating between them. This does not mean that there will be no conflict between interests and goals. On the contrary, secularism starts from the acknowledgement that conflicts between different interests and different people are unavoidable. Yet, they do not have to escalate into violent and harsh confrontations. Secularism is the attempt to construe one community out of all the possible differences that there can be.

The EU's secularism is a break from the history of tragedies produced by religious conflicts. The first step in 1648 did not take religion out of the political equation, but simply divided Europe into regions of homogeneity. Diversity only existed inter-nations but not intra-nations. It is only in the aftermath of the tragedy of World War II that Europe finally embraced a more complex and articulate understanding of diversity, which is now the *leitmotiv* of Europe. The last chapters in this saga, in particular the Charter of Fundamental Rights confirm the EU's commitment to a form of secularism that protects diversity as much as possible. In the next chapter, I will examine the extent to which the ECtHR protects religious diversity by challenging domestic religious monopolies.

# 5

# A Marketplace of Religions

## 5.1. Introduction

Pluralism about religions and world-views is a fairly novel phenomenon in Europe. This may sound too blunt but it is not if one thinks about the principle of *ejus regio, cujus religio* (to each kingdom, its own religion) instituted by the Peace Treaties of Augsburg (1555) and Westphalia (1648). In both cases, the aim was to organize autonomous nation states whose authority would be supported by a homogeneous religious background. Each state would have its own religion, and each religion would have its own states. This amounted to establishing a monopoly of one religious confession within each state.

Europe today is a very different place. As I have already pointed out in the previous chapter, the EU is a supranational organization whose aim is to preserve a great degree of diversity within each member state and across the union. Chapter 4 suggested that the EU's secularism is precisely about the protection and promotion of diversity rather than the relationship between church and state, or the reshaping of the EU's constitutional identity as some would wish. Diversity is also one of the top priorities for the Council of Europe and in particular for the ECtHR. With regards to freedom of religion, I shall argue in this chapter, the ECtHR has worked to dismantle the monopoly of one established religion and to enhance competition between different faiths. In other words, it has begun to set up a marketplace of religions.

Since the landmark decision in *Kokkinakis*,[1] which lifted the anti-proselytizing clause of the Greek Constitution, the Strasbourg Court has attempted to ease the life of minority religions and to create some distance between the state and the predominant religion. To speak of a marketplace is to acknowledge that religion has a role to play in the public sphere, while also stressing that that place is not the privilege of one religion only. The idea of a public

---

[1] ECtHR, 25 May 1993.

role for religion, however, is not an original aim of the Council of Europe. Prior to *Kokkinakis*, the European Commission of Human Rights essentially treated religion as a private concern.

The public and collective dimensions of the right are developed by the ECtHR at a later stage. These elements of the right do not come without major issues. There are three main problems: firstly, if religious voices are protected in the public realm, what exactly is the relationship between religion and democracy? Secondly, if religious groups are allowed to represent the interests of some people, what is the relationship between the state and those groups? And finally, if those groups have their own rules as to how to regulate their community, what is the relationship between those rules and the law of the state?

The marketplace of religions is built along these three lines. It is far from being fully developed and some will resist the very idea; not in the name of monopoly, but in the name of other symbolic ideals that they do not want reduced to the logic of a secular institution such as the market. Here, however, the market is only a metaphor for an organized social practice that is neither completely unregulated nor spontaneously coherent due to the homogeneity of one culture. The marketplace of religions follows three main guiding principles: pluralism, neutrality, and secularity.[2] Each will be examined in turn. Section 5.6. will deal with the limits of the marketplace of religions and section 5.7. will conclude.


## 5.2. Monopoly and Plurality

Religious monopolies can be *de jure* or *de facto*. Both of them should be regulated so that religious pluralism can truly flourish within the legal framework. *De jure* monopolies can at times be very blatant. Any constitution that recognizes an established church or a privileged relation between the state and a church suffers from a presumption of *de jure* monopoly. So for example, the Greek Constitution that recognizes the Greek Orthodox Church as the established church and grants it legal privileges is under a strong presumption of creating a *de jure* monopoly, undermining the possibility of an open society where religious pluralism can thrive. From this viewpoint, the *Kokkinakis* case rightly insisted that the crime of proselytism

---

[2] For a parallel analysis, see Julie Ringelheim, 'Rights, Religion and the Public Sphere: The European Court of Human Rights in Search of a Theory?' in Lorenzo Zucca and Camil Ungureanu (eds), *Law, State, Religion in the New Europe: Debates and Dilemmas* (Cambridge University Press, 2012).

could only be defined in the narrowest sense in order not to affect freedom of religion.

There should be a presumption of *de jure* monopoly also when a constitution entrenches a strong and aggressive secular principle such as *laïcité*, as is the case in France and Turkey. The presumption is confirmed if *laïcité* is interpreted in such a way as to exclude comprehensive religious views and symbols from public life. It was therefore wrong for the French state to impose an absolute ban on the wearing of the Islamic headscarf in public schools. And it was wrong for the TCC to ban the Islamic party, Refah Partisi, from political life. Now it should be possible to distinguish between secularism as a form of *de jure* monopoly (as an entrenched worldview) which culminates in the total exclusion of religious voices in the public sphere, and a secularism that as a default position makes the marketplace of religions possible. The confusion between the two notions of secularism is very clear in *Lautsi*,[3] where the Grand Chamber as well as the concurring Judges Bonello and Power present secularism as an ideology competing amongst many others rather than a legal doctrine for the organization of public space. Neither the Court, nor the concurring opinions of Bonello and Power, highlight that there are several understandings of secularism and the one they chose was far from being uncontroversial to say the least.

*De facto* monopoly can hamper the chances of construing a legal framework in which fundamental rights for all religious and non-religious people are guaranteed and protected. A *de facto* monopoly exists when one church exercises a very strong influence on political and civil society. Few would object to the idea that the Catholic Church exercises a very strong influence in Italy or in Spain, for example. A recent example concerns the presence of religion in the public sphere. Any central square in Italy is dominated by a church. This is often equated much too quickly with the idea that other religions have to ask permission of the Catholic Church if they wish to represent themselves in those places. An example I have in mind concerned a pro-Palestinian demonstration that ended up in Milan's central square at the Muslim time of prayer. They therefore proceeded to pray in front of the Catholic Cathedral, which provoked an outrage in the media. The Catholic Church when interrogated showed a certain degree of understanding. But this only confirms that there is a *de facto* monopoly of one religion in Italy, otherwise there would not be an assumption that the Catholic Church controls the most public of all spaces: the central square of the city.

---

[3] *Lautsi v Italy*, 18 March 2011, ECtHR (Grand Chamber), Application no 30814/06.

Pluralism in this context seems to perform a negative role: the Court wants to lessen the impact of the constitutionally entrenched monopoly of one church. But in reality the pluralism the Court is referring to holds for both religious and non-religious people and it is the pluralism derived from freedom of thought, conscience, and belief. This establishes a deep connection between the marketplace of religions and the more general marketplace of ideas, which is the deep reservoir of, and forum for, democracy. In other words, the marketplace of religions is just a subcategory of the more general marketplace of ideas. It is, however, unclear to what extent and how freely religious people can participate in the broader marketplace of ideas. It is often suggested that religious beliefs can only play a role if appropriately backed up by non-religious reasons available to all the participants in the debate.[4] This suggestion has been played down and criticized in different ways, but it has also been defended by prominent scholars. The most notable defence is by appeal to a distinction between an official and unofficial public sphere: in the latter, religious arguments should be allowed freely.[5]

One lingering question is whether religious beliefs can be used to undermine democracy and secularism. There is no doubt, however, that freedom of thought protects any such belief as long as they do not instigate violence.[6] It is for this reason that it is hard to understand on what basis the Strasbourg Court concludes that the activities of religious parties in purporting to establish parallel legal systems or to replace secular law with religious law are incompatible with the ECHR. The real problem of Refah seems to be its flirting with violence, but not its campaign for increased application of sharia law. Surely the claim is protected, even if the actual implementation of the idea may be problematic.[7] Everyone is entitled to claim that law should be reformed according to one's own convictions; this seems to be a fairly straightforward point. Moreover, Refah never resorted to violent action in practice, so it was very harsh to hold it responsible on that ground alone.

A second problem has to do with the right to ridicule religion in a democracy. Here the position of the Court is questionable as it seems to be prepared to limit free speech when it offends a majority religion.[8] However, one wonders whether the same treatment will be extended to minority

    [4] John Rawls, 'The Idea of Public Reason Revisited' in John Rawls, *The Law of People* (Harvard University Press, 1999), 143–4.
    [5] J Habermas, 'The Place of Religion in the Public Sphere', European Journal of Philosophy, 14 (1) (2006), 1–25.
    [6] *Refah Partisi (The Welfare Party) and ors v Turkey*, 13 February 2003, ECtHR (Grand Chamber), Application nos 41340/98, 41342/98, 41343/98, and 41344/98.
    [7] This will be explored in ch. 6 where some myths about sharia will be dispelled.
    [8] *Otto-Preminger-Institut v Austria*, ECtHR, 20 September 1994, *Serie* A, 295.

religions in the case of the Danish cartoons, where the Prophet Mohammed was associated with Islamic terrorists. A differential treatment in these cases cannot be easily justified aside from the fact that one deals with a Christian religion and the other deals with Islam. It would probably be best to revisit the very *Otto Preminger* case in order to enhance religious pluralism of all stripes, while regulating the relationship between religion and democracy in a way that does not end up in a zero-sum game.

Pluralism is the first axis of the marketplace of religions. It requires the abolition of monopolies on the one hand, and the creation of a link between the marketplaces of religions and ideas. Democracy can and should accommodate the presence of religious voices along all other voices. The weight and place of religious voices can be variable, but this does not mean that it should be non-existing.

## 5.3. Neutrality and the Marketplace of Religions

Religions offer various goods and services to society; the state has an interest in promoting and monitoring those services. Some of them are very valuable for the whole society while others are only valuable to few. A very useful service for the whole society, for example, is the assistance of elderly and vulnerable people. A less valuable function consists in the creation of communities of belief isolated and at loggerheads with other communities. A well-functioning marketplace of religions will help create access to good services, while intervening to curb the negative effects of some practices. More importantly, it will create the preconditions for a productive collaboration between the state and various different religions. The principle that guides that relationship is that of neutrality, which the ECtHR does not interpret in a narrow fashion to mean either strict separation or blind uniform treatment. Instead neutrality implies collaboration on the basis of principled distance.

The ECtHR stated the principle of neutrality in the landmark case *Hasan and Chaush*;[9] it subsequently held that the state must act as 'the neutral and impartial organizer of the exercise of various religions, faiths and beliefs'.[10] At first it was unclear how the Strasbourg Court would articulate this principle. After all, two predominant models of the relationship between church and state closely link strict separation with the idea of neutrality. Thus, the French

---

[9] *Hasan and Chaush v Bulgaria*, 26 October 2000, ECtHR (Grand Chamber), Application no 30985/96, 2000.
[10] *Refah Partisi (The Welfare Party) and ors v Turkey*, note 6 above, para 100.

model insists on separation as unilateral exclusion of any religion from the public sphere. Within this model, the state is neutral in so far as it pushes religion back into the private sphere and protects it only within those bounds. But of course this limits the positive role of religion on the one hand, and on the other it allows for too great interference by the state. The role of the state here is to control and monitor religions so that they do not exceed their bounds. Largely, in practice, this consists of legitimizing a *status quo* whereby majority religions have acquired a very prominent and protected status within societies whereas minorities are constantly and inevitably pushed back and marginalized. For example, in education Catholic schools are very well established whereas other religious schools are not.

A second model of separation is enforced in the USA. In this context, neutrality means that church and state are required by the constitution to abstain from interfering in each other's business. They are meant to inhabit two different spheres of mutual exclusion. The state has no power in matters of religion. The church has no power in matters of state. No doubt this sounds attractive, but the enormous amount of litigation in the US attests to its difficulty to maintain in practice. The main problem with this conception of neutrality is that the state is incapable of intervening in the market to prevent domination of one religion over others. Also, the state is unable to intervene if one religion imposes a great degree of domination from within. Given that the US Market of Religions was set up for an overwhelmingly Christian Protestant population, the system does not cope well with other confessions. In particular, it struggles with religions that claim a bigger role in the public realm, such as Catholicism in the past and Islam today.

The ECtHR does not interpret neutrality in either the French or American way. To start with, separation between church and state is not required by the principle of neutrality as interpreted in Strasbourg. Thus, for example, a measure of establishment is compatible with the Convention system (as for example seen in Greece, the UK, Sweden, Norway, and Denmark). Even though, the Court still pays particular attention to the consequences of systems of establishment, as was attested to in the *Folgerø* decision where the Court declared as incompatible with the ECHR the practice of teaching religious education in a way that gave too much space to the established religion.[11] It nevertheless remains the case that separation is not required and collaboration between church and state is possible.

According to the ECHR the state should refrain from interfering in matters of belief. If a conflict arises between two religions, the state should

---

[11]  *Folgerø v Norway* (2008) 46 EHRR 47.

in principle refrain from taking a side to the dispute (this is one of the central meanings of neutrality). It can nevertheless intervene as a mediator in the dispute in order to foster peaceful and harmonious coexistence. Neutrality can therefore be interpreted as the ability on the part of the state to engage and collaborate with religions at a principled distance from any particular confession, as if the state was an umpire in a sport event or more to the point the organizer of a well-functioning market.

The very idea of the marketplace of religions involves a shift from separation to collaboration. Collaboration implies that religion has an interest for some people as well as for society at large. As stated at the beginning, religion may play a valuable role and in so far as it does, the state must take into account the role of any religions and acknowledge it. Thus it is not necessary for the state to treat all religions in exactly the same way in order to protect neutrality. Also different religions contribute differently to the life of society and should therefore be treated differently but with equal respect. Treating them differently recognizes their specific requirements as well as their specific contribution. Substantive neutrality may even require the state to intervene where a bias is affecting the place of a religion in society.

Neutrality was central in the *Lautsi* case on the crucifix in the classroom. In the first *Lautsi* case, the Second Chamber suggested that neutrality implied that the state is not free to choose religious symbols as its own symbols. The crucifix was presented as being in flat opposition with the rights of the parents to educate their own children according to their own convictions. Even if this was the case, it does not follow without argument that neutrality as principled distance requires a blank wall. It may require a wall with several symbols or a wall with one symbol which represents several important values. Moreover, in the Italian context to impose unilaterally from Strasbourg a ban on crucifixes can be seen to amount to a lack of respect for cultural traditions where local histories are taken into account in order to explain the presence of certain religious symbols. The Grand Chamber put forward a different, albeit equally puzzling, understanding of neutrality which I will examine in the following section.

## 5.4. Exploring the Neutrality Dilemmas

Neutrality is a myth: how can we possibly distance ourselves from ideas we deeply care about, such as the presence of religion in the public sphere? Understood this way, neutrality is neither achievable, nor desirable. Since I wish to say something more about neutrality, it is perhaps necessary to distinguish different ideas of neutrality in order to see its value. The example above refers to theoretical neutrality—that is, neutrality about beliefs and the viewpoint one ought to take when assessing them. In matters of religion and politics, theoretical neutrality is a chimera. It requires people to step out from their set of beliefs altogether in order to take a detached viewpoint— something close to what a scientist achieves when studying an object from a completely detached viewpoint (even on this point there is major disagreement in social sciences as to whether it is possible to detach oneself from the object of study: for example, see the different methodologies used by anthropologists and more quantitative social scientists).

Theoretical neutrality must be kept apart from practical neutrality. The latter is about behaviour and the attitude one ought to take when regulating it in matters of religion and politics. It requires people, and in particular officials, to refrain from inserting their own biases and prejudices into the decisions on particular social problems that involve the overlap of religious and secular norms.

In constitutional matters, practical neutrality is more important than theoretical neutrality. It is about an attitude that officials should take, rather than a more stringent requirement about their beliefs. No doubt constitutional neutrality is a myth if we think of theoretical neutrality. The constitution itself is by definition value-laden in so far as it chooses the best moral values for a given polity. Western constitutions, for example, are biased towards liberal secular democracies (LSD) as a basic political framework. Thus, theoretical neutrality at the constitutional level is off the table. The question is: does practical neutrality make sense within the legal-constitutional framework?

This question is of great importance since neutrality is central to the jurisprudence of Western constitutional states. In the USA neutrality is advocated both in free exercise and establishment cases. In Europe, most constitutional courts have neutrality as their guiding principle and the ECtHR mentions it whenever it deals with freedom of religion. I will focus on the latter experience so as to limit myself to very recent litigation. The aim is not to give an exhaustive account of neutrality, but to understand whether it makes meaningful requests on state officials in charge of policies that affect the lives of religious people.

In order to do that, I shall first attempt to locate neutrality within the web of the constitutional concepts that apply in this field. This may give us greater indication as to its meaning, scope, and strength. Then I shall explore three dilemmas that surround this hazy concept. Firstly, the democratic dilemma: can LSD be neutral between religious and non-religious voices? Secondly, the minority dilemma: can LSD be neutral between minority and majority symbols? Thirdly, the neutrality dilemma properly so called: can the law produced by LSD be neutral between religious and non-religious people? The conclusion will attempt to sketch what it means for a state official to be practically neutral.

## 5.4.1. Neutrality: friends and foes

In order to grasp the contours of neutrality in the legal context, it is useful to examine it in relation to other concepts that populate the universe of constitutional protection of religious freedom. Neutrality can thus be compared to secularism, pluralism, and impartiality: their comparison may tell us a little bit more about the scope and strength of each one. The Grand Chamber decision in *Lautsi* offers an interesting discussion about those concepts and mentions neutrality forty-eight times.

One the one hand, the Italian government argues that secularism must be sharply separated from neutrality. Neutrality is inclusive, secularism is exclusive. The Italian government is firmly committed to neutrality, but not to secularism. In fact neutrality means that the state should refrain from promoting secularism which amounts to a form of proselytism:

The Government also criticized the Chamber's judgment for deriving from the concept of confessional 'neutrality' a principle excluding any relations between the State and a particular religion, whereas neutrality required the public administrative authorities to take all religions into account. The judgment was accordingly based on confusion between 'neutrality' (an 'inclusive concept') and 'secularism' (an 'exclusive concept'). Moreover, in the Government's view, neutrality meant that States should refrain from promoting not only a particular religion but also atheism, 'secularism' on the State's part being no less problematic than proselytising by the State. The Chamber's judgment was thus based on a misunderstanding and amounted to favouring an irreligious or antireligious approach of which the applicant, as a member of the Union of atheists and rationalist agnostics, was asserted to be a militant supporter.[12]

On the other hand Ms Lautsi believed that secularism and neutrality go hand in hand. The applicant argued that secularism mandates neutrality. Neutrality means that the state should adopt the same attitude towards all religious views. Moreover, the state should not interfere with them. In the educational context, neutrality means that the state should create a space that is free from religious symbols:

The applicants contended that every democratic State had a duty to guarantee the freedom of conscience, pluralism, equal treatment of beliefs and the secular nature of

---

[12] *Lautsi v Italy*, note 3 above, para 35.

institutions. The principle of secularism required above all neutrality on the part of the State, which should keep out of the religious sphere and adopt the same attitude with regard to all religious currents. In other words, neutrality obliged the State to establish a neutral space within which everyone could freely live according to his own beliefs. By imposing religious symbols, namely crucifixes, in classrooms, the Italian State was doing the opposite.[13]

Judge Bonello, who wrote a concurring opinion, believes that both neutrality and secularism should not be part of the decision:

In parallel with freedom of religion, there has evolved in civilised societies a catalogue of noteworthy (often laudable) values cognate to, but different from, freedom of religion, like secularism, pluralism, the separation of Church and State, religious neutrality, religious tolerance. All of these represent superior democratic commodities which Contracting States are free to invest in or not to invest in, and many have done just that. *But these are not values protected by the Convention*, and it is fundamentally flawed to juggle these dissimilar concepts as if they were interchangeable with freedom of religion. Sadly, traces of such all but rigorous overspill appear in the Court's case-law too.[14]

Judge Power, who wrote a separate concurring opinion, believes that neutrality has to do with pluralism, but not with secularism. In fact pluralism and secularism are at loggerheads: secularism would be one ideology as opposed to pluralism that protects many different viewpoints:

Neutrality requires a pluralist approach on the part of the State, not a secularist one. It encourages respect for all world views rather than a preference for one. To my mind, the Chamber Judgment was striking in its failure to recognise that secularism (which was the applicant's preferred belief or world view) was, in itself, one ideology among others. A preference for secularism over alternative world views—whether religious, philosophical or otherwise—is not a neutral option.[15]

Neutrality and impartiality are closely linked by the Court and by Judge Rosakis. The two are supposed to be central tenets of the Court in this area:

The keywords deriving from the prior case-law are 'neutrality and impartiality'. As the Court has noted in the present judgment, 'States have responsibility for ensuring, neutrally and impartially, the exercise of various religions, faiths and beliefs. Their role is to help maintain public order, religious harmony and tolerance in a democratic society, particularly between opposing groups.'[16]

As can be seen, there is a real confusion on each one of these notions: neutrality, pluralism, secularism, and impartiality. Much depends on the

---

[13] Ibid, para 43.          [14] Ibid, Bonello concurring opinion, at 2.2.
[15] Ibid, Power concurring opinion.          [16] Ibid, see para 60, *in fine*.

background assumptions that each judge takes as a starting point. If they consider secularism to be an ideology, then they would try to distance it from neutrality. If they consider secularism as a positive world-view, they tend to associate it with neutrality. It seems more difficult to consider secularism as being neutral in itself even if it is what Ms Lautsi believes. It may nevertheless be argued that secularism as a legal doctrine is precisely meant to encapsulate a general duty of the state to neutrality vis-à-vis religion.

Neutrality is one of the values that many constitutions select amongst others. Constitutional courts all over Europe make it their central commitment in matters of religious education as Judge Malinverni reminds us:

> What I find more important, however, is that where they have been required to give a ruling on the issue, the European supreme or constitutional courts have always, without exception, given precedence to the principle of State denominational neutrality: the German Constitutional Court, the Swiss Federal Court, the Polish Constitutional Court and, in a slightly different context, the Italian Court of Cassation.[17]

Courts themselves know very well what neutrality means under the name of impartiality. That is the central virtue they are requested to display in administering justice. Impartiality, just like neutrality, cannot mean that we fully divest ourselves of our background knowledge; we are not blind or deaf (even though justice is often portrayed as the blind goddess). Can a Christian judge still be neutral? She's required to adopt a neutral viewpoint or, better, a neutral attitude towards any form of religion. That is what neutrality means.

Perhaps one way of fleshing out the meaning of neutrality is by reference to the idea of its opposite: bias, commitment, partiality, predisposition, and prejudice. Thus the obligation of neutrality means refraining from being biased, prejudiced, etc. We all have biases and prejudices of course, but in our official capacity we are requested to minimize their effects. This meaning of neutrality is largely negative; it should be complemented with a more positive meaning: once biases and prejudices are overcome, we are left with a number of options that may be at odds one with another. Neutrality cannot possibly mean that officials must be indifferent towards those options. Neutrality must also involve the ability to reach a compromise between polarized positions without succumbing to either one or the other.

Neutrality as a practical attitude has two layers. Firstly, it requires officials to refrain from endorsing biases and prejudices. Secondly, it requires officials to reach compromises that overcome polarized positions. I hope this gives us more indication as to the meaning of neutrality as a practical attitude of state

---

17 Ibid, Malinverni dissenting opinion, see paras 23 and 28.

officials. Neutrality thus defined remains open to a number of thorny quandaries to which I now turn.

## 5.4.2. Three dilemmas

### 5.4.2.1. *The democratic dilemma and neutrality-as-deafness*

LSD are said to be neutral between competing world-views. Religious and non-religious people are free to develop their views and this is guaranteed by their freedom of thought, expression, and religion. In a democracy disagreement about ideas and beliefs is protected so that everyone can flourish according to her own life plans. All this sounds fine, but what does neutrality really mean in this context? In political matters neutrality means that no world-view can aspire to dominate political institutions and public debates. Moreover, neutrality means that political institutions will be deaf to arguments based on partial world-views since it is not possible to shape public norms on the basis of beliefs that cannot be understood, let alone shared, by everyone.

Neutrality as deafness may seem like a wise constraint on everyone's beliefs for the sake of the public interest. But what if LSD themselves encapsulate and promote one biased world-view? What if the framework itself is not neutral? Can it then be neutral towards other world-views? Some argue that secularism is one world-view amongst many others; it is coherent and desirable, but it is just one world-view and there are many others that are equally coherent and desirable. Religious people believe that it is possible for a religious world-view to be the framework for all in a society. Instead of LSD, that would give rise to a theocratic regime, like Iran.

Here's the dilemma: if secularism is a superior world-view, then LSD cannot be neutral between religious and secular world-views. If instead secularism is just a possible world-view, then it is not clear why it takes pride of place within LSD. In practice, this means that one world-view, the secular world-view, is off the democratic table: it is not negotiable and is superior to any other world-view. As a consequence, this means that religious people will find it much more difficult to express their views and their voices since they will always struggle to make them understandable within a framework biased in favour of secular views.

The asymmetry between religious and non-religious people is acknowledged by prominent philosophers and officials but is not fully and satisfactorily dealt with (this may be a sign that we are facing a genuine dilemma, rather than a spurious one). Rawls and Habermas, for example, have their own ways of encouraging religious participation either by loosening the requirements of public reason (Rawls) or by making religious reason a little more appealing (Habermas).

John Rawls displays in his writings a religious temperament. For him the place of religion in a liberal democracy is an open question.[18] In his essay, 'Public Reason Revisited', there are important insights in to the possible contribution of religion to democratic debates. In principle, public reason must be available to everyone, and thus prima facie religion seems to be excluded from participation in the production of norms for the regulation of society. However, Rawls sees the problem in barring religion altogether from the public sphere. He therefore adds a proviso to the restrictions imposed by public reason on the basis of which religion could make its contribution: religious views should be heard by policymakers on the condition that those views will in time be supported and buttressed by underlying public reasons. This way, religious views are not altogether silenced in public, but still a hefty burden is imposed on them.

In his influential work on religion in the public sphere, Jurgen Habermas builds on Rawls's work and attempts to further mitigate the burden imposed on religion.[19] His post-secular position recognizes a greater space for religion and imagination in order to tackle the impoverishment of democracy and public reason. Habermas departs from his Marxist position which saw democracy and religion as enemies. His post-secularism attempts to elucidate the ways in which religion can make a positive contribution to public reason and democracy. Unlike Rawls, Habermas does not require that religious views be supported by underlying public reason, but that religious people engage in a creative process that translates their views into a language that is comprehensible to all. This cognitive process also requires that non-religious people be open to learning from religious views appropriately presented. In this way Habermas hopes to stimulate a virtuous process whereby religious and non-religious people can learn from each other while at the same time reinvigorating the moral fabric of democracy.

Despite these efforts, the problem is not overcome, but its effects merely mitigated. Religious voices are burdened, if not silenced, in the public sphere by the application of a conception of neutrality-as-deafness (NAD). There are four corollaries to NAD:

1. Everyone can cultivate her own world-view provided that it does not claim to influence public policies.

2. If one wants to influence public policies, he has to bracket his world-view and provide reasons that can be understood by everyone.

---

[18] Rawls, 'The Idea of Public Reason Revisited', 143–4.
[19] Habermas, 'The Place of Religion in the Public Sphere'.

3. Religious reasons alone cannot be the basis of a contribution to public debates.

4. Religious people cannot challenge the LSD framework.

A good illustration of the last corollary is provided by the Refah Partisi in Turkey, the first Islamic party to run for public elections back in the 1990s. The Turkish Constitution is staunchly secular and closely mirrors the French *laïcité*, so much so that the Turkish expression for it is *laikly*. The party was dissolved after being elected into government on the ground that its manifesto was incompatible with the secular constitution and did not rule out the possibility of violence to change the political regime. The first charge is the most problematic from our perspective since it highlights the fact that secularism, if constitutionally entrenched, is perceived to be a *conditio sine qua non* for participation in public and, in particular, democratic life. The party was eventually dissolved by the TCC. The case was brought to the ECtHR which eventually decided that the national authorities were better competent to evaluate the compatibility of the party with the Turkish Constitution. In this case, it is clear that Turkish people cannot choose between competing world-views—religious or secular—for the secular world-view is presumed to be entrenched and escapes democratic scrutiny.

Experience shows that the rigidity of LSD had a major backlash. Refah Partisi morphed into a 'moderate' party, advocating superficial support of LSD framework. It changed its name to AKP and won much larger political support. There is a further paradox: the more the party gains political support, the more it is likely to be in a position to change the framework from within. The AKP was recently re-elected and narrowly missed the necessary parliamentary majority required to change the constitution unilaterally. In Hungary, this was achieved by the Fidesz party, which gained two-thirds of seats of parliament and went on to transform the secular Hungarian Constitution into a Christian Constitution.

NAD is problematic and contains two central problems:

1. NAD is based on a myth: the LSD framework is itself neutral. This is debatable since LSD encapsulates secularism as a political world-view.

2. NAD requires officials to adopt a negative attitude towards religion, closing the gates of public reason to religious voices.

Instead of addressing the democratic dilemma, NAD reinforces it and shows that LSD may be struggling with how to give more of a place to religion in the public sphere than is openly acknowledged. The impossibility of challenging the secular political view may explain its own fragility vis-à-vis religion.

## 5.4.2.2. *The minority dilemma and neutrality-as-blindness*

Not only are LSD deaf, they are also blind: they do not want to see religious symbols and buildings (unless they belong to the majority's religion). Neutrality-as-blindness (NAB) is as problematic as NAD, certainly more visibly so. The *Lautsi* case is a striking illustration of the problem. On the one hand, Italy has a laique constitution, and as such it does not embrace any religious symbols. On the other, Italy requires state schools to hang a crucifix in classrooms.

The obvious problem is that the cultural symbols of the majority get preferential treatment over those of the minority; it is therefore hard to claim that LSD are neutral between religious symbols of the majority and those of minorities. A further problem is that such a disparity demotes even further secularism in the eyes of religious people. Not only is secularism but one world-view amongst others, but it may well be a blatant ideology of the majority to impose values and symbols on others. In recent years examples of such disparities have been multiplied: in Switzerland churches are pitted against mosques and their minarets. In Austria blasphemy against the Christian religion is prohibited, while in Denmark blasphemy against Islam is protected. In France, symbols '*ostentatoires*' are prohibited: the problem is that minorities tend to wear the most visible symbols.

The dilemma is I hope clear by now: how can religious minorities embrace majority values and symbols if that comes with the promise of erasing cultural differences? Put in the language of neutrality: how can LSD be neutral between minority and majority cultures, if they turn a blind eye on majority symbols while eradicating minority symbols? This problem is not yet fully acknowledged. LSD's blindness is selective and biased. The risk of double standards is a serious problem besetting all European countries. The dilemma has one corollary and two side effects.

1. The value of secularism (*laïcité*) is compromised by its ideological element. Secularism is not neutral about culture. It is biased towards one local culture.

2. Religious people show distrust towards majority values and symbols.

3. Incapacity to include different cultural practices results in polarization and further problems of integration.

The first corollary has to do with the roots and nature of secularism, which may appear to some as an ideology of the state rather than a benign world-view. This is very much the case in the French experience where *laïcité* has acquired a special status and commands the belief that religion should be relegated to the private sphere. Originally, *laïcité* came into being to resolve a long confrontation between the church and the state. The underlying principle was that of separation and this doctrine does not have any strong ideological connotation. It only became ideological on the interpretation of a section of the society, which saw in it the affirmation of secularism over and above religion.

Olivier Roy, a very perceptive French sociologist, distinguishes between legal *laïcité* and ideological *laïcité*.[20] Legal *laïcité* is the original legal response to the conflict between state and church. It does not attempt to eliminate religion from the public sphere but organizes the public sphere into separate domains. Ideological *laïcité* on the other hand aims at eliminating religion from the public sphere as it considers it detrimental from the viewpoint of public well-being. As an ideology, *laïcité* requires every individual to remove themselves from communitarian attachments when in the public sphere. In the long run this brought us the infamous French statute banning burqas in public. That is only the last step in the long saga of the veil that clearly put France in the spotlight for its treatment of religious minorities. France faces its own minority dilemma: how can the republican state integrate religious people when the republican ideology of *laïcité* requires religious people to divest themselves of any symbol when entering the public sphere?

Instead of waning in the reservoir of bad ideas, the veil debate in France has reached new heights with the ban of *burqa* in public streets. We therefore move from a benign republican state whose intent is to protect pupils from their cultural background, to a paternalist state that is blind to the fact that new immigrants are not integrated and because of that use religious symbols as a last resort to communicate anxieties about their status in an exclusive society. The myth of integration is completely debunked and the French republican state is left with a deeply polarized society of integrated ideological *laicists* and unintegrated religious newcomers.

NAB raises the problem of visibility of religions in the European public sphere. Europe's Christian past is everywhere; there are churches in every town and hamlet. They are living monuments to the existence of religious roots even though religion has gradually loosened its grip on European societies. Christianity nevertheless exercises an influence at varying level and its symbols are still powerful and awe-inspiring. It is in this context that the Grand Chamber develops a very peculiar theory of communication in relation to religious symbols. In order to justify the presence of the crucifix

---

[20] Olivier Roy, *La Laïcité face á l'islam* (Stock, 2005), translated into English, *Secularism Meets Islam* (Columbia University Press, 2007).

in Italian classrooms, the Court argues that the crucifix is a passive symbol, which is a strange conclusion for it to come to. To say this implies that there are active symbols, and this contrast allows you perhaps to see how strange the idea of passivity is, especially as applied to a powerful symbol such as the crucifix. Replace 'passive' with 'neutral' and you will get a glimpse of the odd position of the Italian government, which believes that the crucifix is a symbol for all religious and non-religious people: this is a double bias imposed both on non-Christian religious people and on non-religious people.

NAB is as problematic as NAD and comes with two separate problems:

1. NAB is based on the myth that LSDs have freed themselves from religious cultural roots.

2. NAB requires officials to take a negative attitude towards minority symbols.

The minority dilemma highlights the difficulty LSD have in convincing immigrant minorities that secularism is not an ideological weapon to secure hegemony of the majority's values and symbols. However secularism (and *laïcité*) do not have to be conceived as ideological; they also can be understood as legal doctrines. But even in that case, they will be open to a neutrality dilemma to which we now turn.

### 5.4.2.3. *The neutrality dilemma and secular law*

LSD are ruled by one law for all. This is a standard understanding of the rule of law. One obvious consequence is that secular law is supposed to be neutral at two different levels. First, it is neutral as to its *justification* in so far as it does not embrace any specific world-view (this is open to doubt as we saw before). Because it does not embrace any substantive world-view, then, secular law is the tool to protect equal liberty for all. Secondly, secular law is neutral as to its *effects* since it is not biased in favour of anyone, it does not practically advantage any constituency within the society.

One law for all is at times conflated with one rule for all. This is a grave simplification. Because the law is produced, applied, and interpreted according to one set of procedures and values does not mean it has to be monolithic. A number of rules and exceptions could make the law more responsive to different people and circumstances. Now, the problem is that LSD are not so willing to accept claims of exemption based on religious conscience. If that was the case, then it would mean that religious conscience is somehow more important than other claims of conscience and this would not be neutral between religious and non-religious people.

The problem is, as we saw in the first section, religious voices are not taken into account in the production of norms because of NAD. Other claims of conscience can participate in the democratic production of norms provided that they do not speak with a religious voice. To this extent, they are favoured over religious people.

The dilemma of neutrality is three pronged: how can secular law be neutral between religious and non-religious people:

1. If religious people are not allowed to participate in its production with their voice?

2. If it entrenches a double standard between minority and majority in its application?

3. If the interpreter is biased against religious reason?

Secular law displays a problem with neutrality at all three levels: production, application, and interpretation of norms. As we saw before, NAD has a perverse effect on the way religious people participate in the production of norms. NAB has a perverse effect on the way religious minorities are treated by comparison to religious majorities in the application of certain laws. The combined effect of NAD and NAB no doubt influences the interpreter who is bound by secular law as it is produced and by cultural values as they are practised by the majority.

The only way of rescuing neutrality, it seems to me, is by turning it into a positive attitude towards religion that redresses some of the imbalances at the level of the *effects* of secular laws. At first this type of substantive neutrality may seem paradoxical. How can one be neutral if it favours some people? The rationale for this type of neutrality lies in the fact that those people who are favoured at the level of the effects of secular law are barred from the process of shaping those very laws.

Let me illustrate with an example from each of those three areas. If secular laws are produced in a way that marginalizes religious voices in democratic debate, then the least that one can do is to allow religious people to opt out from ordinary norms that have not been produced with their assent. Accommodation of religious people can also take place at the level of application of rules that are at first sight rigid. Helmets are prescribed by law in order to protect people from serious injuries; however some religious people have successfully claimed an exemption on the basis that their religion requires them to wear a turban which is incompatible with wearing a helmet. Finally, secular law can devise an alternative method of resolution of some cases that takes into account the existence of religious norms. This is already the case in the UK with the Beth Din and the MAT. In each of these three cases, we see that neutrality can be interpreted as a positive attitude that corrects biases entrenched in LSD against religion.

Thus far I have argued that a constitution cannot be neutral because it necessarily chooses values. A constitution is inevitably value-laden, and neutrality may be one of those values that a constitution embraces. If that is the case, neutrality should be understood as practical neutrality, rather than theoretical.

Is the legal viewpoint neutral? The constitution isn't. Neither is policy. Is there a sense in which law is neutral? As we saw, secular law cannot be neutral in its assumptions since it is produced within a framework that is biased in favour of non-religious voices, and it is interpreted by officials who are trained to keep religious reasons at bay. There are a few biases and prejudices built into the picture that secular states present of religious people and voices. Thus, the way in which neutrality can make sense is by actively helping to undo those biases and prejudices and by carving out a place for religion within the LSD framework. Neutrality is usefully conceived as the striving against bias and prejudice. It is not a static conception but a dynamic one. Biases and prejudices are constantly lurking behind legislation and adjudication, and it is the state's duty to unravel them and fight against them as much as possible.

In this sense it is possible to say that law is neutral. Of course, it does not mean that the outcome of law's production is neutral. Norms that are reached by negotiations are the outcome of compromise amongst parties. But some parties, as we saw, are barred from participation in the process. The justification of laws is biased, and its effects are even more so when neutrality is merely understood as blindness or deafness towards religious people. In that way, biases and prejudices are entrenched and a *status quo* is maintained. Thus, the only way in which neutrality can make a meaningful difference is if one understands it in its substantive sense, which is concerned with redress of vulnerable voices and for vulnerable people. For example, the fact that religious voices do not participate in the production of norms can be a ground for requesting an exemption at the level of application and adjudication.

Can adjudication be neutral? As said before the task of the judge is to interpret generally applicable laws. Those laws are meant to be for all, although as we saw they tend to be the expression of those people who are allowed to participate. The way in which one can make them neutral is by, for example, carving out exemptions. Ultimately, judges are trapped in a difficult dilemma. But the law can aspire to neutrality in the relevant sense proposed above. It is not about getting rid of all background assumptions. In its effects however it is possible to *neutralize* adverse policies and unjustified benefits and burdens.

This chapter offers a modest contribution to the understanding of neutrality in the constitutional context. In this context, neutrality should be understood as an attitude rather than a viewpoint. In other words, neutrality has to be understood as a practical requirement rather than a theoretical one. Neutrality is a legal doctrine that requires officials to display a certain type of behaviour that can be broken down into two stages:

1. Neutrality requires officials to unearth biases and prejudices and overcome them through rational analysis of discrete social phenomena.

2. Once biases and prejudices are overcome, officials are left with various options that may be at odds one with another. Neutrality requires officials to overcome polarization through compromise.

Neutrality, in the constitutional context, is best understood as a practical attitude that distances law from bias and prejudice on one hand, and on the other requires legal officials to reach remedies by way of compromise.

## 5.5. Secularity, Law, and the Marketplace of Religions

My suggestion here is that law should make religious freedom and equality possible. To do so, however, law has to be conceived as the ultimate authority, the last resort, and the default framework for the adjudication of conflicting obligations. The idea of a marketplace of religions gives a greater place to religion in public life by providing a forum within which religions and other comprehensive views can express their voices and recommendations as to how best to deal with those conflicts while respecting diverging opinions. When agreement as to a local or alternative method for the resolution of conflicts is impossible, then the law should step in and provide the answer itself. In order to do so, the law cannot rely on neutrality alone but has to posit for itself the goal of protecting and promoting diversity in order to be inclusive of religious and non-religious people.

Conflicts of obligations stemming from the encounter of religious and non-religious people take place at different levels and between different agents. Constitutions and international treaties can at best provide a general framework, and a method of last resort, for adjudicating those conflicts. The point of those frameworks is to guarantee liberty and equality for religious and non-religious people. Conflicts can take place at three different levels: firstly, conflicts of obligations can be the object of resolution of an individual decision; secondly, conflicts of obligations can be between two members of the same community who share the same comprehensive views; thirdly, conflicts of obligations can be between two members of the same community whose comprehensive views differ.

A strong legal framework will enhance liberty in the following ways. First, when an individual is required to reach a decision between conflicting obligations, she is in principle free to decide according to her own self-imposed values or according to the best interpretation of her religion. So, for example, when a woman has to decide whether to undergo an abortion or not, she will have to be free to follow her own judgement, which includes her religious beliefs. When a conflict of obligations takes place between two different persons who happen to share the same comprehensive views, then a strong legal framework oriented in favour of liberty should give them the opportunity to have their disagreement decided by an adjudicator applying the principles that belong to their comprehensive views. So, for example, two Muslim people, who disagree on the best way to apply a financial regulation they agreed, should have the freedom to opt for an adjudicator who is trained in sharia-based finance law. Finally, when two individuals whose comprehensive views differ have to resort to an external adjudicator in order to deal with a conflict of obligations, they should be free to opt for an arbitrator close to their interests. In these three cases, law does not pre-empt the solution of the conflict. Crucially, however, it creates a framework without which the liberty of each of those individuals would be radically limited.

Moreover, law provides a last resort for the adjudication of those conflicts. If in any of those cases, disagreement persists and a solution cannot be found, then the law through its constitutional principles and institutions should provide a last resort for adjudicating the conflict in a way that prevents polarization between different individuals and groups belonging to one society. At times, this will be possible through a carefully reasoned opinion. Other times, a choice will have to be made in favour of a comprehensive view over another. In the latter case, the preference will be given for the situation that enhances the principle of liberty protected by the legal framework. So, for instance, if disagreement is raging between religious and non-religious people over the issue of the beginning and end of life for the purpose of adjudicating matters of abortion and euthanasia, the legal framework will have to prioritize permissibility over impermissibility.

Some may argue that to recognize a public marketplace of religions amounts to unduly legitimizing some religious norms and institutions, thereby entrenching discrimination towards vulnerable people within religious groups. For example, vulnerable women could be pressurized into agreeing to resolve their disputes before religious arbitration tribunals. Needless to say, putting pressure on anyone would be in itself punishable by ordinary law. But the point here is different. The alternative to a marketplace of religions is a black market of religions where religious norms are strictly applied in private away from the scrutinizing eye of the public. Women would equally be discriminated against and denied any access to justice, be it ordinary or based on an alternative dispute resolution. Given this bleak picture I have no doubt about choosing the market-place of religions which recognizes an important place for religions in the public sphere in exchange for greater responsibility to justify the legitimacy of religious norms within secular frameworks.

The ECtHR draws some important limits as to what is permissible in terms of contestation of democracy and the legal system. The central example is still *Refah Partisi*: an Islamic party that challenged the secular foundations of democracy and of the legal system which was deemed incompatible with Turkish constitutional values. This case is a bit of an enigma as it attempts to present in a straightforward non-controversial way two very controversial problems. Firstly, it attempts to suggest that democracy without secularism is not democracy. Secondly, it states that alternative dispute resolution on the basis of religion is incompatible with secular law. The first problem is a real dilemma: how can we possibly embrace democracy fully if we are not prepared to accept unpalatable consequences? The second problem concerns the secular nature of the legal system. The ECtHR seems to suggest that the political project of replacing secular law with religious law is not compatible with the Convention. While the first answer seems to be incorrect, the second seems to be unavoidable. In the case of the relationship between religion and democracy it is not possible to exclude religious parties from participation in democratic life. Indeed the Strasbourg Court acknowledged that 'a political party that is inspired by the moral values imposed by a religion could not be considered in itself as a formation that goes against the fundamental prin-ciples of democracy'.[21] What appears to make the Court side with the TCC is the fact that *Refah* does not rule out employing violence in the goal of establishing a parallel legal system, if not a newly founded legal system on religious foundations.

## 5.6. The Limits of the Marketplace of Religions

The marketplace is a secular institution, no doubt about that. Many religious people would oppose the idea just because of that. This may be due to

---

[21] *Refah Partisi (The Welfare Party) and ors v Turkey*, note 6 above, para 100.

genuine concerns about secular ideologies dominating religious ideas, and in particular the subordination of transcendent visions of the good to immanent institutions such as the market. But it may also be due to spurious concerns that cover up the fact that monopolistic religions do not want to lose their hegemony in a society. The Catholic Church in Italy, for example, would want religious pluralism only in so far as it does not challenge its prominent position in Italian society. That said, there is a deeper and possibly overarching concern: is the secular institution of the marketplace of religions neutral in a way that includes everyone?

In the previous section, I attempted to show that the ECtHR developed a secular foundation for the legal system. It has insisted at various points on the importance of secularism as a constitutional principle (*Refah*). It is therefore puzzling that in *Lautsi*, the Grand Chamber is determined to avoid the issue of secularism. It insists that it is not 'for the Court to rule on the compatibility of the presence of crucifixes in State school classrooms with the principle of secularism as enshrined in Italian law'.[22] This is to firmly disavow the Chamber of the Second Section which had established a violation of the principle of neutrality because the presence of the crucifix was capable of clashing with the secular convictions of Ms Lautsi.

The Court frames the problem in the narrowest possible terms: 'the only question before it concerns the compatibility . . . of the presence of crucifixes with the requirements of Article 2 of Protocol 1'.[23] I am not against judicial minimalism in so far as I believe that the Court does not have to pronounce itself on every possible issue connected with one case. But it is impossible to detach the protection of freedom of and from religion from the idea of the secular state as developed in our modern age. Without secularism, freedom of religion would only be based on the whim of the state who would decide arbitrarily whether or not to tolerate this or that religious group as was the case, for example, in the Act of Toleration 1689 which prohibited the practice of Catholicism in England. It is therefore a mistake to suggest, as Judge Bonello does, that 'secularism, pluralism, the separation of Church and State, religious neutrality, religious tolerance . . . are not values protected by the Convention'.[24] Firstly, Bonello is forced to acknowledge that the Court itself has used these concepts many times before, virtually in every decision on Article 9.[25] Secondly, it is very clear that Article 9 protects freedom of religion

---

[22] *Lautsi v Italy*, note 3 above, para 57.   [23] Ibid.   [24] Ibid. p 40.
[25] See Julie Ringelheim, 'Rights, Religion and the Public Sphere: The European Court of Human Rights in Search of a Theory?' in Lorenzo Zucca and Camil Ungureanu (eds), *Law, State, Religion in the New Europe: New Debates and Dilemmas* (Cambridge University Press, 2012).

as well as freedom from religion; the latter would be hard to understand in isolation from a secular understanding of the state and its law.

The Court adds that secularism is cogent, serious, and coherent enough to qualify as a matter of philosophical conviction that parents can invoke as part of their right to have their children educated in a manner compatible with their own convictions (Article 2, Protocol 1). Secularism is demoted from an overarching principle of the constitutional state to one possible philosophical conviction amongst others. This suggestion is deeply problematic and denotes well the spirit of uncertainty within which we live. It is true that secularism can be understood in many different ways: it is a constitutional doctrine, a philosophical stance, a world-view, and ideology, and even an extreme stance in the hands of scientists who see religion as the arch-enemy. In the European context, however, there is a growing need for a legal response to the presence of religion in the public sphere. Thus, the constitutional understanding of secularism must be distinguished from secularism as a personal philosophical conviction, contrary to what the Court claims here. An individual, like Ms Lautsi, is free to believe that any religion is detrimental and incompatible with her own convictions. The state, on the other hand, should refrain from any such conviction since it is committed to protecting freedom of religion.

Secularism is often understood as an absence: the effacing of religion from the public sphere. But it should be understood as an eminently positive stance which made the values of liberty, equality, and solidarity possible.[26] The French trinity of *liberté, egalité,* and *fraternité* is the underlying theme of secularism. Indeed, secularism as a constitutional approach must protect freedom of belief for both religious and non-religious people; no coercion whatsoever can be justified if it aims to influence people's beliefs. Freedom also covers religious exercise: no one can interfere or curtail the liberty to exercise one's own religion. Equality is also a very important goal: religious and non-religious people have symmetrical rights and duties. Moreover, the state cannot favour any world-view (religious or non-religious) and/or adopt it as its own preferred standpoint. Fraternity requires that the state should hear all the voices of religious and non-religious people when deliberating about its political identity and on the way in which rights and duties should be defined. On top of these political values, which are secular values, there is another goal that emerges from the insistence on democracy and the rule of law that is worth stressing. Both democracy and the rule of law are means to

---

[26] The *Consiglio di Stato*, the highest administrative court in Italy, suggests that the crucifix stands for the same values as the secular state. Indeed, there may well be overlap but there is also a difference in so far as the crucifix cannot be held to represent a shared world-view.

achieving and maintaining a maximum degree of peace and harmony amongst the various constituencies of a society. So the fourth element of secularism as a constitutional approach is the goal of social peace through democratic deliberation and law.[27]

The marketplace of religions is secular in a constitutional sense. It is not a philosophical theory, nor does it stand for a fully fledged world-view. It is essentially a tool or, more precisely, a framework for the organization of diverging views. It may not be neutral in a strict sense. The values it promotes are distinctive and have a strong political connotation. It is nevertheless neutral in a loose sense, in so far as it attempts to be a default position whose goal is to maximize religious diversity, while minimizing tensions between religions themselves and between religious and non-religious people more broadly.

Of course, it is not for the Court to impose one model of church and state relations like in France or the USA. That understanding of secularism is strongly rooted in national experience and was developed at a time in which it was necessary for the state to free itself from the grip of the church: this is particularly true in the French context, where the *Loi de 1905* came into force in order to settle very bitter confrontations between state and church. More generally, that model of secularism is probably outdated. In Europe, the Treaty of Westphalia had established a monopoly on the part of one church in each nation state according to the principle *ejus regio, cujus religio*. That framework created the possibility for a bitter conflict between two competing authorities ultimately aiming towards absolute power in particular areas of life. Today, the relationship between state and church is different and is in most cases one of peaceful collaboration. It therefore does not make much sense anymore to speak of secularism as guaranteeing a strict separation. Secularism in that sense is largely devoid of its original purpose.

It is however possible to distinguish between two models of constitutional secularism.[28] The first is the classical model that deals with the relationship between state and church. The second model of secularism focuses on the role of the secular state in protecting diversity and attempts to go beyond and break free from the cultural and religious homogeneity inherited from the Peace of Westphalia. This does not mean that traditions lose their importance; it simply means that the past should not be used as an excuse not to cope with the contemporary fact of pluralism.

---

[27] For a very similar view, see Charles Taylor, 'The Meaning of Secularism', *The Hedgehog Review*, 12(3) (2010). Of course, this position is in itself open to debates.

[28] See ch. 2.

## 5.7. Conclusion

The marketplace of religions is my preferred way of presenting the position of Strasbourg in relation to the role of religion and its relationship with democracy, state, and law. The marketplace of religions is organized along three principles: pluralism, neutrality, and secularity. Each principle respectively guides the relationship between religion and democracy, state and law.

Pluralism concerns the central function/goal/ambition of the marketplace: to carve out a space for religion in public, in particular within the broader marketplace of ideas that is democracy. Within that space, diversity should be protected and promoted and the monopoly of one religion over others should be avoided. Pluralism applies to world-views and is opposed to cultural homogeneity. Europe does not have a long experience of serious cultural pluralism and is only recently starting to grapple with diversity of a religious and non-religious kind. Pluralism, contrary to conventional wisdom, is not opposed to monism. In fact the two necessarily go hand in hand. There is no pluralism without the identification of a framework within which a plurality of objects can be singled out. Monism and pluralism are two sides of the same coin.

The marketplace of religions also suggests a new relationship between religion and state, which is guided by the idea of neutrality. Conventional secular models of church and state relations insist on a univocal (France) or mutual (USA) idea of separation. Under those models, separation is seen as the pre-condition to securing neutrality of the state vis-à-vis religions. Instead I suggest that separation should give way to collaboration, whereby neutrality is understood as principled distance.

Finally the marketplace of religion concerns the relationship between religion and law. Secularity is the guiding principle in this context. On this issue, the position seems to be stricter in so far as the Strasbourg Court is not prepared to accept anything but secular foundations of the legal system. This is not always straightforward: parallel legal systems are a flawed notion, but this does not have to be confused with the fact that alternative dispute resolution cannot be based on religious principles and practices under precise circumstances. This is what will be examined in the next chapter.

# 6

# What Is the Place of Sharia Law
# in European Legal Systems?

## 6.1. Introduction

Being a Muslim in Europe raises important questions and challenges. The most immediate challenge is what it means to be a European Muslim. Were we to embrace the idea of a Christian Europe with a clear monolithic identity, it would be hard to reconcile the fact of being European with the fact of being Muslim. As we saw in chapter 4, however, being European does not require having a monolithic identity. In fact, being European is about embracing a diversity of religious and non-religious kinds. The truth about identity is that the allegiance it entails cannot be reduced to one form, but has to be pluralistic and composite.

The second challenge concerns the attitude that a state should have towards religious minorities. Should the state favour or disfavour them? Or should it treat them all in a neutral way? Chapter 5 attempted to show that European nation states have a twofold obligation: firstly, they should lessen the monopoly of established churches; secondly, they should set up a marketplace of religions, whereby each religion has equal standing. It is in this sense that secular states treat religious minorities neutrally.

The last challenge concerns the particular nature of Islam, which requires the faithful to guide their behaviour on the basis of religious law (sharia). The extent to which it is possible to reconcile European secular laws with the practice of religious laws is unclear. Some believe that religion should not be the object of special treatment. Others believe that there is room for reasonable accommodation. Some religious people would like to be ruled by their own norms, while others believe that secular laws and religious norms should be sharply separated so as to avoid any type of contamination.

The place of sharia law in European political societies varies. It is incorrect to believe that we can simply turn a blind eye to religious laws or treat them as irrelevant. They are very relevant for a growing number of people, and secular states want to be able to monitor the way in which religious norms affect the lives of people. The fundamental point is that the practice of religious norms has to be compatible with the general framework of legal norms.

Orak Pamuk's *Snow*[1] offers a dramatic example of this problem. In the forgotten city of Kars, young women have started to wear scarves in public as a religious symbol. The state, acting from afar through its army and its police, wants to maintain a strictly secular public space. It therefore forbids women to wear headscarves in public and places pressure on families to educate them in a secular fashion at home. In reaction to this pressure from the state and the family, young women commit suicide, thereby breaching an even more fundamental religious command. The example shows that polarization between secular and religious norms may leave vulnerable people unprotected. Even worse, blind denial of religious norms by the secular state may create a black market where individuals within groups impose religious norms on others that are not publicly acknowledged.

The question posed regarding sharia law thus becomes meaningful given a few assumptions. Firstly, I assume that European legal systems are secular and not religious. Secondly, I assume that religious minorities take religious law as a benchmark for their behaviour. When the Archbishop of Canterbury pointed out that sharia law was already part of the socio-legal landscape, he was correctly starting from two basic factual observations: on the one hand, English law already carves out a place for Muslim Arbitration Tribunals on the basis of the Arbitration Act 1995. On the other, people of the Islamic faith already relied on the opinions of sharia law experts. Thus, by the time of the Archbishop's lecture Islamic law already played both an official and unofficial role in the English and in the European social and legal environment.

This chapter is divided into two parts: the first part analyses the asymmetry between secular law and sharia law and illustrates the fact that they are necessarily imbricated in a more or less explicit way. The second part focuses on the official recognition of sharia law in European legal systems. I discuss several options, each occupying a different place on a spectrum representing forms of relation and interaction between secular and religious laws; from separation to accommodation, engagement, and finally disengagement. The conclusion suggests the most desirable form of engagement between secular and sharia law and delineates the place of sharia law in Europe.

## 6.2. The Asymmetry between Sharia and Secular Law

By comparing secular law and sharia we can learn a great amount about both. There are unexpected similarities and obvious differences that are frequently

---

[1] O Pamuk, *Snow* (Vintage, 2005).

overlooked. Starting with the similarities, both secular law and sharia law are systems of norms backed up by a more-or-less coherent realm of values. It is also possible to hold that many secular values have religious origins in so far as secular morality has been shaped in the mould of religious societies. For example the French trinity of values—*liberté, egalité, fraternité*—is not an exclusive trademark of secularism but arguably has religious roots. In addition, we can say also that both systems of rules define belonging to a community or a group. The similarities at the macro level are striking but they need to be complemented by the differences.

The rules of secular law define belonging to a political society. The rules of sharia law define belonging to a religious community. Overlap exists between the political society and the religious community, but it is not perfect. The rules organizing modern political societies and their institutions escape the reach of sharia law, which was formed in a different historical situation and consequently is not easily adaptable to the specifically modern challenges of contemporary society. This point has an immediate consequence: no matter how committed a society is to sharia law it needs at least one basic secular framework. For example in Nigeria, civil and criminal law is largely informed by religious principles, but political institutions and the Nigerian Constitution are secular in the sense that they do not depend on religious principles. To put it as bluntly as possible, whilst no state can be ruled by sharia law alone, it is theoretically possible to have a purely secular legal system with absolute monopoly of both the sources of law and its implementation.

The absolute monopoly, and subsequent hegemony, of secular law is possible, but not necessarily desirable. To understand this we have to distinguish between two broad tasks of the law: the production and application of norms. Under normal circumstances a division of labour between political institutions exists: thus representative institutions produce norms, administrative institutions apply them in a routinely fashion, and adjudicative institutions interpret them in case of litigation. Monopoly of secular laws means that production, application, and interpretation can only be undertaken by secular institutions and according to secular reasons. Hegemony of secular laws means that secular reasons trump any non-secular voices which have no space in the public sphere as far as the organization of political societies is concerned.

The problem with secular hegemony and the monopoly of secular law is that belonging to the political society becomes more difficult for a certain set of people, namely religious people whose behaviour may at times be at odds with what secular laws require of them. Thus the monopoly of secular law does not leave any space for alternative sources of normativity; in fact it does not even allow non-secular voices to speak their mind as their participation in the debate on common goods is precluded in advance. It appears that the voices of religious people are not adequately represented at the level of the production of norms and cannot ask to be excepted from those norms at the level of implementation. With no voice and no exit strategy, religious people may well feel that belonging to a given political society is very demanding for them.

To be clear, I do not want to argue in favour of abandoning secular law in favour of religious law. As I said before, secular law is necessary and unavoidable for every society, even the most religious society that wishes to be ruled by religious norms in a number of areas. The point I am trying to make is that secular law does not have to be monopolistic or hegemonic in the way it is often claimed to be. In particular, if secular law is monopolistic as to the production of norms, at the level of application of those norms it cannot expect some people not to object on the grounds of conscience and ask for exemption. Now it is true that religious people do not have to have the monopoly on exemption claims, but they nonetheless may be recognized as enjoying a privileged position in so far as they can argue that exemptions at the level of norm application are desirable given that religious voices were excluded from the process of norm production in the first place. Other non-religious people can also put forward claims of conscience, but in their case it is easier to answer that they should have expressed their concerns when the norms were being fashioned rather than object to their application to their particular case.

It seems to me that the imposition of a monopolistic and hegemonic model of secular law is incompatible with the goal of religious and non-religious belonging to the same political society. This would inevitably alienate some religious and non-religious minorities that are not enabled to participate in the process of production and implementation of norms. That said, the level at which participation can be permitted is a very complicated issue that requires careful analysis. In order to do that I have devised a typology of possible interactions between secular law and sharia law which I will discuss in the next section. But before moving to that I shall point out that at the level of production (and modification) of norms, secular law has an obvious advantage in so far as it is a deeply dynamic system of rules that can change quickly and easily by simple application of accepted procedure. Thus, when we talk about religious laws it is at the level of implementation rather than production that one should focus.

## 6.3. A Typology of Relationships

When secular law meets sharia law, there are several possible scenarios that can be imagined. The terms of engagement vary along the stages

Table 6.1. Typology*

|  | No special treatment | Reasonable accommodation | Plural jurisdictions | Parallel legal systems |
|---|---|---|---|---|
| Norm production | X | X | X | V |
| Application | X | V | X | X |
| Adjudication | X | V | V | X |

*X = non-contemplated; V = possible

mentioned above: norm production, application, and adjudication. At each stage it is more-or-less conceivable that religious law plays a role. The role played by religious norms can be measured in terms of participation in or exemption from official processes. We can refer to these as the couple of voice and exit.

In the typology below (see Table 6.1.), there are at least four possible scenarios where secular law's relation to religion ranges from extremely closed to extremely open. In the first scenario religious people are afforded no special treatment, being given no voice or exit strategy. Official law is one and the same for everyone. It is shaped, applied, and interpreted according to purely secular standards. The second scenario is that of reasonable accommodation. This means that religious people still have no voice at the level of production, but they can ask for exemption at the level of application and judges will recognize a certain number of exemptions as being justified. The third scenario is that of plural jurisdictions. Religious voices are still excluded from the production of new norms, but in certain areas they can be exempted from the application of secular law and opt instead for the application of religious law as interpreted by religious adjudicative institutions. This is the case in Britain with the MAT. Finally, the fourth scenario is one in which religious voices are recognized as sources of new regulations. Some speak of parallel legal systems to mean that each community would have authority to shape some independent rules of behaviour. I find the idea of parallel legal systems hard to comprehend since religious law does not aim to produce norms but simply to apply those that are already there. From this viewpoint, any political society needs at least a modicum of secular law in order to regulate those areas that are not touched by religion. To this extent we should not speak of parallel legal systems but instead one legal and political system with a partial implementation of religious law. Let us look at those four scenarios in turn.

### 6.3.1. No special treatment: no voice, no exit

A comprehensive legal system is driven by the ideal of the rule of law. There is one law for all without exceptions or qualifications. To hold anything different would be a breach of the most basic commitment to equality: it is not conceivable to have one law for white people and one for black people; or one law for Jews and one for Christians. This formal equality inherent to the rule of law exists to protect minorities from abuse and domination. But a single law for all can nonetheless impose prohibitions and obligations that are incompatible with some religious norms. For example, a blanket ban on conspicuous symbols is more likely to limit the freedom of religious than non-religious people. The French state's ban on the wearing of the veil is a good illustration of how formally universal law can have disproportionate effects between religious and non-religious communities.

The question is whether the ideal of the rule of law allows for special treatment of religious minorities in certain given circumstances. The answer of a good number of liberals is that religion should not enjoy unique status in the political community and so does not warrant any special treatment.[2] Why should we afford special treatment to religious people but not to non-religious people who may also have grievances with a given law? Note this is not an argument against exemption altogether, but only where it is granted on the grounds of religious belief.

Some believe that secular law should be completely blind vis-à-vis cultural and religious claims for exemption. This is not to say that exemptions are ruled out absolutely, but that they should only be justified on the basis of personal circumstances not related to cultural or religious belonging. For example, an individual with a serious health condition can be exempted from military service if he so wishes. Exemption from military service may also be justifiable where an individual conscientiously objects. This is often the case, and the exemption that is likely to be granted does not depend exclusively upon religious reasons. From this viewpoint, matters of conscience can be both religious and non-religious.

Should religious people be given special treatment? As mentioned above, a strict and rigid separation between state and religion would strongly militate against it. However, as the original example shows, this strict and rigid separation is not free from major problems and dilemmas. Many other cases of deliberate opposition to secular law on the basis of religious conscience can be multiplied. By adopting a blind attitude, the state does not

---

[2] See eg Brian Leiter, *Why Tolerate Religion?* (Princeton University Press, forthcoming 2012).

always achieve the desired results. On the contrary, as the French veil case demonstrates, it seems to reinforce actual or potential discrimination of religious minorities.

European legal systems are largely blind and deaf to religious claims. Religious voices have no access to the production of ordinary laws. Religious people can only participate in the production of ordinary laws by abandoning their religious voices and by resorting to purely secular arguments in favour of their preferred policy choices. Muslim people, for example, must abandon their religious convictions upon entering the political arena. Even if this can be seen as a burden, it nevertheless may be necessary in order to be understood by other people in the public debate who need to be convinced. It remains the case that religious voices are not taken into account at this level, whereas non-religious convictions are heard no matter how irrational or unfounded. Of course, it does not mean that those views will have an influence but at least they can be voiced—they have a channel which is not open to religious people.

In this first scenario, therefore, religious people not only have no voice but also have to accept all the norms produced by secular majorities as their own. In other words, religious people cannot ask for exemption if those norms are incompatible with other religious norms that are central to their life. Now some would say this may be the price to pay to be part of the game. Ordinary laws are meant to be based on reasons available to everyone and as such they can be accepted or criticized freely during the production and application processes. Those norms demand compliance by everyone with no exception.

There seems to be a clear asymmetry here between religious and non-religious people. The latter have the opportunity to influence directly the production of norms, while the former do not. It would seem desirable that the former should benefit at least from a qualified possibility to opt out from ordinary norms that have not been produced with their assent. Whilst this does not make the case for the principled special treatment of claims for exemption on religious grounds, it nevertheless opens the door for the possibility of reasonable accommodation of claims asking for exemption on religious and cultural grounds.

## 6.3.2. Reasonable accommodation: exit without voice

Is it possible to accommodate religious law? From the viewpoint of a comprehensive secular legal system the issue is twofold: should exemptions be granted? If so, who should benefit from exemptions? The fact that the law aims to treat everyone equally is not incompatible with the idea that it should grant exemptions to some people in particular cases. In addition, secular law does not have to impose the same rule for everyone. Sometimes it can give an option. Take marriage for instance: secular law does not have to impose a single contractual regime. The state could easily provide for the regulation of the marriage contract according to different religious norms and institutions on the one hand, and a secular alternative on the other.

When talking about reasonable accommodation, one tends to focus on exemptions from one law for all. But this presents a far too crude picture of the rule of law, which does not have to set one single rule for all. As just mentioned, the law can create a set of options for both religious and non-religious people. Creating options within a single framework is already a way of accommodating for differences. Thus accommodation can take place at the legislative level where religious diversity can be explicitly or implicitly accounted for. States grant explicit powers to religious organizations to establish institutions to provide education for children or make provisions for the homeless; religions also benefit explicitly from tax exemptions when they perform tasks akin to public services. The state may not single out religion for privileged treatment, but by granting tax exemptions and other benefits to institutions involved in certain activities, it implicitly accommodates—if not promotes—the role of religion in the public sphere.

Accommodation can also take place at the level of application of rules, even where they are at first sight rigid. Imagine for example that a Muslim doctor does not want to perform an abortion. This behaviour can be tolerated where the public sector clinic is big enough. Another doctor may perform abortions, while doctors who have religious convictions will perform only operations that he feels comfortable with. Of course, there remains a tension that cannot be completely overcome. But life together allows a margin of tolerance in the day-to-day application of the law. This type of practical accommodation does not have to be tacit or implicit. Administrative regulations and decrees can and do recognize differential treatment for some religious people despite the fact that it is believed to be against their own interest. Thus Sikh people can wear their turbans rather than protective helmets when riding motorbikes. In these situations, the harm of not wearing the turban is purely self-regarding and so the law can reasonably carve out exemptions that do not affect the lives of others. Likewise a Muslim woman should be allowed to wear her headscarf while performing public duties; with doubts only arising in connection with the education of young children susceptible to undue influence in their early development by some forms of clothing. But even the latter point underestimates the ability of children to cope with diversity in a natural way.

It is at the adjudicative level where accommodation is perhaps most contentious. Ordinary courts often face cases in which the rules of two different legal systems clash. Strictly speaking, these are clear examples of legal conflicts; they involve two valid rules that prescribe incompatible behaviours; and courts have to choose between the two, thereby putting one rule to the side. For example, the rules in conflict may concern family law and have religious roots: can courts recognize polygamy?[3]

In principle, European legal systems strictly prohibit polygamy. So, if a second marriage takes place in Europe, it is customarily annulled. But what if the marriage has already taken place in another country where polygamy is allowed? In this case the conflict of rules is the following:

Rule 1 says polygamy is strictly prohibited.

Rule 2 says it is not the case that polygamy is prohibited.

When courts deal with problems of private international law, Rule 2 is a potential candidate for incorporation into the legal system for the purpose of adjudicating the case in litigation. The judge will have to apply the rules of conflict to establish which rule applies. In France, for example, the judge recognized that a polygamous relationship could yield particular legal consequences such as the payment of children's benefits.[4]

In these cases, accommodation is implicit and inescapable. One could even say that sharia law is being introduced through the judicial back door. Courts have to acknowledge private international law as a matter of domestic law. If the foreign law to be applied is sharia law, then there is no other option but to try and accommodate it. It may be argued that European legal systems can block the application of foreign law on the ground of general notions such as public order. But the practice of courts shows that after examining selected aspects of sharia law they do not find it alien to public order. It may still seem that religious law is penetrating the legal system without the explicit consent of society. But what exactly prevents some aspects of sharia law from being incorporated into the legal practice? The answer to that has more to do with prejudice than with informed opposition. The strength of this prejudice in the UK was demonstrated by the reaction to the Archbishop of Canterbury embracing the possibility of a MAT based on the Arbitration Act 1995. Let us look at that debate from a general perspective that deals with the possibility of multiple jurisdictions.

---

[3] See ch. 3 for a discussion of these issues. The example of polygamy is taken from ch. 3.

[4] See Cour de Cassation, Première chambre civile [Cass 1e civ.] [highest court of ordinary jurisdiction, first civil law chamber] 3 June 1998, *Benali v Makhlouf*, Rev. crit. DIP 1998, 652, note Ancel.

### 6.3.3. Engagement: plural jurisdictions?

The life of religious norms does not necessarily stop at the gate of the secular state. We just saw one way in which sharia law may penetrate through the back door as a matter of legal necessity. It may also be allowed through the front door subject to a degree of monitoring on the part of secular institutions. This allows religious practices to exit the realm of the black market of religions and enter the sphere of official legal practice. The existence of alternative methods of resolution for some cases points precisely to the possibility of engagement between secular laws and religious practices in this way. To begin with it is on the basis of secular law that the establishment of those tribunals is authorized: the Arbitration Act guides this engagement. This engagement does not come without conditions. Religious institutions are normally requested to demonstrate a degree of experience and competence.

To a certain extent it is possible to hold that sharia has already been taken into account in European legal systems. This is clearly the case when two parties opt for arbitration instead of ordinary court procedure. Upon agreement, private parties are perfectly entitled to settle their case before a Jewish tribunal, for example.[5] In the case of arbitration, there is no conflict between rules; the parties simply agree to abide by a different set of rules. If the arbitrator does not produce a decision that satisfies both parties, then ordinary courts can step in and decide the case on the basis of national law. In producing a decision, the national courts may very well take into account religious law if it does not conflict with the law of the land.

The debate triggered by the Archbishop of Canterbury's comments, therefore, is premised by a misunderstanding. Critics thought that he was advocating the explicit incorporation of sharia law into English law. However, the Archbishop was merely suggesting that sharia law already plays a role in English law, and that it may play an even greater role in the future. He suggested that Islamic councils could perform a function similar to that of the Jewish courts, and on the same legal basis. This was confirmed very recently in a speech by Lord Phillips, the most senior judge in England and Wales, who stated: 'There is no reason why sharia principles, or any other religious code, should not be the basis for mediation or other forms of alternative dispute resolution.'[6]

---

[5] The Jewish court is called Beth Din, and it operates as a parallel system of adjudication.

[6] Lord Phillips, Address at the East London Muslim Centre in Whitechapel (3 July 2008), <http://news.bbc.co.uk/1/hi/uk/7488790.stm>.

The question of the place of sharia in English law illustrates my twofold strategy. On the one hand, I am advocating that it is necessary to embark on a long-term project to enhance communication and mutual understanding between different groups and individuals in a society. Concretely, this means that it will be necessary to engage in a learning process with regard to sharia law in order to be in a position to evaluate what is acceptable and what is not. On the other hand, I am also arguing for clear rules of the game to settle the conflicts that cannot be solved by appeal to general principles of communication. These rules work as a default position in the case of prolonged and persistent disagreement over specific questions. It is clear, for example, that sharia principles could not be appealed to in order to justify legislation or judicial decisions.

Any political system that cares for its own values does not want them to be violated in ways that are not easily ascertainable. The state exists to ensure that domination is not practised within religious communities. One way to do so is to give more responsibility to local communities in exchange for the possibility of monitoring progress in eliminating practices of domination. This was attempted for example in the UK in cases of forced marriage. The MAT has become one agent, among others, in charge of devising appropriate policies to tackle the practice of forced marriage. Clearly it is more desirable to involve actors who have direct experience of the phenomenon rather than the uninformed speculation of secular officials.

The state can also use its own means to force compliance with religious norms that are perceived to be positive. Ayelet Schachtar uses the example of a Jewish man who promised to give a *get* (divorce under Jewish law) to his wife, only to deny it when legal proceedings had terminated.[7] There is no way in which the state can force him to maintain his promise, but it can impose upon him financial sanctions for its breach.

The case of arbitration cannot be equated with the issue of parallel legal systems. In the case of the Beth Din or the MAT there is no doubt that there is one single legal system which, by one official act (Arbitration Act 1995), authorizes parties to engage alternative methods to settle their disputes. So when scholars talk of plural or parallel legal systems, they are not being very accurate. The fact of having plural jurisdictions which work as arbitration tribunals does not give rise to plural legal systems. The legal system is still one and the same and it has the authority to empower a variety of adjudicators in selected areas of law as long as those areas do not raise matters of public order.

---

[7] Ayelet Schachtar, *Multicultural Jurisdictions: Cultural Differences and Women's Rights* (Cambridge University Press, 2001).

The exit strategy provided by multiple jurisdictions comes with an important caveat. First of all, to have an independent adjudicator—say a MAT—does not amount to giving up one's rights that would normally be protected under ordinary law. Secondly, the arbitrator has a very limited jurisdiction that is defined by ordinary law. Thirdly, parties can still opt out from the arbitration procedure. While multiple jurisdictions operating within a single framework obeying the rule of law is conceivable, it is unclear whether we can talk of parallel or plural legal systems without breaching basic rule of law requirements.

### 6.3.4. Disengagement: parallel legal systems?

There are many ways in which the state can fit religious laws into the secular framework, so much so that religious people may believe that, in the end, it is better to avoid too much engagement with ordinary law so as to prevent contamination of religious norms. An'Naim for example, argues that sharia law has a brighter future away from institutional recognition.[8] State law and religious norms occupy different realms of social existence, the former being concerned with the regulation of political society and the latter with moral guidance. In the end, it is better to let religious norms flourish as a moral guide for behaviour independently from institutionally regimented practice. If sharia law was to adhere too closely to institutional practices it would have to adapt itself to necessary compromises which would undermine its own nature.

Disengagement is for some scholars and religious leaders a welcome form of relationship. But it can lead in two opposite directions: some may militate in favour of disengagement so as to entrench sharia law as the only form of official law. This would go down the extreme path of parallel legal systems, which is highly problematic for many reasons. Others would accept the necessity of secular law as a tool to facilitate gradual reforms within political society, with sharia law being a guiding star of conduct within the private realm. In the latter case, the distinction is that between secular law and religious morality. In the former case, some would like to see a plurality of laws competing for hegemony in the public sphere. In this case, they either talk of plural legal systems or parallel legal systems.

There is a theoretical problem with the very idea of parallel legal systems. The first obvious problem is the way in which we identify legal systems. Is it

---

[8] A An'Naim, *Islam and the Secular State: Negotiating the Future of Shari'a* (Harvard University Press, 2008).

by reference to a rule of recognition? Or is there any other way to do so? If the former, there is never more than one system even if the rule acknowledges competing sources of normativity in the legal system. This is already the case with private international law for example, where foreign rules are applied to resolve disputes in domestic jurisdictions. The rule of recognition can allow for the incorporation of normative sources additional to the ones that are already officially recognized.

The second—related—problem is the notion of parallelism. French and English laws exist in parallel but this is hardly an informative observation. English and Scottish legal systems exist in parallel also. Is this a salient feature of their relationship? I am not sure. I would say no, since each one of those systems claims independence from the other, at least at the formal level. Of course there is cross-contamination, but this does not happen in a formally recognized manner. In any case, parallel here does not mean that for any set of behaviours an individual can choose which law he should submit to (it may be the case elsewhere, for example in India—however, even there it seems that the plurality of laws one can choose from is organized by a single overarching legal system). One may say that in the case of arbitration one switches from ordinary law to another set of norms. In fact this is not accurate, because it is ordinary law that allows you to choose which dispute procedure you want to pursue. No matter what you choose, you are still under the umbrella of ordinary law. This is not the case if actual parallel legal systems existed, in which case one would be able to switch from one system to another. Things are rarely that simple as the choice of law can be subordin-ated to a number of very stringent conditions of belonging to a certain group. Thus in those cases there is a split between citizenship and religious affili-ation. The forms of belonging are plural in the sense that one can belong to one political society while at the same time belong to an exclusive religious community. These two forms of belonging do not overlap in this case. So there is a law for every citizen, but there is also a set of different laws for each religious community in the society. Whilst this situation may be justified in India for contingent reasons, it does not obtain in Europe where the essential mode of belonging is by way of citizenship. All allegiances and attachments are subordinated to one's membership of the political community as a citizen, and are compatible with its official laws only to the extent that it acknowledges them as such.

On this point, it is worth revisiting the position of the ECtHR with regards to the Islamic party in Turkey. The Court objects to the very possibility of parallel legal systems and this position seems to hold for all member states in the Council of Europe. Thus the Refah Partisi had been lawfully dissolved on the basis that it could not reasonably advocate the introduction of a separate legal system on the basis of sharia law. As things stand in Strasbourg, it is impossible to derogate from the secular nature of the legal system to introduce a system of religious laws that stands in opposition to the system of national law. So if we stretch the logic of this case to its limit, then we have to conclude that parallel legal systems are *de jure* impossible.

It is possible also to contest the idea of a parallel legal system from the perspective of formal logic: if two things are perfectly parallel, they would never intersect. In order to intersect they necessarily have to be non-parallel. As we saw, secular law and sharia law cohabit in the same space, and necessarily intersect and at times conflict. So the issue is not whether or not they are parallel; the issue is whether or not conflicts between them can be settled within the secular legal system. At this point, some would realize that I am insisting on a monistic understanding of law. That is correct, and that is also the only way of understanding law. The question one should ask instead is: can there be a plurality of systems? The logical answer to that is that there cannot be since a plurality of systems having authority on the same set of behaviours would defeat the purpose of law which is to give reliable guidance to law-abiding people. If guidelines conflict and there is no single means of resolution then there is no effective guidance, and one will have to decide how to act independently from the existence of law.

This brings us to the last point I want to raise in connection with the Archbishop's speech, what I regard as the sting in the tail. The Archbishop seems to be committed to a criticism of positive law as lacking the resources to understand religious laws. I disagree! Positive secular law is the precondition for the independent flourishing of religious laws. If the rule of law was contaminated by any type of cultural and religious influence it would hardly be capable of coping with diversity in an open and responsible way. Parties would constantly strive for domination of law-making processes, and the chances are that mainstream views would become entrenched, imposing their own positions. The only possibility for religious perspectives to be heard and protected is to have a default secular framework that guarantees principled distance from any world-view of a religious or non-religious character.

## 6.4. Conclusion

The place of sharia law in Europe depends on the relationship between legal and religious norms in general. This chapter discussed four models of interaction: the first model is of total legal indifference towards religious norms. The second model presents possible ways of accommodating religious norms into the ordinary legal system. The third model discusses the possibility of multiple jurisdictions of religious and non-religious kinds. Finally, the fourth model presents the challenge posed by the idea of parallel legal systems whereby religious norms have a life independent from secular norms.

The first and fourth options do not offer very attractive solutions: either the law is blind to religion or religion is blind to law. The first scenario displays a very crude understanding of the rule of law, one that mistakes the idea of 'one law for all' with the idea 'one rule for all'. The fact that law aims to give guidance to everyone without discrimination does not mean that the law cannot offer different options to different people. One single legal framework can easily encompass a plurality of rules that apply differentially. The fourth option is also too crude in that it preaches the possibility of a perfect disentanglement between secular and religious laws. Also it flirts with the idea that one legal system cannot cater for diversity, and that instead a plurality of legal sources would be more desirable than an organized system of sources. This cannot be but wishful thinking of the worst kind. The nature of law is to authoritatively guide behaviour either directly or indirectly by establishing space for alternative application or alternative adjudication in the name of one law. In reality, the very notion of plural authorities would be undermined by the absence of a monistic framework. In such a situation, there would not be a plurality of authorities coexisting side by side, but a pure and simple struggle for hegemony between competing authorities that are incapable of full affirmation.

In each of these extreme cases, the risk is either of letting a black market of religious norms flourish in the background or of promoting the polarization of religious and non-religious people. Neither of those two scenarios is desirable for vulnerable private parties such as women and children. It is not desirable either for public actors who would fail to promote a system that is capable of coping with the practice of diversity. It is essential that in public as much as in private relations the black market of religion does not perpetrate values that are at odds with those of secular societies. As long as they do not, they have a right to participate in the shaping of public policies that contribute to the betterment of the whole of society.

For this reason, the second and third options can both be considered compatible with a secular legal system under certain conditions. In addition, these two models are compatible with one another, meaning that each European state could elect a blend of each in order to cope best with the fact of religious and cultural diversity. To begin with, reasonable accommodation is desirable in so far as it corrects the imbalance between secular and religious voices in the shaping of public policies. To the extent that religious voices are not able to participate in the shaping of those policies, they should at least have the possibility of claiming exemption and exit those schemes they have not consented to. Reasonable accommodation is not only desirable but also necessary in so far as migrants bring with them pre-existing legal obligations that may stem from the application of religious laws in their original countries. In these cases, secular courts have to grapple with and accommodate religious norms that become relevant in private law disputes such as family law. Secular courts may or may not be capable of giving religious norms their proper interpretation and that is why the third option—which allows for an organized system of multiple jurisdictions—is not an altogether foolish option.

Option three is more desirable than people think. It is a good thing to delegate areas of adjudication to people at the community level in exchange for the possibility of monitoring the compatibility of that system of adjudication with the basic legal and political requirements of the secular system. The alternative is to let local communities apply their own norms in a secretive and obscure fashion. Option three becomes desirable in comparison to the alternative: a black market of sharia law.

The place of sharia law in European legal systems is a highly volatile debate, but it would be a mistake to simply sweep under the secular carpet the fact that migrants bring with them cultural practices imbued with religious norms that must be acknowledged and understood in order to avoid any perverse effects incompatible with European understandings of basic rights. It is a fact that some people are subject to the implementation of sharia law in Europe. Secular law cannot ignore such facts, and to that extent it has to take it into account. It is hard to see how it can avoid a certain degree of accommodation. In fact, I attempt to show that there is ground for mutual exchange where the state would probably gain more insight and control over the practice of religious norms. Engagement may turn out to be so advantageous for the state that religion may even consider opting for disengagement so as to avoid unnecessary contamination of its moral norms with secular institutional practices. Secular states have an important and difficult task in balancing engagement between secular and religious norms whilst preventing the creation of a purely exclusive system where either religious or non-religious people are not welcome.

# PART III
# PARADISE

The third part of the book concludes the journey from Dante's transcendental monism to a secular immanent monism. Dante's world is Christian and transcendental. In his conception of Paradise, man's nature is idealized; all men are angels and there is no conflict, no expression of negative emotions, while in hell man is shown with all his human vices. Dante's trajectory is to move away from human chaos to reach an eternal order in the afterlife.

The secular Paradise in this book attempts a completely different journey, although it starts from the same premise. Human vices and passions are part and parcel of human nature. They cannot be straightened or bent; a virtuous man is not someone who suppresses his passions, but he's someone who knows them, understands them and is able to give to them the appropriate weight. This basic view of human nature has three implications: one political, one ethical, and one legal. The political implication is that European institutions at every level have to promote education so as to enhance rational mastery as well as mutual knowledge with a view to a life in common (chapter 7). The ethical implication is that human diversity should be regarded as a paramount value rather than suppressed and side-lined in favour of more conventional ways of life (chapter 8). The legal implication is that human societies are better off when they devise legal frameworks that maximize diversity, whilst minimizing violent and coercive ways of life. Secular law is therefore inclusive, not exclusive, and provides a monistic framework to deal with conflicts stemming from diversity (chapter 9).

# 7

# The Classroom as a Tolerance Lab[1]

## 7.1. Introduction

I grew up in Italy and attended a state school where a crucifix was hung on the wall of the classroom. I am in the unique position of being a potential victim and a potential perpetrator of that situation. I am a potential victim since I am a secularist and I always opted out from the weekly religious education class taught by someone appointed by the Roman Catholic Church. Yet, at the same time I am a potential perpetrator because I was raised as a Catholic and belong to the majority of people who do not find the crucifix (or, for that matter, any of the other Christian symbols in Italian public places) particularly intrusive simply because it was part of our daily life. The explanation lies in Italy's cultural and social homogeneity, which held true until the end of the 1980s. Under these conditions, integration was not a central preoccupation. Why would one promote integration in a place that is already very cohesive? Integration becomes necessary when there is a social, cultural, or ethnic diversity that makes it increasingly difficult to live together peacefully. If that is the case, then one may speak of a progressive disintegration of the social fabric. Any state that experiences disintegration has to respond with a politics that promotes integration.

Integration is, however, not always regarded as the best remedy to a lack of social and cultural cohesion. This is because states believe socio-cultural homogeneity to be desirable; many states are committed to an ordered political realm that leaves ample room for the development of socio-cultural pluralism. In this case, instead of integration one speaks of accommodation.

The realm of education, I shall argue, is the main laboratory wherein the state can test its policies concerning the harmonious organization of a society and the recognition of the place of religion within it. States committed to integration promote one school for everyone, in which pupils are turned into

---

[1] This chapter is a revised version of my essay 'The Classroom as a Tolerance Lab' in M Hunter Henin (ed.), *Law, Religious Freedom and Education in Europe* (Ashgate, 2012).

full citizens of a society. States committed to accommodation, instead, allow a certain leeway for religious communities to organize and deliver education through faith schools or other private schools funded by the state. Since I believe both approaches to have strengths and weaknesses, the model I present seeks to steer a middle course between the two. In particular, I shall suggest that, in order for the state to improve social cohesion, it has to create the preconditions for mutual understanding and solidarity between members of different socio-cultural groups. In other words, the classroom should be a laboratory for engaging in the practice of tolerance.

My analysis will be theoretical and comparative. In section 7.2., I begin with a brief inquiry into the notion of integration and contrast it with the notion of accommodation. My position—which I term 'the classroom as a tolerance lab'—steers a middle way between integration and accommodation. In section 7.3., I focus on three major European states: Italy, France, and the UK. Italy is an obvious choice because it was involved in the high-profile *Lautsi* case before the ECtHR which prompted this discussion.[2] France, at the beginning of the Third Republic, put religious education at the core of its political project through the laws of Jules Ferry entrenching a right to free education.[3] The UK is also an interesting case as it sponsors multicultural-ism through state-funded faith schools. These three states are under pressure as they struggle to square religious claims with liberal and republican prin-ciples. In each of them, there have been very high-profile cases: the saga of the *foulard islamique* has captivated France during the past twenty years and the UK Supreme Court opened its first judicial year with a case on discrimin-ation in faith schools.[4] I end with a discussion of the *Lautsi* case as a possible illustration of how the state should promote education as a tolerance lab.

## 7.2. Integration

The most general notion of integration portrays society as a whole and individuals, or groups, as its parts. A harmonious whole includes every individual and every group. If someone is left out, then integration is

---

[2] *Lautsi v Italy*, ECtHR (Grand Chamber), 18 March 2011, Application no 30814/06.

[3] Loi du 16 juin 1881 établissant la gratuité absolue de l'enseignement primaire dans les écoles publiques. Loi dite 'Jules Ferry' et 'Bert Paul', <http://mjp.univ-perp.fr/france/1882enseignement. htm>. Lois du 28 mars 1882 sur l'enseignement primaire obligatoire, <http://www.r-lecole.freesurf. fr/doc-hist/loiferry.html>.

[4] C McCrudden, 'Multiculturalism, Freedom of Religion, Equality, and the British Constitution: The JFS Case Considered', International Journal of Constitutional Law, 9(1) (2011), 200–29.

necessary to bridge that gap. Understood in this broad sense, I can hardly think of anyone opposed to integration. In theory, the purpose of a common society is to integrate everyone regardless of class, sex, or religion. In practice, however, there are tensions that make integration quite a difficult business—and not always desirable. In relation to the whole, there are centripetal and centrifugal forces. The most important centripetal force is equality: since no one enjoys being negatively discriminated against, religious minorities will demand recognition of the same privileges granted to religious groups of the majority. The strongest centrifugal force is freedom: everyone wants their thoughts and beliefs recognized and protected and religious groups in particular ask for the respect of their own beliefs. One can readily see that liberty and equality, as understood above, pull in opposite directions.

Integration, in the most general sense, is an aim or goal of the state and it is close to what some call the goal of social cohesion. In all European states, people are encouraged to develop bonds that keep them together, bonds that go beyond mere respect of the same law to form a set of principles guiding life in common. 'Integration as an aim' should be distinguished from 'integration as a process'. The latter is what a state deploys as a means to attain the goal of integration. For example, in order to promote the goal of integration—that is, in order to turn individuals into republican citizens—France deploys a strategy of integration by setting conditions of belonging to the republican nation. Integration as a process is not universally embraced; many states prefer to promote the goal of integration (or, more precisely, social cohesion) through the process of accommodation.[5]

Integration as a process is centripetal: it attracts everyone to one socio-cultural centre as in France. Accommodation as a process is centrifugal: it allows for divergence in order to avoid disintegration.

Both strategies of integration and accommodation have risks and problems (see Table 7.1.). Integration, for example, can easily slip from a virtuous process towards assimilation at best and uniformity at worst. The problem

Table 7.1. Integration and accommodation processes

|  | Ideal | Corruption | Evil |
|---|---|---|---|
| Integration | Centripetal | Assimilation (eg France) | Uniformity (eg Soviet Russia) |
| Accommodation | Centrifugal | Atomized separation (eg UK) | Segregation (eg USA pre-*Brown v Board*) |

[5] S Choudri (ed), *Constitutional Design for Divided Societies: Integration or Accommodation* (Oxford University Press, 2008).

with assimilation is that it is not responsive to the needs of cultural minorities. Either they take it or they leave it. Uniformity is even worse because it
not only requires parts to adapt to the whole but it also requires the whole to
minimize its internal diversity as much as possible. An example of blind
uniformity is that imposed by Soviet Russia in which cultural and religious
differences were repressed by an overarching, egalitarian ethos.

Accommodation presents parallel risks and problems. Accommodation
without a plan can easily result in aimless diversification, which may result
in atomized societies. Everyone and every group is accepted provided that it
does not impinge upon the life of others. We live like boats passing one
another in the night; we are not interested in others and others should refrain
from becoming interested in our lives. Diversification of this kind is not
intrinsically bad but is a perilous slippery slope that sometimes leads to
segregation whereby a society is ruled by the motto 'separate but equal'.
The USA pre-*Brown v Board of Education* exemplifies such a risk.[6]

This should not allow one to forget that the aim of both is to promote
integration. I am not sure whether one strategy is better than the other
overall. Essentially, I think that it is contingent upon history and other
local variables. However, I hope it is clear that both processes are potentially
problematic and have to be closely monitored—in particular, in relation to
the treatment of religious minorities.

Republican states such as France have always spoken primarily of integration. Multicultural states such as the UK prefer to talk about accommodation. The difference between the two lies chiefly in their conceptions of the
whole. In France, the whole is static and the parts must be fitted into that
whole. In the UK, the whole is dynamic and the parts contribute to a
reframing of the whole. Thus, 'republicanism' and 'multiculturalism' stand
at opposite ends of the spectrum. French republicans, who favour a formal
conception of equality, speak of the need to integrate discriminated people
into mainstream society. British multiculturalists, who favour freedom as
non-interference, speak instead of accommodation of minorities as parts of a
larger whole.

Buried behind those theories lie some assumptions as to what a society
should look like. France, for example, believes that there should not be any
intermediary between individuals and the state. Groups and communities
cannot be regarded as speaking for a set of people and are not considered
to be legitimate representatives of a world-view that differs from that of the
state. Thus, religious communities cannot present themselves as having a

---

[6] *Brown v Board of Education of Topeka*, 347 US 483 (1954).

collective voice in the public sphere. Equality in the French republican sense amounts to a very formal ideal according to which the state is blind vis-à-vis any sexual, religious, or ethnic difference. This ideal of equality presents some obvious problems and stands in opposition to the ideal of liberty as non-interference defended by multicultural states such as Britain who believe in the desirability of giving to groups and communities a voice and recognizing them as representing a valuable diversity. Even if laudable, the mere recognition of diversity does not guarantee a peaceful and cohesive coexistence because it does not guarantee that diversity will be taken into account when deliberation takes place. Moreover, it is likely that socio-cultural and economic gaps between groups make mutual understanding increasingly more difficult.

Both republican and multicultural strategies seem to be ill-equipped to face the challenges of religious pluralism.[7] In particular, their insistence on abstract understandings of liberty and equality is deeply problematic as they aim at imposing controversial understandings of how society should be— only to blame individuals and groups when they do not conform to this or that model of an ideal society. Moreover, those ideal understandings seem very little concerned with the value of solidarity between individuals and groups of different socio-cultural origins. Solidarity as a value greatly differs from liberty and equality as it can only be understood, nurtured, and promoted on the ground rather than from the abstract perspective of the state looking down on its citizens.

The state has an obligation to secure the preconditions for solidarity between individuals and groups. In order for this to be possible, individuals and groups need to disregard prejudices and stereotypes regarding their neighbours whose origins and roots are poorly known. Living side by side harmoniously requires a certain amount of mutual trust that can only come if one's neighbour is not regarded as an agent of disturbance but as an individual, like any other, with his/her own religious, political, cultural background.

The only possible way to promote a certain measure of trust and mutual knowledge is by giving individuals and groups a chance to experience parts of a life in common. Education provides the necessary space where people can attain mutual understanding and dispel prejudices and stereotypes about each other. The classroom can perform the vital role of bridging socio-cultural gaps by exposing people to different cultures within a common environment. Sadly, the possibility of this experience is doomed if from the outset some

---

[7] For the French debate, see C Laborde, *Critical Republicanism: The Hijab Debate and Political Philosophy* (Oxford University Press, 2007). For the British debate, see Tariq Modood, *Still Not Easy Being British: Struggles for a Multicultural Citizenship* (Trentham Books, 2010).

people are excluded from classes as is the case, for example, with Muslim pupils wearing the headscarf in French schools. The experiment is also doomed if the state encourages groups and communities to organize themselves autonomously, as with faith schools in Britain.

The classroom should be a real tolerance lab where everyone engages in an experiment from the start. At stake is the very possibility of coexistence and cohabitation, so every state should take this experiment very seriously and promote the practice of tolerance on the ground instead of imposing an idealized and moralizing vision of an ideal society starting from an abstract understanding of the values of liberty or equality. In the next section, I will explore the extent to which European states have an obligation to promote a tolerant environment through education from the viewpoint of the right of education protected by Article 2 of Protocol 1 of the ECHR.

## 7.3. State, Religion, and Education

In the past twenty years since the first *foulard* case in 1989,[8] courts in all European states have been flooded with cases about the place of religion in primary and secondary education. The cases can be divided into three broad categories. Firstly, they concern religious symbols in the classroom. Secondly, they concern religious syllabuses in public schools. Thirdly, they concern the way in which states organize systems of state, private, and religious schools (see Figure 7.1.). Much has been said about the first, less about the last two. Here, I want to say something about all of them through a discussion on the general right to education protected by Article 2 of Protocol 1 of the ECHR and the way in which it influences the mission of the state as promoter of tolerance.

This section offers some considerations on the nature of the right to education, the role of the state in its implementation, and the place of religion in schools. The point I am trying to buttress is that education is the first building block to promote a genuinely plural and tolerant society. There are several issues blurring the general picture, the first of which is the distracting power of religious symbols. In *Lautsi*, the issue of the crucifix may be the most visible concern, but the most important problem is the nature of the right to education and the corresponding obligation of the state to organize a system of education that is inclusive and that allows for different

---

[8] Avis du Conseil d'Etat Section de l'intérieur, 27 November 1989, no 346893, Avis 'Port du foulard islamique', <http://www.rajf.org/spip.php?article1065>.

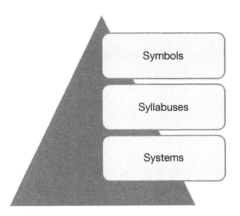

**Figure** 7.1. Three categories of concern

individuals and groups to come together in a tolerant environment. The question is the following: what is the role of the state in regulating education in order to promote tolerance? Article 2 of Protocol 1 ('right to education') of the ECHR reads as follows: 'No person shall be denied the right to education. In the exercise of any functions which it assumes in relation to education and to teaching, the State shall respect the right of parents to ensure such education and teaching in conformity with their own religious and philosophical convictions.' The interpretation of this Article immediately raises three problems. Firstly, it does not clarify who the right-holders are. It is ambiguous, for example, whether from the viewpoint of the children education is a right or an obligation. Secondly, it is necessary to understand the scope of the obligation of the state in providing education. Thirdly, it raises the issue of conformity between the education offered by the state and the religious and philosophical convictions of parents.

The Second Chamber of the ECtHR in *Lautsi* outlined some clarifications in a formulaic way.[9] Firstly, the main fundamental right is that of education and is held by children. In this context, parents have an ancillary right to respect of their religious and philosophical convictions. Secondly, the obligation of the state is to guarantee that education provided to students be objective, critical, and impartial. The Court draws a distinction between 'education' and 'indoctrination' and strictly prohibits the latter. Finally, the state has a duty of neutrality and impartiality; for the Court, neutrality guarantees in particular the right to believe or not to believe of all parents

---

[9] *Lautsi v Italy*, ECtHR, 3 November 2009, Application no 30814/06, para 47.

and children. The ECtHR adds that Article 2 of Protocol 1 should be read in conjunction with Articles 8, 9, and 10. In other words, it does not seem to be a self-standing right but a subsidiary duty like the prohibition of discrimination under Article 14. The central idea seems to be that of neutrality as a necessary precondition for pluralism. The Grand Chamber breaks free from the idea of neutrality as a central duty of the state and claims instead that Italy has a wide margin of appreciation concerning symbols in the classroom since the presence of a religious symbol does not amount to indoctrination. To reach this conclusion, the Grand Chamber uses the controversial notion of a 'passive symbol'. It is hard to make sense of this idea since passive symbols cannot be opposed to active symbols; a symbol always being passive. What the Court seems to hint at is that the teaching of religion is more intrusive and can amount to indoctrination. Moreover, the person teaching the class should be free from religious symbols.[10]

None of those principles are free from controversy. Moreover, there remain some unanswered questions as to the so-called 'right to education'. In most European states, education is regarded as a duty for children. The age requirements vary but may go up to the age of majority. Yet, at the same time, education must also be a right of children. If the state did not make any provision for education, children through their parents would have a claim against the state. But what exactly are the rights of parents vis-à-vis the state? Is it about the state offering a choice between state and private schools? Or is it about the state offering a system of state schools that meet some high standards of education?

The scope of the obligation of the state raises even more important problems. The crucial issue is the *quality* of education provided by the state. If you only have a right to something mediocre, then you may just as well waive it in order to have a better education provided by the private sector. Regrettably, the poor quality of state education entrenches class differences based upon economic means.

I believe the UK *JFS* case[11] could be read from the alternative viewpoint of the state's obligation to provide a quality education. UK state schools offer a very basic service when it comes to education. It is no secret that private schools provide a better start in life and entrench class differences based on economic means. The rich will be rich and well educated; the poor will be poor and poorly educated. One way of overcoming the class divide in

---

[10] The court prohibits the wearing of an Islamic scarf on the part of the teacher. See *Dahlab v Switzerland*, ECtHR, 15 Febuary 2001, Application no 42393/98.
[11] *R(E) v Governing Body of JFS* [2009] UKSC 15.

education provision is to attend faith schools that are often very well ranked in national tables and offer a very high standard of education.

The Jewish Free School (JFS), for example, is often classed amongst the very best schools in the country. Despite being funded by the state, by making admission dependent upon religious criteria faith schools practise discrimination. If one belongs to the religion of the school, then in principle one is eligible for a place. The applicant (M) had been raised by his father and his mother, an Italian Catholic who converted to Judaism in Israel. The problem in the case was that the criterion employed by the school followed an Orthodox understanding of Judaism that excluded M because his mother had not converted according to standards required by the school. The criterion was criticized on the basis that it introduced racial discrimination under the cloak of religion.

This case, regarded from the viewpoint of the right to education, raises the issue of whether the state should fund faith schools that will inevitably exclude some on religious, if not apparently racial, grounds. Is there a right to education in a religious institution? Article 2 of Protocol 1 does not seem to give a conclusive answer as it states that: 'the State shall respect the right of parents to ensure such education and teaching in conformity with their own religious and philosophical convictions'. Does this mean that the state should simply permit the existence of faith and other private schools? Or does it mean that the state should fund those schools? The ECtHR in *Lautsi* held that the provision does not discriminate between public and private schools. This probably means that the state is free to choose on how best to structure and fund education provided that it does not prohibit faith and other private schools. This seems to be reasonable, but it does not tell us the exact scope of the state's obligation to guarantee education.

France has put education at the heart of its republican project since the nineteenth century. In the law of 1881 Prime Minister Jules Ferry established the principle of free state schools.[12] In 1882, he made them both compulsory and *laïques*—that is, ostensibly free from any religious element.[13] The motivating ideal was to promote social advancement and integration of all through public education. If education is to be understood as an instrument for individual development and improvement of social status, then the right to education only makes sense if it imposes a strong duty on the state to guarantee the highest possible standard of education for everyone. This is not incompatible with having faith schools or other private schools. However, the state should give priority to the funding of state schools in order to ensure

---

[12] *Loi du 16 juin 1881*, note 3 above.        [13] *Lois du 28 mars 1882*, note 3 above.

they are as competitive as possible. Any other standard would simply defeat the purpose of public schools as the great social levellers.

As part of their obligation to secure the right to education, states need to send a clear message to state schools and private schools in order for them to strive to create a pluralistic environment in which tolerance can flourish. By banning the veil, France betrayed its original republican values. To put Muslim students in a situation of having to choose between wearing the *hijab* or leaving school militates against the result originally intended by Jules Ferry: it pressures them to give up their right to education in a public school in order to find a more tolerant environment in which they can feel at ease with their identity. Most of the Muslim pupils who wear a scarf seek refuge in Catholic schools that are more tolerant than state schools towards both religious people and religious symbols.

Tolerance in the religious context is a difficult value to practice because it requires striking a balance between opposite reactions of acceptance of and opposition to diversity.[14] Such a value is, by definition, very unstable as the context can often tip the balance in one way (mostly in the direction of opposition) or the other. In order to be consciously tolerant, it is necessary to know the object towards which we direct our acceptance or opposition. This requires much nurturing that can best be achieved through education. The state should introduce in state schools a mandatory class in civic education for the purpose of creating the preconditions for toleration. Such a course should include teaching knowledge of civic and political institutions as well as religious institutions understood in the broadest possible sense.

Given this premise, it is open to discussion whether the ECtHR rightly sanctioned Norway for introducing a compulsory course on 'Christian Knowledge and Religious and Ethical Education' in 1997. The Grand Chamber in *Folgerø* considered that the curriculum was insufficiently critical, objective, and pluralistic to justify its mandatory character.[15] The intent of the course was, among other things, to promote dialogue between faiths. However, the Court believed that it was not *objective* enough and as such it had to be made optional. It is difficult, however, to delineate the precise standards of objectivity required by the ECHR. It is safer to assume that, on these issues, local knowledge would help to shape the best possible curriculum. It does not seem to be the prerogative of a supranational court in any event.[16]

[14] See ch. 1 for a discussion of tolerance as opposed to toleration. See also ch. 8 for a discussion of the ethics of diversity.
[15] *Folgerø v Norway* (2008) 46 EHRR 47.
[16] Ian Leigh, 'Objective, Critical and Pluralistic? Religious Education and Human Rights in the European Public Sphere' in Lorenzo Zucca and Camil Ungureanu (eds), *Law, State and Religion in the New Europe: Debates and Dilemmas* (Cambridge University Press, 2012).

The importance of education on religious and civic matters has to do with the cognitive dimension of tolerance. When we extend our knowledge of the external world and we come to the conclusion that there is nothing dangerous with a group or a practice, then we give up opposition to that practice even if we are not prepared to embrace it. Moreover, knowledge through a balanced education helps to form much more stable and reasonable judgements. Even when one disagrees with someone, this does not constitute a ground for opposition. On the contrary, it may well prompt cultural enrichment. Of course, after deliberation and disagreement one may rightly consider another person's opinion to be wrong. Yet, even that cannot constitute a good reason for opposition as 'wrong' opinions do not curtail freedom of thought or action.

## 7.4. Back to Symbols: *Lautsi* and the Crucifix in the Classroom

In *Lautsi v Italy*,[17] the Chamber of the Second Section of the ECtHR found that the presence of the crucifix in Italian state schools violated the right to education in conjunction with the right to freedom of conscience, thought, and religion (Article 9 ECHR). This case provoked a strong and passionate reaction from the Catholic Church as well as the majority of politicians and a substantial number of private citizens in Italy. As is often the case, the heat of those debates was inversely proportional to the light shed by them. The government filed a request to hear the case before the Grand Chamber, which was accepted on 2 March 2010. On 18 March 2011, the Grand Chamber reversed the decision of the Second Section and concluded that the presence of the crucifix was not incompatible with the right of parents to have their children educated in line with their own philosophical convictions.[18]

As mentioned above, the issue of religious symbols is only the tip of the iceberg. European states are now facing significant tensions in the regulation of religion in public schools. One of the explanations for this is the crystallization of a conception of secularism that prohibits religion from interfering in the public sphere.[19] This position is often inconsistent with compromises the state has reached with dominant religions in each country. The changing cultural, social, and political landscape in Europe casts light on the arbitrary compromises that the secular state has reached with local religions. Emerging

---

[17] *Lautsi v Italy*, note 2 above, para 47.     [18] *Lautsi v Italy*, note 2 above.
[19] See ch. 2 for a discussion of two opposite conceptions of constitutional secularism.

from this finding is a competing understanding of secularism as a default framework within which religious and non-religious people can both contribute to the shaping of public policies.[20]

Education is the first laboratory and experimental space for the difficult practice of tolerance. The state, as we saw, has to invest in state schools in order to promote greater mutual knowledge, which is the best instrument for allowing tolerance to flourish. Moreover, opposition is bred by the socio-economic gaps that education is meant to bridge in the first place. A state that does not successfully promote social advancement through education is already failing in its mission to overcome social and cultural conflicts.

Religious and civic education is a necessary element of any state school curriculum. How can we possibly study the history, philosophy, literature, and art of our countries without understanding the role religion played and how, along with other intellectual sources, it shaped our moral and political landscape? Armed with these points, we can go back to the initial issues: is the presence of the crucifix interfering with the right to education of children? Is it interfering with the philosophical and religious convictions of their parents? And more importantly, is the presence of the crucifix preventing the creation of a more tolerant environment? First, as I suggested, the criterion to judge state schools is the overall quality of their curriculum. There is no doubt that Italian schools offer a high standard education for everyone and for free. It is still possible to choose a private school if parents so desire. Post-war experience has shown that the presence of the crucifix in Italian state schools has never interfered with the critical, objective, and pluralistic nature of public education. The main limit of that system lies in the presence of a course of religious education which is run by a teacher appointed by the Vatican. That course, however, is not mandatory and is easily possible to opt out from. In line with my previous points, it would be desirable that the state replaces that course with a compulsory course on pluralistic religious education.

The idea that the state must be 'neutral' in the sense of completely expunging religion from public schools is based on a contested notion of exclusive secularism that is in sharp opposition to more inclusive conceptions.[21] The ECtHR in *Lautsi* seems to have embraced an understanding of exclusive secularism that is more likely than not to lead to major confrontations between states and religions. The Grand Chamber had a great chance to formulate a more inclusive understanding of secularism that allows a place

---

[20] Lorenzo Zucca, 'The Crisis of the Secular State: A Reply to Prof. Sajó', International Journal of Constitutional Law, 7(3), 494–514.
[21] See ch. 5 for a discussion of neutrality.

for religions in the classroom and in the public sphere—a secularism that truly promotes tolerance and pluralism in the best tradition of the Court itself. However, the Grand Chamber decided to frame the problem in the narrowest possible terms, holding that the issue only concerned the compatibility of the crucifix with the right of education and freedom of religion. It controversially held that the decision had nothing to do with the compatibility of the crucifix with the principle of secularism.[22]

I believe that the Grand Chamber's decision lacks subtleness and articulation. In the remaining pages I want to discuss my preferred solution, taking as a cue the pleadings presented by Professor Weiler before the Court in its general hearings. I address here both the general principles raised by the *Lautsi* case[23] and Professor Weiler's brief.[24] In the interest of space, I will only mention the most essential arguments.

In its decision, the Chamber dealt with the nature and scope of the right to education as encapsulated in Article 2 of Protocol 1. Therein lies an important tension between the *obligation* of the state to provide equal access to education for all and the *obligation* of the state to guarantee pluralism and diversity through respect for the parents' convictions. To achieve the latter aim, it has to promote an environment where everyone can identify with the school—including its syllabus and its symbols. The central question, as I understand it, is the following: how can the state treat people with different religious and philosophical convictions in a way that guarantees equal concern and respect? This tension is encapsulated in the Chamber's judgment:

Respect for parents' convictions must be possible in the context of education and capable of ensuring an open school environment which encourages inclusion rather than exclusion, regardless of the pupils' social background, religious beliefs, or ethnic origins. Schools should not be the arena for missionary activities or preaching; they should be a meeting place for different religions and philosophical convictions, in which pupils can acquire knowledge about their respective thoughts and traditions.[25]

When faced with such a fundamental conflict, judges should exercise a good degree of empathy—that is, the natural human capacity of putting oneself in someone else's shoes, and in the process trying to avoid the trap of dividing the camp into two sharply divided camps of the secular and the religious. This is often difficult in legal settings where the binary logic tends

---

[22] *Lautsi*, note 2 above, para 57.
[23] *Lautsi*, note 2 above, para 47.
[24] JHH Weiler, 'Editorial—State and Nation: Church, Mosque, and Synagogue—the Trailer', *International Journal of Constitutional Law*, 8(2) (2009), 157–66.
[25] *Lautsi*, note 2 above, para 47c.

to polarize discussion. I firmly believe that in order to deal with conflicts one needs to go beyond that binary logic in order to find a better compromise.

Weiler's analysis is thought-provoking and engaging but falls in the legalistic trap of dividing the world into two halves for the purpose of showing that choosing a side is never a neutral decision. His discussion follows three main lines that mirror the three legal principles he draws out from the case. The first principle is the affirmation of the right to freedom of religion and freedom from religion, which, though hardly an object of contention, is often difficult in its application. The second principle concerns the need for a classroom that inculcates tolerance and pluralism and is bereft of religious coercion. Here, I would like to briefly say that prima facie everyone may agree with that idea but the practical implications are far from clear. As explored above, the ECtHR conceives of schools as meeting places for different religions and philosophical convictions. In order to create this environment, the state has to deal with three main policy issues that are all interlinked. Firstly, the state has to set up a system in which equal access to education is promoted; this requires a judgement as to whether, for example, faith schools should be funded by the state. Secondly, the state should make sure that the school's syllabus promotes a sufficient knowledge of diversity so that it cannot simply impose a religious course of a given confession without providing the opportunity for opting out. Ideally, the course would promote pluralism by presenting a diversity of religious and secular positions on ethical issues. Thirdly, and I want to stress here that this is only the tip of a much bigger iceberg concerning the place of religion in education, the state should decide which symbols to display and refrain from embracing symbols that may hamper equal membership and diversity.

It is the third principle that chiefly concerns Weiler. This is the principle of neutrality as articulated by the Court: 'The State's duty of neutrality and impartiality is incompatible with any kind of power on its part to assess the legitimacy of religious convictions or the ways of expressing those convictions.'[26] He criticizes the rationale of neutrality proposed by the Court by using one conceptual argument and two sets of dichotomies. The conceptual argument has to do with the understanding of 'freedom of religion'; Weiler suggests that the individual freedom of and from religion is complemented by the freedom of the state to define its own national identity by selecting, among other things, its religious symbols. The two sets of dichotomies concern the definition of a *laïc* /non-*laïc* state and the factual situation of having a symbol or not having one. Here, I will attempt to argue against what

---

[26] *Lautsi*, note 2 above, para 47.

I regard as a conceptual mistake and as false dichotomies. More generally, I will criticize the binary logic that splits society into secular and religious camps and which, albeit typical of legal reasoning, is very detrimental when one attempts to solve social and legal conflicts.

The first conceptual mistake concerns the distinction between the individual freedom of religion and the freedom of the state 'when it comes to the place of religion or religious heritage in the collective identity of the nation and the symbology of the State'.[27] Freedom in constitutional terms is defined in relation to the established constitutional authority of the state. The state has the power to change legal relations in ordinary law but finds its limit in the existence of individual freedom which signposts immunity from regulation on the part of the individual as well as a disability to regulate on the part of the state. So to say that the state 'has freedom' is inaccurate. The state has the power to determine the place of religion or religious heritage in its own collective identity by choosing the symbols it prefers but this power can be limited by the exercise of freedom on the part of an individual or a group who can reasonably show that they have been discriminated against.

Weiler argues that in Europe the state is not obliged to follow a given model of church–state relationship. This is correct but even in this context it is inaccurate to claim that the state has a freedom to decide its own model as this would suggest that the ECtHR has the ultimate authority to decide these issues and the state only has residual authority. However, the truth is that the ECtHR can only point to a violation of Convention rights whilst the authority to determine the collective identity of the state remains in the hands of the state itself. The Grand Chamber takes up this suggestion and avoids imposing a single model of the state–church relationship. Today, that is not an issue anymore. What is at stake is the way in which the secular state deals with diversity in a society that is increasingly pluralist and less and less homogeneous. Unfortunately, the Grand Chamber shirks from taking a position as to the obligation of the state to show genuine respect for those people that are not comfortable with Christian religious symbols exposed in a public place. That said, the main responsibility still lies with the state.

What kind of choice can the state make? Here, Professor Weiler uses the first false dichotomy between *laïc* and non-*laïc* states. French *laïcité* represents one paradigmatic form of secularism whereas England is described as a typical non-*laïc* state. There are two problems with this dichotomy. The first is that *laïcité* is far from being a representative form of secularism; if anything, it is a radical (and often ideological) exception in Europe.[28] It is radical because

---

[27] Weiler, 'Editorial—State and nation; church, mosque, and synagogue—the trailer', p 161.
[28] Olivier Roy, *La Laïcité face á l'islam* (Stock, 2005).

it has imposed, since 1905, a very strict separation between church and state which was created after a bitter conflict between the French state and the Catholic Church. More problematically, it is ideological as it claims to provide the foundation for a set of values common to all the citizens of France. But of course the suggestion that, once stripped of religious beliefs, we would all converge towards a common national identity defined in purely political terms is just an illusion. *Laïcité*, in this ideological sense, is not compatible with freedom of belief.

The second problem with the dichotomy is that the polar opposite of a *laïc* state is defined in purely negative terms: non-*laïc* states. This is hardly accurate and as a consequence not very helpful. England, the example used by Weiler, is a very complex case. It certainly cannot be defined as *laïc* but it has many secular elements along with elements of establishment. In brief, as Julian Rivers points out, the English system encapsulates a tension between establishment and secularism.[29] Instead of positing a dichotomy between *laïc* and non-*laïc* states, it would be more stimulating to propose a typology of the variety of secularisms in Europe.[30]

I want to raise, in passing, another problem for Weiler's argument. The Italian Constitutional Court singles out *laïcité* as one of the constitutional principles embedded in the foundational text (although not explicitly mentioned). Concerning the crucifix in the classroom, it refused to rule on this issue because it lacks the jurisdiction to review an administrative decree. But the constitutional judge decided as a matter of internal regulation to remove the crucifix from the courtroom, thereby taking a side in the debate. It would seem that, from a constitutional viewpoint, were we to draw the appropriate consequences of the principle of *laïcité* as recognized by the Constitutional Court, crucifixes would have no place in school classrooms. However, Italy is for the moment an in-between case that shows a tension between its secular (or more precisely *laïque*) character and the acceptance of certain elements of religion in public institutions. I believe that the Italian state holds inconsistent positions as to the place of religion in the public sphere. But I also believe that it is for the state to decide what form of secularism suits it and to draw from it all the necessary conclusions. Conversely, it is not the mission of an international court to suggest which form of secularism is the most appropriate at the local level. An international court can, however, pinpoint

---

[29] J Rivers, *The Law of Organized Religions: Between Establishment and Secularism* (Oxford University Press, 2010).

[30] See for an interesting debate, M Waner, J Van Antwerpen, and C Calhoun (eds), *Varieties of Secularism in a Secular Age* (Harvard University Press, 2010).

a contradiction between existing principle and practice, while attempting to formulate a minimum common definition of secularism.

The final and most important false dichotomy is that between a wall with a symbol and one without. Weiler's parable of Marco and Leonardo, two children who are equally perplexed by the presence and absence of the crucifix, aims to illustrate that neither of these two choices is neutral. It may be true that a naked wall is not a neutral solution in this particular case where emptiness would be the expression of an act of rejection. It does not follow, however, that the presence and absence of the crucifix are equivalent. Moreover, those two options do not exhaust the realm of the possible. I do believe that a solution can be found in an alternative arrangement.

Besides the two polar opposites, there are at least two more positions. The first option is well known and consists of having several symbols rather than one. Having several symbols would be more consistent with a more inclusive ethics since one symbol is to be reasonably interpreted as expressing an exclusive position. Moreover, the solution in favour of a plurality of symbols was the position initially adopted by the Italian state which used to require having on the wall a picture of the valiant king, Vittorio Emanuele I, along with a crucifix. It can then be argued that Italian walls should not be emptied but filled with other symbols that may capture the increasing diversity within the classroom. Alternatively, one could of course have a picture of the president or the prime minister but it is doubtful that this would be acceptable to all.

There is another completely different position to consider which requires the active engagement of all interested parties. Given that one, two, or more symbols—or none at all—are alternative positions, it would be desirable to spark a debate about which option most pleases the local community of parents, teachers, and pupils in the school. One problem remains: where to start? Should the debate take place from scratch or should it take account of the status quo? This decision is better left to the state as the constitutional authority charged with the selection of national symbols. This may mean that we would have to start with the default position of the crucifix, even though as I said this is inconsistent with a self-avowed commitment to *laïcité*. However, the point here is not to bow down to or resist state authority but to take this tension as an opportunity for local deliberation and mutual learning. On this point, the Grand Chamber ends up leaving too wide a margin of appreciation for the nation state. The ECtHR should have put more pressure on Italy to engage in a serious national debate as to the desirability of the crucifix in the classroom. As things stand, Italy will simply ignore this issue until the next major litigation.

I am not arguing that the symbol should be removed as a matter of principle. One can well imagine a scenario in which the rule for everyone would remain unchanged: the Italian state elects the crucifix as a symbol to be hung in classrooms. However, it should be possible to apply for an exemption to this rule. The exception could work according to a deliberative model. The debate could have two stages: first, parents (and/or pupils depending on their age) would have to present reasons for and against the crucifix in the classroom. If they agreed to keep the crucifix, then the deliberation would end there. If they agreed to have an exemption to the general rule, then they would have to decide what best arrangement to put in place instead: another symbol, several symbols, or a white wall. In this way, the power of the state to determine its own national symbols would be preserved and not overruled by the ECtHR. The second is that freedom of and from religion would equally be enhanced although not in a way that is openly polarized and exclusive but in a way that is inclusive, pluralistic, and tolerant. Individual freedom is a powerful weapon that may be abused by some individuals who are not able to accept that compromises are at the core of democratic societies. Thus, the Grand Chamber had the opportunity to put forward an understanding of the right to education that is sensitive to the idea that classrooms should be the laboratory of tolerance in so far as they are the best places wherein one can experience pluralism and develop mutual understanding. The presence of the crucifix in Italian classrooms is not always incompatible with the respect of parents' convictions. However, and this is what is missing in the Grand Chamber's decision, the state has to show a real concern and respect for those parents that disagree with that rule by giving the possibility of an exemption mechanism. If the state can devise a system whereby the crucifix can be regarded as a starting point for a local debate on what symbols bind us together then it will perhaps be acceptable. The overarching goal is not to impose unilaterally a secular or a religious view of what the symbols in the classroom should look like. The aim should be to provide an environment within which the exchange between religious and non-religious people is possible, creative, and productive. The classroom as a tolerance lab does not require as a matter of principle the removal of the crucifix once and forever. Instead, it demands that the decision on what symbols should be displayed in a classroom be dependent on mutual understanding and respect. Unfortunately the Grand Chamber treats the notion of respect very ambiguously.

The Grand Chamber regards the second sentence of Article 2 of Protocol 1 as being central to the case. In particular, it focuses on the notion of respect towards parental convictions. For the Grand Chamber: 'The word respect in Article 2 means more than "acknowledge" or "take into account" . . . it implies some positive obligation on the part of the State.'[31] So the Court distinguishes between two conceptions of respect. One is about acknowledgement, the other is about esteem. We merely acknowledge someone else's views when we can see the difference between two views without wanting to learn from the other person's perspective. In the case of respect as esteem we can see the difference and yet we are ready to make the other person's viewpoint part of our world-view; this attitude involves a greater willingness to learn and compromise.[32] In theory, the Grand Chamber opts for the latter understanding of respect, although, in practice, it applies the former. The Court holds that the philosophical convictions of the parents must be respected by the state. It is noted by the Court here that respect requires a more demanding attitude than simple acknowledgement. Legally, this means that the state has a positive obligation to take into account parents' convictions.[33] Nevertheless, what the Court gives with one hand it manages to take away with the other in the very same paragraph, and, in a feast of poor logic, holds that the notion of respect will vary from country to country. In other words, the Court says that respect is a stringent universal moral and legal requirement, yet it also holds that it is not all that stringent as it depends on the context and on European consensus.[34] Surely, to show respect to parents' convictions involves a great deal of effort on the part of the state! Not at all, says the Court, since respect depends on whether there is consensus on certain practices at the European level. This is like saying that I respect everyone's opinion, but I am happy to silence those thoughts that are not approved by the majority consensus. Or one can turn the table against the Court itself: I respect the ECHR, but I am prepared to disregard it completely if there is no consensus on its authority. Those are the kind of problems that the Court entered into by engaging (poorly!) with the notion of respect.

The Grand Chamber fails to show respect for the notion of respect. Unfortunately, it gives the state a blank cheque which does not require any extra step to be taken. This is not ideal as there remains a big tension between those people who regard the crucifix as desirable and those who see it as an unacceptable presence.

---

[31] *Lautsi*, note 2 above, para 61.

[32] For a defence of this position, see Martha Nussbaum, *Liberty of Conscience: In Defense of America's Tradition of Religious Equality* (Basic Books, 2008). See also Brian Leiter's response, *Why Tolerate Religion?* (Princeton University Press, forthcoming 2012).

[33] *Lautsi*, note 2 above, para 61.

[34] Either respect is universal or contingent; the two are mutually exclusive.

## 7.5. Conclusion

Symbols should not occupy us for too long. The state has a general obligation to organize a system of education which values religious communities without giving them the opportunity to isolate themselves from other religious and non-religious people. In other words, the system of education that a state devises should protect pluralism while promoting a vision of education as an experiment—a laboratory—in the practice of tolerance. In the UK, it is highly doubtful that faith schools can create a diverse environment in which mutual understanding and tolerance can be fostered. It is all the more suspect when a school excludes pupils on debatable religious grounds, as was the case in *JFS School*.[35] The state should not subsidize educational environments where socio-cultural, not to mention ethnic, homogeneity is the norm and diversity only the exception. In France, republican schools that are engaged in the mission of forming republican citizens cannot pretend that everyone who enters the educational environment blindly accepts republican values. If those values are strong, education will be able to pass them on by requiring individuals to reflect upon them and allowing them to embrace them because they are desirable—not because they are imposed.

European states that are seeking to enhance social cohesion cannot rely on strategies of integration or accommodation that reinforce and entrench assumptions about ideal societies. I have sought to demonstrate in this chapter that states are better advised to take into account the fact of pluralism on the ground and to organize it in such a way that mutual understanding between various groups in a society is possible. Of course, tensions between individuals and groups will not be totally dispelled; this would in fact be very worrying as it would be a sign of uniformity. On the contrary, those tensions could play an important role in pushing people to reflect upon their own commitments and on the necessity of recognizing diversity. This could be the lesson of the crucifix if taken as a starting point for engaging with others in order to better understand oneself.

I started by saying that I was both a potential victim and a potential perpetrator of the presence of the crucifix in Italian classrooms. I would like to suggest that this is not because I am inherently irrational or lack the ability to take a clear stance. It is because I can see a tension between my secularist position and my sense of belonging to a culture that is imbued with religious elements and symbols. To feel that tension is to be able to see that

---

[35]  *R(E) v Governing Body of JFS.*

there are important reasons that militate in favour of either position and I do not want to simply prioritize one above another. Instead, I believe that that tension is a starting point for further reflection on the secular state and the presence of religions within it. It is in the classroom that such a reflection should start and can only take place if we conceive of the classroom as a tolerance lab. Needless to say, the presence of religion in wider society is not only a matter for the state to address but requires virtuous behaviour on the part of all citizens: in other words, it requires a proper ethics of diversity, which will be examined in the next chapter.

# 8

# Religion and the Ethics of Diversity

## 8.1. Introduction

Religious diversity has not been a feature of European nation states. Its suppression and the wilful imposition of religious homogeneity have characterized much social and political experience. Of course, as pointed out in chapter 1, religious diversity was grudgingly tolerated, but there was no effort to understand it. More importantly, diversity was controlled and policed by the state: only approved religions could be part of the social fabric. As a result, religious diversity was stifled within nation states but also across nation states.

This chapter is not only about religious diversity: it deals with diversity in general. It attempts to suggest that diversity matters as a fact from two viewpoints: the natural and the cultural. Its importance as a natural fact cannot be underestimated at the macro and micro level: biodiversity matters across and within species. Its importance as a socio-cultural fact matters across and within Europe, especially given the growing presence of immigrant minorities. The relation between natural and cultural diversity is also important here: cultural diversity can be explained by reference to the environment in which one lives.[1]

Diversity has often been underrated by philosophers, who regard it at best as a subspecies of other values, or at worst as a hindrance to individual autonomy.[2] By the latter, they mean that individual development should not be curtailed by cultural traditions. But autonomy insists on an ideal, a less than real image of human beings as happy separate islands, while diversity is a relational concept that explains why individual minds flourish alone *and* when they form social bonds. This chapter puts diversity at the centre of

---

[1] As Montesquieu attempted to show in his most important work *The Spirit of the Laws.* Cultural diversity is rooted in a given environment. This means that it has a limited exportability.

[2] See KA Appiah, *The Ethics of Identity* (Princeton University Press, 2005). Appiah discusses this problem, but then goes on to adopt a very classical liberal (Millian) position.

the search of the good life.[3] Within this account, virtuous behaviour means to maximize one's own natural diversity within the cultural environment we are living in.

The ethics of diversity departs from religious and non-religious ethics. The ethical theory defended in this chapter is naturalistic in the sense that it claims to present an alternative picture of human beings as firmly rooted in the natural world. The ethics of diversity is heteronomous, since the basis of the moral law is independent from individual will in two ways: firstly, natural diversity is rooted in the idea that human beings live a good life if it is in line with their instinct for survival and maximization of control over the external world. Secondly, cultural diversity is rooted in the idea that individuals—and institutions for that matter—flourish alone *and* when they form strong socio-cultural bonds. What defines a good life mirrors both sides of diversity, whereas autonomy reflects a purely individualistic viewpoint.

This chapter begins by distinguishing the ethics of diversity from other ethics of religious and non-religious kinds. It then goes on to place diversity at the centre of a naturalistic ethics. Section 8.3. explains the secular character of the naturalistic ethics. Section 8.4. explains the difference between the ethics of diversity and value pluralism. Section 8.5. concludes by highlighting the implications for religion.

## 8.2. Foundations

Religion provides the strongest possible foundation for ethics: human beings would live a good life if they scrupulously followed God's commands.[4] Life on earth would not be immediately improved by that but it was clear that the recompense would come with life after death.[5] Compared with such a powerful position, secular ethics have always struggled to impose themselves as they only promised a good life in this contingent world and nothing more than that.[6] For those whose life is a struggle, there is little hope of redemption or salvation. Life is just dull and horrible and a secular ethics would only confirm the most dreaded fear: some people are born lucky and blessed with

---

[3] Diversity should be distinguished from individual autonomy on which is based JS Mill's experiment in living expounded in his *Autobiography* (Penguin Books, 1989).

[4] For a recent religious ethics that stresses the importance of diversity, see Jonathan Sacks, *The Dignity of Difference: How to Avoid the Clash of Civilizations* (Continuum, 2003).

[5] St Thomas Aquinas, *Summa Theologica* (Christian Classics, 1981).

[6] T Nagel, *Secular Philosophy and the Religious Temperament* (Oxford University Press, 2010).

terrestrial goods, while others have to endure the burden of a poor and meaningless life on earth.

The price of religious ethics is their transcendental metaphysics. By creating a sharp divide—a dualism—between this world and the afterlife, the whole search of meaning in our life is postponed or simply dreamed up as we have no means to access nor to ascertain metaphysical truths of religious kind apart from what the Holy Scriptures tell us. Dante is a perfect example of this dualist structure: nothing makes real sense on earth, not even human laws or human justice.[7] The only perfect understanding of justice is divine and Paradise is strictly and rigidly organized according to the most precise principles of justice.

Descartes embraces a dualist understanding of reality.[8] The physical world follows earthly laws that are written in stone in the sense that they are not mutable and are scientifically ascertainable. The place of science is carved out and put on a strong pedestal. That understanding does not challenge the parallel query about the life of the soul, which follows laws completely different from earthly laws. The interaction between the soul and the physical world seems to be dependent on non-scientific laws that some call divine laws. Divine laws are also written in stone, although in a different sense: they have been given to man by God who dictated his words to the prophets. Divine laws do not follow earthly patterns like scientific laws, but they instead dictate the right ways to follow in order to gain entrance into the realm of heaven. Scientific and divine laws are different in nature and point, and are to be studied with completely different sets of minds and methodologies.

Spinoza, possibly the first secular philosopher, resisted that suggestion.[9] For the first time, he applied his encyclopaedic knowledge of the Bible to show that the words of God could not be taken at face value because there are many points at which the Holy Scripture contradicts itself. This would either mean that God is fallible or that the word of God is incoherent. Faced with this paradox, the only conclusion was to suggest that the words of God as inscribed in the Holy Scripture are only reported by human voices. They contain important moral messages, but should not be taken as literally encapsulating the ultimate words of God. Human fallibility is a necessary trait of the understanding and interpretation of divine laws. As a humanly transcribed text, the Bible has to be submitted to the conventional

---

[7]  E Auerbach, *Dante: Poet of the Secular world* (NYRB Classics, 2007).

[8]  R Descartes, 'Meditation VI' in *Meditations on the First Philosophy* [1641], trans J Cottingham (Cambridge University Press, 1996).

[9]  For a study of Spinoza as starting the Secular Age, see Steven Nadler, *A Book Forged in Hell: Spinoza's Scandalous Treatise and the Birth of the Secular Age* (Princeton University Press, 2011).

scientific method of inquiry. The conclusion was devastating: there is no difference in nature between the study of the Bible and the study of any other phenomena in the world.[10]

Spinoza's position was even deeper than that: he resisted the very dualism between body and mind at the centre of Cartesian philosophy.[11] Spinoza's *Ethics* is a monumental attempt to demonstrate that the laws of the body and the laws of the mind are one and the same.[12] If we want to understand human behaviour we have to understand scientific laws. And even further than that: if we want to understand God we have to understand nature (*Deus sive Natura*):[13] divine laws are not separate from natural laws, they are the same. Spinoza thus brings God back to earth and puts him at the centre of the natural world. By so doing, he dismisses centuries of learned Judeo-Christian metaphysics. His metaphysics is rooted in this immanent world, and so is his *Ethics*.

Spinoza's *Ethics* was firmly rooted in this world. It was the first secular ethics.[14] It reconciled the individual with the natural world and created no barriers to what we can know and do.[15] We do not really know what we are capable of, because we scarcely know what our body and our mind are capable of. Spinoza wants us to find within ourselves our grain of eternity. We are God-like in so far as we all originate in one and the same divine source which coincides with nature. To understand ourselves is to understand one part of nature. It is also to understand what place each one of us has within nature and what are the deep connections between natural laws and our behaviour.[16] The good life is about a deep understanding of the functioning of our bodies and minds within the natural world. Spinoza's *Ethics* requires us to push the boundaries of conventional knowledge and to free ourselves from prejudices and other burdens that prevent us from getting closer to real understanding.

What is the foundation of ethics for Spinoza? This was clear in his mind: 'No virtue can be conceived as prior to this endeavour to preserve one's own being.'[17] The supreme virtue is that of striving to preserve oneself and

[10] B Spinoza, *Theological-Political Treatise*, trans Samuel Shirley, 2nd edn (Hackett Publishing, 2001).

[11] For a modern criticism of dualism, see J Searle, *Mind* (Oxford University Press, 2005).

[12] Spinoza, *Ethics* in *The Collected Writings of Spinoza*, trans Edwin Curley (Princeton University Press, 1985).

[13] Spinoza, *Ethics*, Part IV, Preface.

[14] J Israel, *A Revolution of the Mind* (Princeton University Press, 2009). See also, Nadler, *A Book Forged in Hell*.

[15] Stuart Hampshire, *Spinoza and Spinozism* (Clarendon Press, 2005).

[16] Montesquieu, *The Spirit of the Laws*, trans Thomas Nugent (MacMillan, 1949).

[17] Spinoza, *Ethics*, Proposition XXII, Book 4.

to extend one's own control over the external world. The real motivating factor of a life worth living is based *avant tout* on the protection of that very life without which we would not even ask the question of what is a good life. To have a good life one has to have a life—there is no bypassing this basic fact. Life is about the human striving to preserve oneself and to increase the control over the external world.[18] So something is good or virtuous if it maximizes the preservation of life and control over the external world. Something is bad or vicious if it minimizes self-preservation and control.[19]

Despite the vocabulary, the ethics of diversity, which builds upon Spinoza's *Ethics*, has nothing to do with a utilitarian viewpoint. Utilitarianism posits an ideal goal that is vague and remote from life as we experience it. For example, happiness is certainly a common, although vague, aspiration for us all. Yet, it is not stable and constant enough to provide the very basic standard for the evaluation of our life. It is not an easy task to establish what maximizes our happiness if we have no idea of what happiness may be. Also, utilitarian maximization does not take seriously the separateness of individuals; while a naturalistic ethics as I understand it starts from the recognition of separateness based on self-interest and self-preservation.

What does this tell us about the obligations we have to one another? Enlightened self-interest includes the idea that we are stronger in body and mind if we unite with other people: the greater the union of people, the stronger the resulting commonwealth. From this viewpoint, it is against self-interest to isolate oneself and live in autarchy.[20] It is in line with self-interest to form strong bonds with other individuals in order to form a harmonious union of people that strives to protect and promote a common good under a system of laws. The common good is defined by the pursuit of rational good for each individual. When an individual identifies a rational good, she will wish it for everyone. For example, once we come to realize that freedom from coercion is a rational good for each one of us, it must follow that this rational good must be the same for every other being. Thus, it is fully consistent with self-interest to pursue the drive to unite with other people in order to live in harmony and free from conflicts between people that may undermine the individual's pursuit of self-interest.

The ethics of diversity is well beyond and above the divide between liberals and communitarians. Self-interest is consistent with the drive to unite with other people in a stable and strong community governed by a system of laws.

---

[18] The parallel with Hobbes ends here.

[19] Gilles Deleuze, *Spinoza: philosophie pratique* (Les éditions de minuit, 1995).

[20] Many liberals would disagree about this. If one believes in individual autonomy, then one possible option is autarchy or solipsism.

Our self-interest finds its higher expression in the common good. The basis for obedience to general laws stems from our own self-interest understood rationally as the endeavour to preserve oneself and to extend control over the external world. Both things are better achieved together with other human beings rather than in isolation.

The latter observation goes beyond the damning question of what unites us all—the glue that keeps us together. In a fully rational commonwealth whose intent is to preserve itself and increase its power, the glue is provided by the rational realization of the fact that together we are stronger. We do not need to ask what keeps us together; if anything we should ask what divides us. The problem arises from the fact that we are not fully rational and we are scarcely capable of drawing all appropriate conclusions from our fallible nature. We are driven more by negative passions and desires and are therefore prone to experience negative feelings towards other human beings, including those who belong to our community.

Conflicts ensue from negative emotions that prevent a full use of rationality and we are therefore pushed back to the question of what may keep us together despite all our feelings of opposition towards other people. At this point, one often refers to an external source of ethics and morality as towering over us and oppressing us into behaving in harmony with other people. One is often tempted to believe that religion alone keeps us together and prevents the worst behaviour of people towards one another. Religion would thus play a civic role, keeping the basest desires of human beings in check. Religion may play such a central role because we often despair about the capacity of human beings to order their life according to the strictest mandates of reason.[21]

It is clear, however, that religion is regarded as a second-best form of cohesion by secular thinkers: because people are fallible and irrational, it is necessary to provide an easy-to-use glue to keep things together. Religion, however, comes packaged in a powerful comprehensive perspective which claims to be the only source of good life to the exclusion of secular ethics. This does not mean that religion and a secular ethics cannot coexist—they can to the extent that religion accepts its rational bounds.[22] Where religion claims a foundational status not open to rational investigation, it asserts itself as empty theology that is principally interested in power and control over all else. Of course, it is in the interest of religious institutions to increase their

---

[21] Machiavelli and Spinoza agree on this point.
[22] Immanuel Kant, *Religion within the Boundaries of Mere Reason* (Cambridge University Press, 1998).

power in that way, but that power is not consistent with the powers of individuals alone and in community among themselves.

The ethics of diversity, on the other hand, does not represent a fully-fledged world-view to the exclusion of any other world-views, be they religious or non-religious. The ethics of diversity can only offer a default common position, the point of which is to maximize the thriving of as many world-views as possible. The ethics of diversity opens up the space for freedom of thought rather than imposing one view that limits any other world-view. To maximize the thriving of world-views, however, requires the positing of at least some limits to avoid clashes between world-views that will turn into violent confrontations between religious and non-religious people. To put it slightly differently, the ethics of diversity aims at maximizing diversity while minimizing mutual domination and aggression.

## 8.3. Diversity: Micro and Macro

In a nation state, there is a tendency to stress the unity of the legal-political system while glossing over all the different types of diversity present in the society. In Europe the rise and fall of the nation-state model was premised by a strong sense of national unity. The myth of national identity has kept nation states together even if in the last fifty years or so nation states have ceded power to devolved entities as well as supranational organizations such as the EU. The tension between diversity and identity is one of the characteristic traits of contemporary Europe: so much so that the very motto of the EU is 'Unity in Diversity'. Diversity and identity, however, are two faces of the same coin rather than two completely separate notions. My personal identity as an individual makes me different from anyone else in the world: there is nobody like me. It is therefore necessary to distinguish between different levels at which diversity can play an important role.

### 8.3.1. Biodiversity

Diversity has many layers and encapsulates a number of creative tensions. At the most general level, it is possible to talk about biodiversity—that is, diversity of life in the natural world. The idea of biodiversity is crucial to challenge the liberal myth of man's special place in the world. The ethics of diversity does not start from that myth. Instead it holds that human societies can be understood and explained against the background of a wider natural order which follows the same laws for all species. Within that order the preservation of diversity is paramount, as it equates to the very preservation of life: when human beings lessen diversity in the world, they also undermine a source of life and survival. The human race cannot grow indefinitely without causing the death of other species and eventually its own.[23]

## 8.3.2. Diversity v Identity

Human diversity can usefully be contrasted with monolithic identity, that is when one aspect of identity takes the lion's share and cast shadows on all other aspects. Religious identity, for example, rides roughshod over many other local cultural identities that are somehow weaker than the one single unifying power of religious identity. When religious identity loosens its grip because of a progressive secularization, then local diversities emerge. The secularization of the mind began with Spinoza's *Tractatus Theologico-Politicus*; the idea was to free individuals from a number of prejudices and received ideas from the Bible that prevented human beings from thinking freely unencumbered by those ideas. That kind of emancipation has not yet fully materialized, nor will it ever, since the masses are not free from their fears, prejudices, and other barriers to real knowledge. The possibility of rational mastery is there for everyone to build on, but it is no mean feat and has not always been promoted by political or religious institutions. After all one of the central points of religion is to render individuals obedient and this interest goes hand in hand with that of political power. Rational mastery is often at odds with the exercise of power. In addition to that, there is great scepticism about the capability of the masses to achieve rational mastery. In a secularized world the instruments of mass deception change and not always in the best possible direction. The media create a set of beliefs and models to which the masses aspire. Media-organized brainwashing is one of the greatest obstacles to the deployment of rational mastery on the part of a great chunk of the population.

We all have different minds but they are constantly interfered with and brought to imitate a mass-media model of the individual-consumerist. To this extent, control of the masses by religion is perhaps more desirable, which insists on important social virtues. Ideally, those weapons of mass deception would not be used to transform individuals into meek obedient sheep. It is however unlikely that religious and political institutions would promote free individuals on a large scale. Perhaps this is because it is impossible. Perhaps this is because it is not in the interests of rulers. This makes life for the individual who breaks free from mass prejudices very hard. Individual

---

[23] Edward O Wilson, *The Diversity of Life* (Norton, 1999).

diversity based on a genuine freedom of thought is always regarded with great suspicion by ruling powers. Spinoza, for example, had to live in anonymity as his views would have led to his persecution. His original ideas had already forced his expulsion from the Jewish community of Amsterdam.

## 8.3.3. Individual diversity

As just indicated, each one of us has an identity that makes us different from one another. We have different minds and bodies, each one of which enjoys the potential for self-mastery and great understanding of the external world. The capacity for self-mastery is something that we all have, but it does not mean that we all exercise it. Often external influences make us believe and behave in a way that is very similar to anyone else belonging to a given community. Religion is a strong external power that makes us believe and behave in a meek and obedient way to the commands of a religious or political leader. To this extent, religion is an impediment to freedom of thought because it does not allow for individuals to form their own beliefs from scratch. Instead, it induces them to believe in a series of ideas that are imposed from above.

When religion is too strong an external influence, it shapes identity in a way that does not leave any room for serious individual development. One's individuality blends into the mould of religious identity and leaves no room for serious free-thinking away from received ideas. In other words, religious identity has the lion's share and blocks or limits any other source of individual identity that characterizes any person at birth. In a pre-globalized world, religious and cultural identity would coincide in a way that made us all very similar albeit not identical. Italian identity, for example, was deeply rooted in a Christian world-view which largely coincided with our cultural identity. Language, art, symbols, and so on are still shaped in the Christian mould and this explains for example why the Italian Supreme Administrative Court (*Consiglio di Stato*) defines the crucifix as a secular symbol, standing for values shared across the religious/non-religious spectrum.

Diversity needs to be distinguished from individual autonomy.[24] The latter derives from a liberal conception of the special place of man on earth, which cannot solely be explained by non-human laws. In the liberal-contractualist model when man enters society he does not altogether give up

---

[24] Appiah acknowledges the tension between autonomy and diversity but tends to play it down, see Appiah, *The Ethics of Identity*. Someone who sees an inevitable tension is W Galston, *Liberal Pluralism: The Implications of Value Pluralism for Polititcal Theory and Practice* (Cambridge University Press, 2002).

his autonomy, which is preserved as his ultimate natural right. However natural autonomy is a strong passion and is likely to come into conflict with the autonomy of other individuals. In Hobbes, this is the reason for having a strong centralized government that adjudicates on conflicts between individuals. Another crucial upshot of natural autonomy is the idea of radical equality between individuals who are considered to be equally endowed with that faculty from birth, so their rise and fall should only be measured by how well they use their special human faculty of autonomy.

Diversity is not compatible with the idea of the radical equality of autonomous individuals, since the basic belief is that each one of us has different minds and different potential. More importantly, the way in which we develop our own individuality depends very much on how well one has been trained and educated in pursuing an individual path unencumbered by external pressures. Finally, just as the eternal order of nature explained by scientific laws is organized hierarchically and with a great diversity of species, so the human order is nothing but a reflection of the order of nature. It is an illusion to believe that man has a special place within nature, as much as it is an illusion that human beings are endowed with a special faculty called autonomy which makes them all equal at birth (and all different at death). Each one of us is different from the beginning and our natural differences should be taken more seriously when we attempt to understand political societies in which natural differences matter politically. Individual diversity militates in favour of a political regime that maximizes diversity (of thought to begin with), and allows for a great room of dissent. This does not mean that all opinions are strictly speaking equal; diversity implies that some ideas will be better suited to promote the common good than others.

The ethics of diversity is first about individual diversity. It claims that in order to flourish each one of us has to free herself from prejudices and barriers to genuine knowledge. The path to this emancipation is nonetheless very arduous as it faces continuous attempts to interfere with individual minds. Moreover, as explained above, individuals pursue their self-interest best if they associate themselves with others so as to pursue common interests together. So when individual minds join the network of minds they have to strike a difficult balance between self-assertion and acceptance of others, which is not an easy task given the complexity of social, cultural, and legal norms.

### 8.3.4. Group diversity

Diversity also has a collective dimension. The way in which communities form their identity and articulate their difference from other communities is similar to the way in which each individual develops. Montesquieu developed a pioneering project in *The Spirit of the Laws*, showing that cultural differences in the world have a very empirical basis that can often be explained by appeal to a scientific methodology.[25] From that viewpoint, human laws are not fundamentally different from other laws. The varieties of human laws can therefore be explained by appeal to empirical data and local factors ranging from the climate to the economic background of a society. The diversity of human laws on the ground does not preclude the idea that human laws also have a deep common structure. It also shows that cultural diversity is a contingent and contextual fact; it is the product of a particular environment and cannot be easily transplanted.

Religion plays an important role in shaping local communities; most communities around the world gather around religious institutions. Hence the importance of religious buildings as symbols and the resistance of countries like Switzerland to the construction of minarets. Small, independent Swiss communities have far too strong a Christian identity to allow direct competitors without fighting. The presence of minarets is not a matter of individual rights, but a much deeper matter of the dilution of identity. So in this case, a strong local identity is deeply resistant in the face of religious diversity. Religious diversity sounds almost like an oxymoron. From within the community, the point is to create homogeneity and identity where there is little room for individual diversity. Diversity is only present by comparison to other religious groups.

There is a very difficult problem here: how can different religious groups live together in the same space? If their identity is at the same time cohesive and exclusive, then there is little room for living together with other communities that are equally as cohesive and exclusive. Things are made worst by the fact that each community develops social norms that are dependent on religious identity. This is particularly the case for Jewish and Muslim people, whose religions include a strong belief in the religious roots of law. To be a good Jew is to follow Jewish law as set out in the Torah. For example, the Torah requires Jews to rest on a Friday—how can this social norm be squared with the fact that in Western states everyone works on a Friday?

The answer to the problem of life in common between religious groups is secular law.[26] It cannot possibly be anything else unless one was to presuppose social homogeneity within which everyone would accept as default one dominant religious norm as a social norm. Thus, in Italy the day of rest is

---

[25] E Durkheim, *Montesquieu et Rousseau, précurseurs de la sociologie* (Librairie Marcel Rivière et Cie, 1966).
[26] See ch. 9.

Sunday which happens to be the Christian day of rest. But of course, as already pointed out, social homogeneity is just a well-engineered myth and one that has often been imposed on a society by the nation state. The recognition and protection of diversity is a much more demanding ideal that stems from the basic fact that as individuals and as groups we are diverse.

Social norms do not have to become legal norms. One common example of a social norm is that of the man who attends mass and is required to take off his hat. This social norm applies only to those individuals who decide to enter a church; moreover, there is no need of an official sanction since peer pressure is crucial to securing compliance with social norms. These types of social norms can live side by side with the existence of legal norms without ever coming into conflict. In Europe, moreover, ordinary laws entrench Christian norms in many ways. For diversity to become possible, it is necessary for European laws to become less Christian and more secular in a way that makes religious and non-religious diversity greater.

## 8.3.5. Individual v Group diversity

Individual and group diversity are at times compatible and at times in conflict. If group diversity is used as a means to instil homogeneity and obedience within one group, then it is likely to create a double tension as not only is individual diversity stifled but also group diversity as it comes to be seen as a threat and thus a reason for fencing interests rather than for contributing to a common good of the whole society. Belonging to a group, however, does not have to be grounds for an exclusive identity anymore. A plurality of belongings, where each belonging is compatible one with another, can also be compatible with the fact of individual diversity. In fact, it may be said that individual differences are enhanced and communicated through plural affiliations and attachments.

Individual and group diversity are to be respected within one legal and political framework that defines the terms of mutual engagement. For example, it is clear that each individual can enjoy freedom of thought without limits since his beliefs kept to himself cannot possibly interfere with anyone else. The expression of those thoughts poses already a slightly different issue. It is possible to think of the limitation of the expression of certain thoughts when they happen to be destructive of the social peace. For social peace is the precondition for the exercise of freedom of thought and one would undermine the very basis of his own freedom by engaging in the disruption of social peace. Of course, regulation of speech comes at a great price and should be conducted carefully, but it is easier to see that the great advantage of freedom of expression can be outweighed by competing individual and social interests.

Crucially, the ethics of diversity is secular in so far as it does not embrace any religious viewpoint and has a naturalistic foundation as its starting point. So the ethics of diversity is not only negative but has a positive dimension. It does not stand for any world-view in particular, but makes religious and non-religious world-views possible to the extent that they are compatible with the legal and political system of the relevant unit. The ethics of diversity has a single implication for the legal-political system: diversity of minds is paramount and should be respected at any price. Diversity of groups should be respected in so far as it does not impinge on the diversity of minds.

## 8.4. The Ethics of Diversity and Secular Philosophies

The ethics of diversity is not a fully fledged secular philosophy if by secular philosophy one understands a philosophy that does away with the cosmic question: what gives meaning to our life in this universe?[27] Most certainly, some philosophers have displayed a clear secular temperament.[28] The cosmic question disappears and is not a central concern anymore, perhaps not even a minor worry. It is clearly possible to have this temperament and some examples of this temperament are increasingly frequent. Hume is perhaps the first philosopher to have a sincere and full-blown secular temperament: he simply did not worry about the cosmic question and was therefore totally uninterested in it.[29]

Secular philosophies, however, are not capable of addressing the worries of those who do happen to have a religious temperament. By and large, subsequent attempts to construe an ethics after the death of God have not provided satisfactory answers for religious people. At best, they came up with further queries, dilemmas, and questions. Thomas Nagel, after examining a wide range of secular philosophies, concludes that his own position regarding the cosmic question is nothing else than the recognition of a general feeling of the absurd. Life is not full of meaning, life is absurd: we have to make the most of our life here and now, but we cannot expect to find internal or external guidance.

---

[27] Nagel, *Secular Philosophy and the Religious Temperament*.

[28] D Hume, *An Enquiry Concerning Human Understanding* (Oxford University Press, 2008).

[29] For a pithy debate between a secular and a religious philosopher, see Daniel Dennet and Alvin Plantinga, *Science and Religion: Are They Compatible?* (Oxford University Press, 2011).

The peculiarity of Spinoza's *Ethics* is that it is a secular ethics with a deep religious temperament. God is the sole source of thought and matter; God and nature are one and the same. The work of a scientist or a philosopher who is seeking to understand the world as it is by way of the application of scientific method is perfectly compatible with a belief in an ultimate unitary being. In fact, that belief constitutes the very starting point of any scientific/philosophical inquiry. To know God/nature is to know all the causes and effects that explain natural phenomena starting from the original cause with an increasing level of sophistication and detail. The causal chain is not broken and the quest of knowledge is precisely about discovering all the links that bring us back to the original cause.

Spinoza's *Ethics* is perfectly compatible with scientific attitudes which claim that there is only one way to understand the world; that is, the scientific method is the only reliable source of knowledge of this world. The scientific perspective alone, however, can hardly account for—and much less answer—the damning ethical question of what is the good life. Most attempts to discredit religion are largely negative—they display an enormous effort in showing that religion is just a set of fanciful claims with no evidence whatsoever. Those theories hardly attempt a positive exercise that tries to explain to us why human beings feel a deep tendency towards religious beliefs.

A notable exception to this is a positive attempt to explain religious experience as we feel it in James's *The Varieties of Religious Experience*.[30] Not surprisingly, James himself is a great admirer of Spinoza and builds on one of his many insights: the religious experience must be understood at the physiological level as a form of exalted feeling that can be explained through scientific analysis. The life of prophets and the perception of miracles can be explained as an experience close to a special type of pathology. A prophet is someone who first and foremost feels differently from anyone else at the physiological level. James's psychological inquiry provides a solid basis for understanding the religious experience as well as the religious temperament—which is totally unexplained by fully fledged secular philosophies such as Hume's, Nietzsche's, or Sartre's.

The ethics of diversity does not attempt to provide one exclusive interpretation of the good life but, rather, to free the path from the obstacles that prevent us all from seeking a good life. Prejudice, fear, and other negative passions cloud our rational capacity to increase satisfaction of our self-interest and control over the external world. The primary aim of such ethics

---

30 W James, *The Variety of the Religious Experience* (Penguin Classics, 1983).

is to clear the path in order to enable everyone to seek her own flourishing. The way in which everyone seeks their own advantage is multiple and variegated. Since we are all different there is no single path and we simply have to make the most of who we are after we discard all the burdens and obstacles that prevent us from full emancipation. In this sense at least, the ethics of diversity has nothing to do with secular philosophies that have populated our moral landscape in the last four centuries. Those secular philosophies can provide one possible world-view, although it would be just a world-view alongside other religious world-views that have an equal claim to validity in guiding people's quest for a good life.

The ethics of diversity paves the way to a better life for individuals, even if it recognizes that that task is extremely ambitious. The ethics of diversity starts from self-interest but recognizes the basic fact of life that we are better off promoting our interest in association with others. The greater the association, the greater is the interest protected. Self-interest is the basis for a genuine pursuit of the common good. In order to do so, then, one has to accept to be ruled by norms produced in the common interest within the framework of a properly functioning legal system. The ethics of diversity does not have a normative foundation, but begins with the fact of diversity at the individual and community level. This fact in turn provides a yardstick by which we can measure the success of legal and political systems constructed by human beings. To the extent that those legal and political systems protect diversity of thought, those systems are healthy and are consistent with the self-interest of every individual. To the extent that those legal and political systems curb diversity of thought and attempt to cloud the minds of citizens, those systems are corrupt and decadent and will sooner or later face an internal implosion, as was the case for example with Arab dictatorships. For those reasons, the most consistent political system with a naturalistic ethics is democracy, since it is the one system that is constructed in order to make diversity of thought possible. The fact that democracy itself can be corrupted to the extent that the masses can be brainwashed is not an argument against democracy, but is an argument against the manipulation of democracy.

The ethics of diversity does not have a normative bias in favour of this or that life, be it religious or non-religious. Religious and non-religious people have a common interest in building a legal and political system that is based on naturalistic ethics since the central point of those ethics is to maximize diversity of thought as much as possible while minimizing aggression. This leaves the legal and political system with the burden of dealing with pluralism.[31]

---

[31] See ch. 9.

## 8.5. Monism, Value Pluralism, and Diversity

Diversity and value pluralism go hand in hand. Contrary to what many believe at first, they are both compatible with the idea of a monist framework. In fact, it would be impossible to value diversity of minds without a monist framework within which hierarchies and differences are organized. The same can be said for value pluralism: it requires a monist framework in order to establish which values are in and which values are out.

The difference between value pluralism and diversity lies in the notion of radical incommensurability. Pluralism is committed to ranking all values at the same level *in abstracto*. Starting from that premise, value pluralism implies the existence of a sacrifice when adjudicating between competing values. Sacrifice is never justified as there is no meta-value guiding adjudication, and so there is no principled reason to prefer one value over another. On the other hand, diversity does not follow the logic of incommensurability. Diversity is committed to the fact that in the natural order there are rankings and hierarchies that are mirrored by human societies.

Diversity as understood here does not imply a radical sense of equality between different people and ideas. If anything, it mirrors the radical diversity defined so far and is compatible with the idea that within the natural order there are hierarchies and rankings between different people and ideas. Diversity in human societies mirrors diversity at the macro natural level, what we referred to as biodiversity. Human societies cannot stifle pluralism, and nor should they. Yet they can channel its potential by protecting diversity, while mitigating in practice some of its perverse consequences as to socioeconomic inequalities. In other words, to put diversity at the centre is more likely than not to promote equality *in concreto*.

It is somehow curious that value pluralism as understood by many contemporary philosophers would imply that everyone's opinions and ideas have the same rank within liberal democracies. For most contemporary philosophers diversity is a derivative value at best and a hindrance to individual autonomy at worst. As we saw in previous sections, liberals assume that individual autonomy is the most important property of human beings as members of a political society. Since everyone is endowed with individual autonomy, then it is everyone's equal responsibility to make the most out of one's life experiment. The fact that one life experiment ends up being very different to another is just a consequence of a deep-seated initial equality.

To take diversity seriously, means to challenge that very assumption of initial radical equality between human beings. Diversity means that people do not start from the same running block and that people's thoughts and opinions cannot be equally ranked. An individual's fully formed and adequate ideas are superior over the ideas of someone who has formed them through passive indoctrination by mass media, for example.

European liberal democracies are not very serious about religious diversity, which is protected on paper, but in many ways limited in practice. To start with, liberal democracies attempt to erase from public view religious symbols, in particular those of minorities; hence, veils, minarets, and other symbols are regulated more or less strictly. Moreover, liberal democracies are deaf to religious voices that cannot participate in public debates with religious arguments. This does not mean that all voices are equal and equally import-ant for the life of the polity. Religious voices may or may not have an impact on the shaping of policies; this can be evaluated once they have been given a hearing. Diversity requires that those voices should not be silenced without a fair hearing, but does not require that they should be taken into account on the same basis as any other reason since no voice can claim authority without being able to be shared by everyone, that is religious and non-religious people alike.

## 8.6. Conclusion

The ethics of diversity takes diversity—including religious diversity—seriously, but is itself a secular ethics. Human beings are stripped bare and left with their natural passions. Their Judaeo-Christian clothes that wrapped them up giving them a virtuous appearance are dismissed. The rejection of Christian ethics leads to two different paths. On the one hand, most liberal philoso-phers opted to put man at the centre of the ethical world as a special being endowed with full consciousness, individuality, and the power to regulate his life according to his own autonomy. Everyone would begin in a position of radical equality, only to flourish in her own way during her life. Foundational diversity would be discarded in the name of the egalitarian picture of humanity which Hobbes posits as a consequence of the social contract. On the other hand, it is possible to put the natural world at the centre of ethical thinking, and consider human beings as one being amongst many others. According to this ethical picture, man is not special or endowed with super powers, but he is just another inhabitant of the natural world. The diversity of each human being in terms of the balance between his passions and his varying ability to control them mirrors the diversity of the natural world itself. The idea of radical equality is replaced by diversity, which is both a natural and a cultural fact that needs to be preserved against the imposition of homogeneous standards of thinking and behaviour.

The ethics of diversity does not have a normative foundation like consequentialism or deontology, nor a religious foundation either. Its starting point is the natural fact of diversity expressed as the varying ability to strive for survival and to maximize control over the external world. This natural premise is nevertheless compatible with the idea of living together, since human beings maximize their prospects of survival and control by grouping with others. In turn the fact of teaming up with other individuals requires a certain amount of regulation of behaviour in order to avoid undermining the beneficial effects of community. It is in this light that democracy as the expression of everyone's diverse wills comes into focus. The final product of democratic deliberation would of course be secular law, which should truly strive to be one law for all.

The ethics of diversity is secular in that it values diversity of both religious and non-religious types. Religion has a role to play in the public sphere and its voice should be heard at every stage of democratic deliberation, except in the final product—that is, secular law—which necessarily has to employ a language that is understandable by religious and non-religious people alike. In some cases where the religious position cannot be fitted within secular law, there will be the possibility of exempting those who do not see their voice represented by secular law. It nonetheless remains the case that secular law is the default framework within which disagreement between religious and non-religious people can take place. The nature and role of secular law will be explored in the following chapter.

# 9

# The Rule of Secular Law in Europe

## 9.1. Introduction

Diversity breeds conflicts between individuals and groups. Law's task is to deal with those conflicts in order to preserve social peace. However, to deal with conflicts does not mean to solve them or explain them away.[1] In fact social peace may well amount to the capability of coping with conflicts without eliminating them. In a Westphalian Europe—where social homogeneity was the paradigm—to preserve social peace meant to minimize (religious) diversity and its violent consequences. Law didn't need to be secular since it could ally itself with the dominant religion for the sake of social control and stability. Socially engineered homogeneity is a chimera and so diversity re-emerged in Europe and required an appropriate response which had to go beyond religious factions.[2] It is at this time that the idea of secular law gains scientific and social recognition.

In this chapter, I end the journey that began with Dante's vision of Europe in medieval times.[3] Back then, the only way to make sense of Europe as a political space was to postulate a deep unity that mirrored closely the transcendent Christian moral order.[4] In the kingdom of heaven everything is ruled on the basis of universal and a-temporal laws. Sins and vices of the secular world—as opposed to the celestial one—had to be explained as the human inability to live according to revealed laws. However, the terrestrial limits of human life do not preclude the existence of a deep monistic unity of all the laws of a religious, political, or scientific kind. This deeply monist and

---

[1] See Lorenzo Zucca, *Constitutional Dilemmas: Conflicts of Fundamental Legal Rights in Europe and the USA* (Oxford University Press, 2007).

[2] Benjamin Kaplan, *Divided by Faith: Religious Conflict and the Practice of Toleration in Early Modern Europe* (Harvard University Press, 2007).

[3] Some take the central question of political philosophy from Dante to modern days to be the so-called Theologico-Political question, see Leo Strauss, *Spinoza's Critique of Religion*, trans Elsa M Sinclair (Schocken, 1965).

[4] For Dante's vision combining an Aritstotelian position with a Thomistic one, see Dante, *De Monarchia* (Rizzoli, 2007).

orderly world-view is to be contrasted with the view common in the enlightenment of the seventeenth century which posited a dualism between the world of religion and the world of science: natural laws belong to a different domain from religious laws.

There is a third domain that can be carved out which maintains a distance from both religious laws and natural laws. It is the domain of secular laws. Laws are secular in two senses. They are secular in opposition to religious laws, in so far as they do not rely on divine authority. They are also secular in contrast to natural laws, in so far as they are created by humans. Secular laws are not moralizing in the way religious laws are, albeit they have a minimum teleological dimension in so far as secular laws aim at social peace as a desirable, and overarching, end. They are not naturalizing in the way natural laws are, albeit they have a naturalistic dimension since human laws are responses to human needs deeply rooted in human nature.

The journey ends with a return to monism, although of a very different nature. If in Dante's world, monism was transcendent through and through, here monism is immanent through and through.[5] Secular law represents the never-ending human attempt to create a stable monistic framework within which every human being is capable of living without fear for her life or for her means of survival. Within such a monistic framework, diversity is protected and maximized at least to the extent that everyone is free to flourish in their own way; at the same time, aggression from other individuals and groups is minimized, otherwise the framework would be pointless.

Sections 9.2. and 9.3. carve out the domain of secular laws in opposition to religious and natural laws. Section 9.4. argues that secular law necessarily construes a monistic framework that makes social diversity possible and manageable. Section 9.5. attempts to show the way in which secular law applies in the European context. Section 9.6. concludes this chapter.


## 9.2. Secular Laws: Between Natural and Religious Laws

Secular laws are not easy to positively define, but may well be defined in the negative: they are neither religious laws nor are they natural laws. Religious laws are those laws that are ultimately rooted in the Holy Scriptures from which they draw their authority. Their main difference with secular laws is evident. Religious laws are not produced by deliberation and compromise.

---

[5] The trajectory from a transcendental view to the immanent frame is convincingly elaborated by C Taylor, *A Secular Age* (Harvard University Press, 2008).

They cannot change since the will of God is immutable. Secular laws, in opposition to religious laws, are changeable and contingent. They are the product of compromise and deliberation with a view to obtaining a reasonable degree of social harmony and peace.

Natural laws are also immutable in the sense that natural, phenomena follow a discernible pattern that can be encapsulated in a scientific formula. Natural laws are not posited by God or any other supernatural entity; natural laws have their own inner logic which has no ascertainable purpose from the scientific perspective. In other words, natural laws are not teleological. By this I mean that evolutionary biology, for example, does not explain the way in which species evolve by reference to a given starting point and by pointing to a necessary path followed by all the species. Evolution happens in a chaotic way in the sense that accidents determine the survival of some species and the disappearance of others.

The tripartite distinction between religious, natural, and secular laws corresponds to three discrete domains of analysis: the sacred, the natural, and the juridical. Religious laws pertain to the sacred domain, that which cannot be proved;[6] natural laws belong to the natural domain, that which can be proved; the two are opposed in this sense. For a long time, this dualism characterized the way in which we organized knowledge in the Western world. Theology would inquire into the sacred domain, whereas science would inquire into the natural domain. But as stated there is another set of laws that is different from religious laws in so far as they are not given by a supreme being. They are also different from natural laws in so far as they are a human creation. Secular laws pertain to the juridical domain that can be studied in its own right. Montesquieu in *The Spirit of the Laws* was the first to insist on the autonomy of the juridical domain. Not only that, Montesquieu also insisted that despite the apparent chaos of secular laws, there was a deeper order. All secular laws follow a common pattern which is not immediately ascertainable, but is nevertheless available and open to human cognition. Secular laws, for Montesquieu, are human responses to external problems that arise in connection with human sociability (human relations) or in connection with the human relation with nature. In both cases, it is possible to identify orderly patterns of human behaviour that depend on our (ever so limited) understanding of human nature or of nature itself. Secular laws are therefore not simply contingent and chaotic, but are deeply ordered because they are necessary responses to objective problems that can be apprehended through the understanding of natural laws. Once the common order is

6 E Durkheim, *The Elementary Forms of the Religious Life* (Free Press, 1995).

unravelled, Montesquieu goes on to explain what makes secular laws different from one another; the diversity of secular laws lies in the changing circumstances in which we live. For example, if we live in a country where the soil is particularly fertile, then secular laws will protect and promote agricultural interests as a matter of necessity. If the country is kept alive by a strong financial system, then secular laws will hardly impinge on that system.

The relationship between the three domains can also be looked at from the viewpoint of primacy of the juridical domain. When religious groups clash with one another, the only possible tool to resolve their disagreement is secular law since they cannot possibly compromise on their tenets of faith. It is also the case that when scientists clash about diverging scientific paradigms they have to resort to quasi-juridical forms of adjudication in order to establish whose version is more authoritative in the scientific community.[7] Finally, when religious laws clash with natural laws, experience shows that religious tribunals are not well suited to adjudicate on these issues as the case of Galileo reminds us. Even in this case, the juridical domain of secular laws is necessarily superior to the other two.

Secular law's point and purpose is to create a framework within which all individuals living in a territory can organize their life in a way that is orderly and peaceful. To this extent, secular laws are not in competition with or opposition to either religious or natural laws. If anything secular laws are there to find ways in which conflicts between religious and non-religious people as well as between religious and scientific world-views are dealt with, with a view to preserving the stability of the community.

The recognition of a juridical domain independent from the sacred and the natural domains goes beyond the dualism of the fields of knowledge posited by Descartes.[8] The dualist picture was an attempt to save theology from the corrosive and all-consuming attack of scientific knowledge. To posit a dualism would preserve the dignity of the sacred domain from the intrusive interrogation of the natural scientific approach. Prior to that dualism, the world was neatly and clearly organized along the lines of a theological monism. Everything depended on the original will of God, including natural laws.

Dante's world, for example, represented the ultimate depiction of the order of God's world as opposed to the vicious chaos of a human world that could only aspire to the perfection of the real transcendent world, where prices and penalties were decided and distributed with unforgiving regularity. In Dante's world, the juridical domain coincides with the sacred domain and

---

[7] Thomas S Kuhn, *The Structure of Scientific Revolutions,* University of Chicago Press, 1996.
[8] See ch. 8.

is crisply expressed in the image of the last judgement. From a purely transcendent viewpoint, one that clearly ranked the sacred above any other domain, we move all the way to a secularized world where the sacred domain is a peripheral universe whose importance is limited and only influences those who wish to be so.[9] In today's world, the natural and the juridical domain have long established their independence. The natural domain did so in opposition to the sacred domain. The juridical domain of secular laws proved to be the model for dealing with conflicts of any type between religious and non-religious people.

Secular laws, and in particular the study of the juridical domain, resist both moralizing and naturalizing tendencies. However, it is probably not possible to hold, as Kelsen did, that a pure theory of law can be formulated in a way that excludes every influence from religious and natural laws.[10] Secular laws belong to a discrete domain—it is true—but this does not mean that secular laws do not borrow elements from religious laws. They are influenced by natural laws which affect human behaviour and have to be taken into account when formulating sound policies to maintain the social peace. I need to say more about the non-moralizing and the non-naturalizing character of secular laws.

## 9.3. Secular Laws: Non-moralizing/Non-naturalizing?

Secular laws do not exist in a vacuum. They exist in a world with natural laws. They are crafted for a given society in order to address specific problems. In addition to that, those who create secular laws respond to and are influenced by the variables that pertain to the natural world in which we live. Montesquieu understood that some contingent variables such as the climate, the nature of the soil etc, do influence the way in which societies regulate themselves. Those variables must be taken into account in order to explain the apparent chaos of secular laws across the world.

Secular laws have a deterministic dimension like religious laws: their goal is to achieve and maintain a well-ordered society, a sort of paradise on earth. Whilst they may be more or less coercive or more or less paternalist secular laws all have the same goal which is itself immutable: to stabilize competing forces in a society for as long as possible. To this extent, secular laws are

---

[9] Charles Taylor, *A Secular Age* (Harvard University Press, 2008).

[10] Hans Kelsen, *Pure Theory of Law*, trans M Knight (University of California Press, 1960/1967). See also Hans Kelsen, *Secular Religion* (Springer, 2011) (posthumous publication) for a polemic against the rise of theology in the West.

teleological like religious laws. Religious laws, however, have a strongly moralizing teleology: to aim and aspire towards the order willed by God as the ultimate and the greatest possible good. Secular laws, on the other hand, can aim at the goal of a well-ordered society while preserving an infinite number of paths that can lead there. Moreover, a well-ordered society may take various forms; its chief rationale is instrumental: in a well-ordered society humans can flourish to an extent that is not possible under a strongly moralizing society. Secular laws in this sense do not have a strong moralizing character.

Secular laws, like natural laws, also have a materialistic dimension.[11] They are not completely independent from natural laws since they are framed to respond to human needs and problems arising in a world with natural laws. Even so, secular laws are not merely a response to those problems—an attempt to catch up with what nature provides for us. Secular laws escape a fully naturalized explanation since they address problems that arise from the artificial organization of human societies. Humans group together in societies in order to cope with natural needs and problems, but then realize that the very fact of coming together creates problems of a different order which humans have to address in order to keep society well ordered. To this extent, secular laws have a materialistic dimension.

Secular laws are not moralizing, but it would be churlish to say that they do not mirror some constitutive values of the community they regulate. Indeed, the ultimate goal of social peace is a shell that can be filled with a number of abstract values that often overlap with the French trinity of *liberté*, *egalité*, and *fraternité*, all understood loosely. The axiological dimension of secular laws, however, is not to be founded on the existence of God, or the imitation of nature. The French trinity is a set of values that points to the truth of moral conflicts. Instead of limiting the realm of morality, the French trinity opens it up to infinite value choices since it is impossible to determine a priori what the right combination of values for each society will be. The axiological dimension of secular laws has to do with both their materialist and the determinist character defined above. Secular laws, in order to fulfil their promise, have to track the material necessities of humans as well as respond to the deep human concern for a common goal, a clear teleology that underpins secular laws. Yet secular laws do not simply mirror natural laws; they only reflect some of the materialist elements of natural laws; if this was not the case, it is likely that secular laws would not last long. Also secular laws do not posit a transcendental goal, but simply reflect the goal that human

---

[11] This is clear in Part 2 of *The Spirit of the Laws*.

societies embrace at their outset: to maximize survival for the greatest number of people. This does not entail the suppression of all conflicts. To the contrary, social peace is a situation whereby conflicts are dealt with on a constant basis rather than suppressed.

## 9.4. (Legal) Unity and (Socio-cultural) Diversity

To the extent that secular laws tend towards the single goal of social peace, they also promote social unity. Unity should not be understood as opposed to diversity. If anything, in this context the unity of the social body is a precondition for the protection of diversity. Let me explain. Religious and non-religious people may disagree on several issues ranging from the value of life to more concrete issues such as what to teach at school. Disagreement about abstract and concrete problems is to be welcome in any society: doubt and critical analysis allow for better thinking and better policies. However, moral, social, and religious diversity in particular have been shown to be dangerous at times, in the sense that they may lead to social breakdown, strife, and ultimately to violence.

To preserve diversity, it is therefore necessary to have a unified framework that sets out procedures intended to cope with the escalation of disagreement to breaking point. Law works to provide a framework beyond diversity, a framework that maximizes diversity while preserving the unity of the whole society. It is thus that the juridical domain establishes its own autonomy and, from this viewpoint, its superiority over religious and natural laws.

Undoubtedly, secular laws do not always maximize diversity. There are two opposite paths to attain the goal of social peace. The Treaty of Westphalia is one way of achieving peace at the price of diversity: nation states were carved out in a way that religious homogeneity within a discrete territory would be protected and promoted. In this context, diversity was minimized and the only token it was granted was that of tolerance for minority groups that happened to upset the engineered social homogeneity.[12]

There is another way of attaining social peace by guaranteeing the protection of diversity within a heterogeneous society while maintaining some basic principles such as the respect for the legal constitutional framework which attempts to preserve and equal distance from any world-view represented in the society. Europe today has no other choice but to invest in a common legal framework that maximizes diversity while preserving its own unity. This does

---

[12] See ch. 1.

not mean that it should only deal with disagreement through procedural rules. Secular laws themselves promote a number of plural values (starting with the French trinity); being plural values that are likely to conflict one with another, secular laws have to be always open to renegotiation and compromise about what those values require from all members of society. In particular, those values must respond equally well, if not better, to the demands of the most vulnerable people in society.

Law can therefore aim at the unity inherent in social peace either by suppressing diversity or by maximizing it. The second option is more difficult and demanding and constantly requires difficult choices by institutions and more virtuous behaviour from citizens. It is nonetheless the only way in Europe given the way our societies have *de facto* moved away from homogeneity and are now mirroring diversity at its highest degree. Unity is not opposed to diversity but is opposed to a monolithic identity, in its substantive sense.[13] Nation states have maintained and promoted social homogeneity through the myth of monolithic identity. The myth banks on the idea that people living in the same territory and with a similar history, share a profound bond which makes them all part of the same nation. The salient features of their belonging to a nation are meant to be summarized in a set of simple conditions that everyone meets by virtue of being born into a given society. For centuries the myth of a monolithic identity has played down the expression of diversity by those people living in a given society. The pressure one is under to show one's peers that one belongs has often suppressed the need for communicating divergent beliefs and intuitions.

Unity of the legal-constitutional framework does not require, indeed it resists, the myth of a monolithic identity. Legal-constitutional unity accepts the basic facts that there are, and there always have been, plural identities with different world-views and that it is only a forced simplification to insist on a single identity that takes the lion's share and rides roughshod over other features of human beings that require protection in the name of their difference. The decadence of the nation state and the struggle for European integration signifies that unity has nothing to do with monolithic identity.

## 9.5. Law, Religion, and the State in Europe

The unity provided by secular law is to be distinguished from the unity provided by the state. It has often been normal to associate the law and the

---

[13] A Sen, *Identity and Violence: The Illusion of Destiny* (Allen Lane, 2006).

state as if they were synonymous, as if they coincided. In the Westphalian context, it was indeed how the partition of Europe was engineered. Each state enjoyed independent authority backed up by a homogeneous religious situation. Thus, the creation of a nation state with one dominant Christian religion came hand in hand with the monopoly of authority on the part of the state. Religion was then a source of legitimacy for the nation state: one state, one religion, and one law characterized the rise of the nation state in the early modern stage. The process of secularization created a split between state and religion, but at first it seemed to further strengthen the relationship between the state and the law.

Secular law, however, is more than the simple expression of the will of the secular state. As we have seen hitherto, secular law carved out an independent domain from the sacred and the natural one. It became an object of study, and a powerful tool with which the society could be managed and conflicts dealt with. Secular law's aim is to preserve and promote social peace in any given community; the state has only a contingent role to play here to the extent that the form of the nation state represented for some time the primary form of organized political community. But the link between state and political community is not a necessary one, as can be shown by an historical example. In the Middle Ages, cities were the dominant political form; for example, the concept of citizenship comes from the idea of belonging to a city. It was then obvious that the ultimate authority of the law was the duke or prince of the city. And it was also clear that there was an open struggle between the authority of the duke and that of the church.[14] This means that the authority, independence, and unity of secular laws do not originate with the modern nation state. To the contrary, it applies to any form of organized power that happens to be predominant: the city in the late Middle Ages, the nation state from the late seventeenth century, and regional organizations in the twenty-first century.

The model of the nation state is on the decline in Europe. True, there is still an overwhelming insistence on national power, but recent financial crises have demonstrated very well how powerless a medium-sized nation state is in a globalized economic environment. In this context, the main source of secular law regulating the markets and the debts is not national anymore but European or international. The nation state must abide by the strict requirements of the international rule-givers if they want to survive financially. This example aims to show that the site of production of secular law is

---

[14] A symbolic example is the competition between the secular authority represented by the Palazzo della Signoria and the religious authority represented by the Duomo in Florence.

not exclusively the state and perhaps that site has shifted beyond the state altogether.

The unity of secular law cannot be explained by reference to the unity of the state. The unity of secular law can instead be explained by reference to the purpose of secular law, which is ultimately to preserve and promote social peace in highly diversified societies. It may be said that our world displays a growing degree of fragmentation rather than unity. And it is true that different institutions and regulations pursue competing projects in terms of values and sometimes in terms of rules. I nevertheless believe that pluralism of values requires, rather than undermines, unity at the legal level. The more we acknowledge value pluralism, the more evident the need for a unitary legal framework when it is not already in place. So what about the regulation of religion beyond the state?

Religion in Europe goes well beyond the realm of national regulation. No doubt it tries to influence law and politics wherever possible, especially when one church is firmly entrenched in one society, as is the case of the Catholic Church in Italy for example. But that doesn't capture the re-emergence of other religions in the public sphere.[15] New religions in the West, like Islam or Pentecostalism for example, cannot hope to control the production of national law and politics from their minority position.[16] They do not even want to, since their project is not to win over the West through use of the conventional channels of domestic public life. The project of new religions is to create a community of the faithful beyond the nation state: a community linked by new technologies and through faith, beyond linguistic and cultural barriers.[17] Religion is back and aims to fill the hole in the lives of many people living in Europe.

New religions have quickly learned to use the language of rights and discrimination as a Trojan horse in the European public realm. The ECtHR, for instance, is bound to be very responsive to the violation of minority rights and the rise of claims concerning freedom of religion (Article 9) in the last fifteen years amply confirms a growing worry at the international level. Domestic institutions, in particular domestic courts, are likely to protect national traditions linked with local religion more forcefully than the ECtHR. The *Lautsi* decision was a good illustration of this problem. The Italian State Council attempted to defend the crucifix in the classroom, arguing that it had become a secular symbol for all, conveying secular values such as liberty, equality, and fraternity. At the other extreme of the spectrum

---

[15] Joel Casanova, *Public Religions in the Modern World* (University of Chicago Press, 1994).
[16] O Roy, *Holy Ignorance* (Oxford University Press, 2011).
[17] Roy, *Holy Ignorance*.

is the ECtHR in its second section. Its first decision in the *Lautsi* case was an adamant defence of a strong secularism of the ideological type in Europe. Given this premise, the conclusion of the second section of the Court was inevitable: the crucifix in the classroom is in breach of the Convention because it does not respect the principle of secularism which is embedded in the Convention.

The Grand Chamber decision in *Lautsi*, however, in trying to please everyone ended up disappointing everyone. The Grand Chamber addressed the second-section decision in *Lautsi* and dismissed quite bluntly and without serious reflection the suggestion that secularism is a precondition for the realization of individual rights; the Grand Chamber insists that individual rights have to be understood and protected in a vacuum. The Grand Chamber states, for example, that freedom of religion cannot be linked to the principle of secularism.[18] This is a highly problematic statement since it is clear that if a society was not secular, but religious, the equal protection of non-dominant religions would be dependent on the arbitrary will of those religious leaders in power. New religions understand that national and international institutions can be exploited strategically to protect their own position on a case-by-case basis, since there seems to be great uncertainty as to the secular model that Europe should embrace, there being so many varieties of it and no evident consensus to select one position.[19]

## 9.6. Conclusion

Secular law is the tool with which conflicts between people and ideas are dealt with. Conflicts between religious and non-religious people cannot be solved, avoided, or defined away. Secular law pursues the overarching goal of social peace which is not posited from the outside as an ideal goal, but is instead intrinsic to the very formation of communities: secular law aims at a unitary framework which is not transcendent, but immanent. The framework provided by secular law is a default arrangement within which diversity thrives. Religion has to be fitted within this framework and not outside of it. This is particularly the case once we embrace religious diversity and recognize that no religious claim can trump any other for the purpose of ruling society. Each individual is free to believe that salvation lies in the afterlife, but all of them live in this immanent world.

---

[18] *Lautsi v Italy*, 18 March 2011, Application no 30814/06. See in particular the concurring opinion of Judge Bonello of Malta.

[19] In the last chapter I will argue that a European model of secularism is possible.

Secular law makes religious freedom possible. It does not subordinate it to the arbitrary will of ideological authorities, but allows it for all claims. Secular law in Europe protects and promotes freedom of religion by setting up what I called a marketplace of religions. The marketplace of religions is itself part of the marketplace of democracy; this means that it fully participates in it, while being subject to restrictions that apply in that market plus some other specific restrictions applicable to the marketplace of religions. It is not possible, nor is it desirable, to relegate religion to the private sphere. It is however possible to regulate the role of religion in the public sphere so as to mitigate adverse effects and police extreme behaviour. The same ideas are applicable to sharia law as well. There is no serious reason to rule out sharia from a regulated contribution to the life of those people who regard it as a valid source of authority; thus sharia law is eligible for a discrete well-defined process of arbitration between private persons willing to have its rules applied to their case, in family disputes for example.

Secular law promotes stability, which is at times threatened and fragile due to negative emotions such as fear. Fear of diversity in particular is often the cause of polarization between various groups and of alienation of minorities. Secular law is the tool through which secular institutions can dispel phobia by promoting mutual knowledge, and by protecting religious and non-religious voices. Secular law is not strictly rooted in the existence of a secular state, and applies also to international institutions. At the supranational level, the commitment of the EU to secular law means it cannot embrace a Christian identity as the sole source of identity and of values. It is obviously necessary for the EU to be open to the Christian claim of identity as to any other religious and non-religious claim. Secular law is not meant to be a rejection of any world-view, because secular law does not constitute a fully fledged world-view. In sum, secular law is the voice through which a secular Europe speaks and the special way in which it deals with diversity. In the next and final chapter I will conclude the journey that took us from a Europe split by religious conflicts to a Europe united in the name of a new model of supranational secularism.

# 10

# Law and Religion in a Secular Europe[1]

Is there a conflict between law and religion? And if so, what can be done about it? To answer these questions one can take several paths. A very arduous, if not impossible, path would be to define what law is, what religion is, and what conflict amounts to given the nature of the two objects. Each of those tasks could easily take the space of several treatises, without much hope of success. This book takes a different path. It deliberately narrows down the question and looks at both law and religion as normative systems that vie for the regulation of power. From this viewpoint, law and religion necessarily conflict, since by stipulation they are competing systems of regulation of behaviour. So the question becomes: what place do they occupy in European political societies and do they overlap in such a way that conflict cannot be avoided?

The answer to that question is that conflict between law and religion cannot be avoided, but it can be apprehended and dealt with. To apprehend the conflict I offer a broad-brush genealogical approach; to deal with it I propose an ameliorative perspective. In other words, it is necessary to understand the problem before we can hope to improve on it.

## 10.1. A Genealogical Approach

Let me explain the genealogical approach first. The place of both law and religion evolved beyond imagination from medieval Europe to contemporary Europe. From a world where religion was the pole star of any belief and behaviour we have arrived to a position where religion is a private matter of individual conscience.[2] To arrive where we are in Europe, we went through a number of tremendous conflicts, which came in three waves. To begin with,

---

[1] This chapter is a revised version of my essay 'Law and Religion in a Secular Europe', *The World Financial Review* (May–June 2012), 28–31.

[2] For a full genealogical exercise, see Charles Taylor, *A Secular Age* (Harvard University Press, 2007).

in a fully religious world like seventeenth century Europe, the struggle for power and regulation of behaviour was between competing religious factions. The answer to religious wars was to eliminate conflicts between religions by separating them from each other and by giving each priority within the territory of a nation state. The presence of other religions would then be subject to moralizing toleration. The confusion between power and religion within the nation state had set up a ticking bomb that was merely waiting to explode.

The second inevitable wave of conflicts came when the nation state attempted to free itself from the domination of one church. This was particularly true in France, where the revolution had asserted state power in opposition to the privileges of the church and the aristocracy. The nineteenth century saw a remarkable escalation of tension between state and church. The tension culminated in the *Loi de 1905* establishing a legal principle of *laïcité*, which amounted to a unilateral separation between the state and the church, where the state was the dominating element. For the rest of the twentieth century, most nation states in Europe attempted to find ways to police the boundary between church and state either by separating the two, like France, or by entrenching the privileges of an established church, like the UK.

The third wave is more recent and has to do with the growing immigration of religious minorities in particular Muslim people from North Africa, the Middle East, and the Far East. The presence of vocal religious minorities in turn rekindled the interest in mainstream religion. Religious minorities and majorities united to argue in favour of a bigger place for religion in the society. They also divided people between those who believe that Europe can only be Christian because of its roots and those who believe that Europe is secular. The two questions are linked but the way in which they are linked is unclear. My aim is to shed light on the last wave of conflict between law as the secular expression of power and religion. I do so by proposing a new model of secularism which goes beyond the church-and-state debate. To a large extent, the way in which European states deal with Christian churches has been settled. What is controversial is the place of religions within the public sphere at the national, European, and international level: secular law faces an uphill struggle when regulating the presence of new religious voices that claim for more protection, more participation, and exemption wherever secular law is incompatible with religious commands.

The new model can be described as inclusive secularism;[3] it is inclusive because it carves out a place for religion in the public sphere, while striving to

---

[3] I will say more about it in the next section.

maintain law free from any discrete world-view so that as many world-views as possible will manage to flourish.

## 10.2. An Ameliorative Approach

The second aspect of the theory is what I call an ameliorative approach. Conflicts between law and religion cannot simply be removed or avoided. They are bound to resurface and reappear in different guises. I aim to understand those conflicts rather than to suppress them or define them away. The way in which we have to deal with them is not by abandoning secular law and compromising it with other forms of regulation of behaviour. Secular law stands for the necessity of a legal political framework that does not depend on a transcendental world-view, but is firmly rooted in our immanent world. Secular law is also the instrument through which the legal-political framework can be policed so as to guarantee human flourishing and social peace.

It nevertheless remains the case that the place of religion within the secular legal-political framework is contested, sometimes bitterly so. One predominant view seems to suggest that religion should be protected only in so far as it does not venture out of the private domain. According to this view, when crossing the rigid boundary between private and public, one is requested to divest herself of religious symbols and views and join the public sphere as a neutral participant.

Secularism in the twentieth century is at times described as requiring the absence of religion from the public sphere. Law would then have to police the boundaries between the public and the private sphere. This dichotomy would also resolve the conflict between law and religion, since the former would be sovereign in the public sphere while the latter would be free in the private sphere. Secularism-as-absence has a side-effect: it empties the public sphere of all vitality; public debates become largely technical and procedural. The quality of political discourse diminishes greatly.[4] Mutual understanding between religious and non-religious people is more and more difficult. But it can be even worse: only technicians would be able to participate in public debate. The corruption of democracy begins here.

The new model of inclusive secularism I propose attempts a Copernican revolution along three dimensions: ethical, political, and legal.

---

[4] S Smith, *The Disenchantment of Secular Discourse* (Harvard University Press, 2010).

## 10.2.1. The ethical dimension

First, it is necessary to elaborate a naturalistic ethics that distinguishes between toleration and tolerance. Toleration is regarded as a moralizing attitude that depends on a prior commitment to one religious truth; from that vantage point, other religions can *only* be tolerated as false but not dangerous. Tolerance is a natural human attitude that allows us to apprehend diversity of any type without preconceived opposition or full-hearted acceptance. Tolerance as a natural attitude is possible if, and only if, individuals are not overwhelmed by negative emotions—such as fear—towards diversity that are often misinformed images of a less-than-fully-known external object or person.

Following from that understanding of tolerance, we can place diversity-as-a-fact at the core of our concerns and attempt to build on it a new way of conceiving ethics that is no longer centred on notions such as autonomy and individualism. Individuals and groups cannot be autonomous in a strong sense because they cannot be the sole source of their norms of behaviour. Their behaviour is governed by heteronomous sources: by that I mean that the way in which each one of us develops is deeply dependent on external cultural and religious norms which we come to assimilate and take for granted. Thus to believe that individuals rely on their individual autonomy to guide their own behaviour presupposes a false, idealized picture of human nature; a more promising depiction of human nature starts from the basic fact of diversity and attempts to reconcile this fact with the human necessity of living together under shared norms. For a long time, religion offered the basic unifying glue for individuals in a given socio-political space. But with the demise of religion in Europe, it was necessary to ground law and politics on different foundations.

## 10.2.2. The political dimension

Europe is still struggling to find a rationale for secular politics. Many avenues have been attempted without real success; in fact some secular strategies can even backlash in so far as they polarize the society into those who believe in a secular ideology and those who don't. I distinguish between two conceptions of secularism that encapsulate competing attitudes to religious diversity. On the one hand, exclusive secularism believes in the idea that religion should be relegated to the private sphere, as it cannot offer reasons that can be shared by everyone for the purpose of public regulation. On the other, inclusive secularism believes that religion can offer a lot to political discourse even if the reasons it offers will eventually have to be translated into legal instruments that can be understood by both religious and non-religious people.

Public institutions at the national, supranational, and international level play a crucial role in promoting mutual understanding between religious and non-religious people. The best way to bridge the gap between polarized groups is by promoting a model of education that does not exclude a priori religious reason from its premises and its syllabuses. For example, the school classroom should become a tolerance lab where religious and non-religious people test their beliefs and come to understand one another.

## 10.2.3. The legal dimension

The most difficult aspect of the relationship between law and religion is where to draw the boundary between the two. I suggest that both law and religion have reasons not to be reciprocally contaminated in order to prevent their mutual dilution. Secular law must always strive to be the law for everyone, while religious law is by definition only the law of a group culturally defined. Any attempt to impose the latter would smack of a unilateral negation of the value of other religious views as well as of the secular view. That said, secular law must always take the challenge that it is biased in favour of non-religious people seriously, and must always try to neutralize that bias if it exists.

Secular law is culturally specific but it also has a universal dimension, in so far as it constitutes a tool for the resolution of conflicts and the attainment of social peace. Secular law is neither an expression of religion nor science. It mediates the conflict between the two as well as the conflict between competing religious world-views and those between competing scientific world-views. Both religion and science mimic law when they need to deal with their own conflicts. In this sense, law's institutional and procedural dimension makes it different from naturalistic and religious systems of thought. The risk of collapsing into one or the other is always present, but secular law needs to constantly strive to preserve its independence and primacy.

The absence of a clear overarching secularism at the European level leaves the door open to any type of religious argument in the public sphere. In this confused atmosphere, various claims as to the religious identity of the European political project are put forward so that they can gain dominance. There are, in fact, four different models that have been put forward to describe the nature of the European political project: a Christian Europe, a post-secular Europe, a laic Europe, and a secular Europe, *tout court*. We are going to have a look at each one of those in order to single out the benefits of the last model that I defend.

## 10.3. Four Models for Europe

### 10.3.1. A Christian Europe

The Vatican and some other scholars would like to propose a Christian foundation to the European polity.[5] The idea is that Europe grew into a secularized set of states without ever shaking off its Christian roots. At the basis of European morality lie Christian values, which are the necessary building-blocks and glue that keep all Europeans together. There is nothing else as strong and as widespread as Christian values, so the only winning bet for Europeans is to accept that beyond their doctrinal differences they are all Christians at base level. From this viewpoint, there is no need for a constitutional framework, since we already have an underlying ethos which penetrates all social institutions, including, of course, law. This model is simple and backward-looking: it is about finding in the past the roots of our future, however slimmed down and adapted to the present context. The next model wants to move forward rather than backward, but it may overestimate the power of reason to achieve a compromise between law and religion.

### 10.3.2. A post-secular Europe

Some philosophers see Europe as being at the end of its secular trajectory.[6] They equate the rise and decadence of secularism to the rise and demise of reason, as the sole leading principle of the Western world.[7] Habermas, for example, attributes in his later work a great importance to imagination and religion as sources of inspiration and knowledge. The secular project, according to Habermas, shows its limitations in that it arbitrarily expels from our understanding ways of life and world-views that should be given more attention, also given the fact that life in a secular world has not necessarily brought 'salvation' beyond apparent material progress. It is therefore necessary to move to a post-secular world in which reason and religion

---

[5] Joseph Ratzinger and Marcello Pera, *Without Roots: Europe, Relativism, Christianity and Islam* (Basic Books, 2007); see also Joseph Weiler, *Un'Esuropa Cristiana* (Rizzoli, 2003).

[6] Jurgen Habermas, *Between Naturalism and Religion* (Polity, 2008).

[7] For a debate between Ratzinger and Habermas, see Joseph Ratzinger and Jurgen Habermas, *The Dialectics of Secularization: On Reason and Religion* (Ignatius Press, 2007).

are capable of communicating one with another. Europe would have to embrace post-secularism and come up with ways of regulating religion that are much more open and responsive to the contribution of religion in the public sphere.

### 10.3.3. A laic Europe

In response to both those who defend a Christian Europe and a post-secular Europe, there are those who want to maintain a status quo biased in favour of ideological secularism, which I associate with a specific conception of French *laïcité*.[8] Of course, Europe cannot possibly embrace one national understanding to the exclusion of all the others, so the approach offered by laic Europe doesn't cut any ice. Plus, it is clear that the social phenomenon of new religions in Europe is not something that can simply be dismissed or regulated out of view. It is something that needs to be addressed and understood. The laic approach does not aim at understanding but it simply wishes to impose one view, which is itself a historical relic. Law in this model would follow a precise plan to outlaw whatever form of religion, and the recent French prohibition of burqas in public streets confirms this point.

### 10.3.4. A secular Europe

The model I defend is neither Christian, nor post-secular, nor laic, but simply secular. It may be argued that to insist on such terminology is not likely to advance the debate as much as desired, since the notion of secularism is too loaded anyhow. I disagree. I believe that we haven't done enough to defend and promote a view of secularism which is not ideological or exclusive. A secular Europe does not have to rule out religion from the public sphere, since it can be confident of its achievement and openly address other perspectives without the fear of collapsing or giving in. If there is a problem it is that secularism has always been too implicated with religion, even if official secular ideology wanted to portray itself as pure and neutral. There is no need, and no real possibility, for strict separation between religion and law, religion and politics. The relation can be ascertained and even cherished to the extent that religion is in the business of preserving a well-ordered community within which peace reigns. It has an overlapping interest with secular law to this extent. Today's business of secular law is to celebrate

---

[8] Agustin Menendez, 'A Christian or a Laïc Europe? Christian Values and European Identity', Ratio Juris, 18(2) (2005), 179–205.

diversity while maintaining a unitary framework within which disagreements between different people can be dealt with peacefully.

A secular Europe respects the domain of the sacred as well as the domain of the natural. But the language in which secularism speaks is neither religious nor scientific, although it has links with them both. The language of secularism is that of the juridical domain, which goes beyond the national realm and informs all European institutions which are attempting more than ever to find a common framework where litigation can be coordinated. In terms of the protection of religion, the ECtHR has a leading role, although it has shunned its responsibility to expand a conception of secularism that can provide a frame for understanding and adjudication of individual rights. It is to be hoped that the Strasbourg Court will reconsider its position in *Lautsi* and will formulate a sound conception of secularism along the lines offered in these few pages. Secularism at the European level should go beyond the church and state debate and should be geared towards the protection of diversity. It is not because each state has a different conception of secularism that it is not possible to find a minimum common denominator at the European level.

Today's Europe does not seek a deep unitary moral order, as was the case in Dante's medieval Europe. We learned that the deep moral order preserved and promoted by religion comes at the price of violent strife between various religious sects who hold the truth about morality and rectitude. Religious conflicts were at the root of the creation of the nation state, which embraced one discrete religious view over others. In turn the nation state rebelled against the established church and became the secular state by positing a degree of separation between itself and religion. The separation between one state and one church allowed religious diversity to flourish again and to prosper at the national and international level. In contemporary Europe, the problem is no longer the relationship between the state and its church. The problem concerns the relationship between politics and religious diversity. I attempted to suggest that we have to move on from church–state debates and change our perspective on the relationship between law and religion. Secular law should be regarded as the tool to build a framework within which religious and non-religious people are able to live together.

# Index

**United States of America**
  church–state relationship  98, 118
  equal citizenship  8
  rational consensus  8
  religious freedom  8
  religious pluralism  4
  segregation  134–40

**value pluralism**
  competing values  174
  diversity distinguished  174
  ethics of diversity  160
  law versus religion  64
  radical incommensurability  174

**Vatican**
  Christian values  194
  conflict of laws  57–8
  *Corpus Vaticanum*  57
  moral and political issues  45, 57–8
  practical authority  45
  separation of church and state  57
  sovereign status  57
  theoretical authority  45
  transposition of Italian laws  45

**Weiler, Joseph**  69–71, 84–8, 149–53

**Zwingli, Huldrych**  17